THE LAW OF THEFT

A

THE LAW OF THEFT

SECOND EDITION

By

J. C. SMITH, M.A., LL.B.,

of Lincoln's Inn, Barrister;
Professor of Common Law and Head of
the Department of Law, University of Nottingham

LONDON
BUTTERWORTHS
1972

ENGLAND: BUTTERWORTH & CO. (PUBLISHERS) LTD.
                LONDON: 88 KINGSWAY, WC2B 6AB
AUSTRALIA: BUTTERWORTH & CO. (AUSTRALIA) LTD.
                SYDNEY: 586 PACIFIC HIGHWAY, CHATSWOOD, NSW 2067
                MELBOURNE: 343 LITTLE COLLINS STREET, 3000
                BRISBANE: 240 QUEEN STREET, 4000
CANADA: BUTTERWORTH & CO. (CANADA) LTD.
                TORONTO: 14 CURITY AVENUE, 374
NEW ZEALAND: BUTTERWORTH & CO. (NEW ZEALAND) LTD.
                WELLINGTON: 26-28 WARING TAYLOR STREET, I
SOUTH AFRICA: BUTTERWORTH & CO. (SOUTH AFRICA) (PTY.) LTD
                DURBAN: 152-154 GALE STREET

ISBN Casebound: 0 406 37902 5
Limp: 0 406 37903 3

MADE AND PRINTED IN GREAT BRITAIN
BY THE BISHOPSGATE PRESS LIMITED,
21 NEW STREET, LONDON, EC2M 4UN.

PREFACE

Three years have elapsed since the Theft Act came into force and its provisions are now beginning to be overlaid by case law. Criticising the decisions under the Larceny Acts was for many years a favourite sport of academic lawyers, and some of the writings suggested that the appellate courts had made few, if any, correct decisions in half a century. If is gratifying to find a much closer accord between judicial interpretation and academic opinion in the vital early days of the construction of the Theft Act. Only in connection with the notorious section 16 have serious criticisms been made of the decisions of the courts; and that baffling section was bound to give rise to differences of opinion. It is to be hoped that Lord Justice Edmund Davies's call for the replacement of this "judicial nightmare" (*Royle*, [1971] 3 All E.R. 1359 at 1363) will soon be heeded.

Generally, the decisions have tended to clarify and confirm the law; but an exception is *Lawrence* v. *Commissioner of Police for the Metropolis* ([1971] 2 All E.R. 1253) which leaves the relationship between theft and obtaining by deception in such an uncertain state as greatly to add to the difficulty of stating the law. Judicial reluctance to go beyond the point necessary for the decision is well known; but the whole reason for the existence of the appeal to the House of Lords is to settle points of law of *general* public importance. Even when their Lordships decide the case on a narrow point, might they not be expected to tell us whether a broad principle acted on in the court below is right or wrong?

I considered carefully whether the time had come to jettison the comparisons with the law under the Larceny Acts and decided that it had not. The old concepts and the old case-law still seem to be prominently in the minds of many of those engaged in the practice and in the teaching of the law; and, so long as this is so, it seems useful to demonstrate the new solutions to the old problems. Perhaps it cannot be repeated too often, however, that with rare exceptions, the old cases are cited as illustrations and not as authorities.

In this new edition I have endeavoured to take account not only of developments in the courts but also of other commentaries on the Act or parts of it. No writer on the subject can fail to be influenced by Mr. Edward Griew's very perceptive book, *The Theft Act* 1968. In the few areas where I disagree with Mr. Griew's views I have tried to state my reasons for doing so. Several reviewers scrutinised the first edition very carefully and I have made changes in the light of their observations. If I have failed to respond, it is probably not because I have overlooked the criticism but because, having considered it, I have obstinately adhered to my original view. I am particularly grateful to Mr. Peter Glazebrook for a long list of points which he thought too trivial to include in his published review but which were of great assistance to me. I am indebted to all those who have made comments and criticisms, particularly to Mr. Roy Rudd for taking so much trouble to give me the benefit of his very careful scrutiny of the first edition; to Mr. Alan Prichard for some valuable suggestions; and to Mr. Ian Hooker who has read the whole of the proofs. Through their assistance, numerous improvements have been made and errors corrected. The faults that remain are my responsibility.

I have endeavoured to state the law as at January 1, 1972.

January 1, 1972

J. C. Smith

CONTENTS

CHAPTER I

INTRODUCTION

CHAPTER II

STEALING UNDER THE THEFT ACT

CHAPTER III

ROBBERY

CHAPTER IV

CRIMINAL DECEPTION

Contents

CHAPTER V
OTHER OFFENCES INVOLVING FRAUD

Contents

APPENDIX

THE THEFT ACT 1968

(For a detailed list of contents of the Act see page 194, below.)

INDEX

TABLE OF STATUTES

References to *"Statutes"* are to Halsbury's Statutes (Third Edition)
showing the volume and page at which the annotated text of the Act
will be found. All references are to paragraph numbers. For the
Theft Act 1968 see the Appendix where the full text of the Act is set
out with cross-references following the principal sections indicating
where those sections are discussed in the narrative part of the book.

TABLE OF CASES

NOTE. Cases are listed under the name of the accused whenever the usual method
of citation would cause them to be preceded by the abbreviation "R. v." signifying
that the prosecution was undertaken by the Crown.

PARA.

A

B

PARA.

ABBREVIATIONS

The following are the abbreviations used for the principal text-books and legal journals cited in this book. References are to the latest editions, as shown below, unless it is specifically stated otherwise. The particulars of other works referred to in the text are set out in the relevant footnotes.

Archbold	*Criminal Pleading, Evidence and Practice*, by John Frederick Archbold. 37th ed. (1969) by T. R. Fitzwalter Butler and Marston Garsia.
Blackstone, *Commentaries*, I	*Commentaries on the laws of England*, by Sir William Blackstone, Vol. 1 (4 Vols.). 17th ed. (1830) by E. Christian
C.L.J.	Cambridge Law Jorunal
Griew	*The Theft Act* 1968 (1968) by Edward Griew
Hale, 1.P.C.	*The History of the Pleas of the Crown*, by Sir Matthew Hale, Vol. 1 [2 Vols.] (1682)
J.Cr.L.	Journal of Criminal Law (English)
Kenny, *Outlines*	*Outlines of Criminal Law*, by C. S. Kenny. 19th ed. (1965) by J. W. C. Turner
L.Q.R.	Law Quarterly Review
M.L.R.	Modern Law Review
N.L.J.	New Law Journal
The *Report*, Cmnd. 2977	Criminal Law Revision Committee, Eighth Report, "Theft and Related Offences." (1966) Cmnd. 2977
Russell	*Crime*, by Sir W. O. Russell. 12th ed. (1964) by J. W. C. Turner [2 Vols.]
Smith and Hogan	*Criminal Law*, by J. C. Smith and Brian Hogan (2nd ed., 1969)
Williams, C.L.G.P.	*Criminal Law: The General Part*, by Glanville L. Williams (2nd ed., 1961)

CHAPTER I

INTRODUCTION

[**1**] Until 1968 the English law of stealing developed in a piecemeal and haphazard fashion over several centuries. The common law began with a very elementary and crude notion of stealing which covered only the most obvious and direct deprivations by one person of property which was in the possession of another. As the inadequacies of the law were exposed by the ingenuity of rogues, so the courts and, later, Parliament extended the law to punish more sophisticated forms of dishonesty. The courts generally achieved their purpose by extending the ambit of the original crime of larceny by means of fictions and strained interpretations of the concepts which constitute the definition of that crime—particularly the concept of possession. Parliament's method was to create a new crime to supplement the old.

[**2**] In one way or another most varieties of dishonest appropriation of the property of another were brought within the ambit of the criminal law and, with one or two exceptions,[1] the gaps through which the dishonest might slip were narrow and did not present a serious problem. But this was at the price of tolerating an immensely and unnecessarily complicated structure, full of difficult distinctions of a purely technical character and bristling with traps for the judges, magistrates, prosecutors and police who had to administer the law.

[**3**] The Theft Act 1968 has swept all this away and given us a completely fresh start with a new definition of theft which embraces all—or virtually all— of the kinds of dishonest conduct which came within the definitions of the old crime of larceny (in all its multifarious forms), embezzlement and fraudulent conversion. This is, in itself, an immense simplification, for the boundaries between these offences were difficult to draw precisely and, right up to the time of their repeal, were the subject of controversy. With the repeal of the old law, the fictions and strained interpretations also pass into legal history.

[**4**] It would be dangerously misleading to suggest, however, that the law of stealing has been, or can be, made childishly simple. Stealing consists in interference with other persons' rights in property, their rights of ownership, whether legal or equitable, their possession and control over chattels and things in action—intangible property. These rights are regulated by the civil law and, in an advanced society, their structure is inevitably complicated. This is something of which the reformer of the criminal law must take account in the legislation which he proposes, but which he cannot alter. The concepts of the civil law must be utilised in the definition of the crime. Moreover, while many borderlines are eliminated by the use of a broadly based definition of theft,

---

[1] E.g. the situation in *Fisher* v. *Raven*, [1964] A.C. 210 and (as some would think), that in *Moynes* v. *Coopper*, [1956] 1 Q.B. 439.

there must always remain the borderline between interferences with another's property which are criminal and those which are not. It is difficult to define this line in the first place and whatever definition is adopted will lead to difficulties of interpretation.

[**5**] The old law of stealing was contained in the Larceny Acts of 1861 and 1916. These Acts contained the vice generally to be found in nineteenth and early twentieth century criminal statutes—the creation of a multitude of separate crimes to provide an aggravated punishment because of the presence of a single circumstance of aggravation. Simple larceny was punishable with five years imprisonment, but there were many types of stealing with greater or less penalties according to the nature of the property stolen, the place where it was stolen and the relationship between the thief and the owner. The fact that the subject of the larceny was a will, title deeds or a mail-bag was a sufficient circumstance of aggravation to raise the maximum to life. Other single circumstances which allowed of an enhanced punishment were that the larceny was of cattle or goods in the process of manufacture, from the person, from a ship, by a clerk or servant, or by a tenant or lodger. On the other hand, lesser punishments were provided, for example, if the larceny was of ore from a mine or of a dog. Any court in sentencing a thief today will take account, in determining the sentence, of very many factors in addition to such single elements of aggravation or mitigation—indeed it is very unlikely that the factors enumerated will be the most important in the court's decision.

[**6**] In place of all these aggravated forms of larceny we now have the single offence of theft with a single penalty. As the definition comprehends within it offences which were formerly punishable with imprisonment for life and for fourteen years, it was inevitable that the maximum penalty provided should be more than the five years available for simple larceny. The ten year maximum which is provided by the Theft Act[2] should not therefore be regarded as an invitation to impose higher penalties for what would formerly have been simple larceny; if anything, the contrary should be the case for, overall, penalties have been reduced. It has been suggested that the question the sentencing judge should ask himself is: "What proportion does the crime before me bear to the greatest possible crime coming under the same name; if, for example, fourteen years is the maximum penalty, what ought to be the penalty for the crime before me?"[3] This view is supported by decisions of the Court of Criminal Appeal that the statutory maximum must be reserved for the worst conceivable cases and that the imposition of the maximum where a worse case can be imagined is wrong in principle.[4]

[**7**] Less easy to justify is the provision of a maximum of ten years for obtaining property by deception, for the scope of this new offence is substantially the same as the old crime of obtaining by false pretences which carried only five. The explanation is that deception has been expanded to include cases which were formerly larceny by a trick and which are also within the scope of theft. It would have been slightly anomalous to have had different penalties for these

---

[2] Section 7.

[3] Fry, J. (1883), 52 *Nineteenth Century* 848.

[4] *Edwards* (1910), 5 Cr. App. Rep. 229; *Austin*, [1961] Crim. L.R. 416; *Da Silva*, [1964] Crim. L. R. 68.

acts, according to the section under which they happened to be charged[5] and, if theft had carried a higher penalty, prosecutors might have felt obliged to charge acts which were larceny by a trick under the old law as theft whereas, as will appear,[6] it is highly desirable that they should be charged as obtaining by deception. In any event, it is submitted that the Act provides no justification for any increase in the penalties for acts which would formerly have been obtaining by false pretences or larceny by a trick.

1 THE INTERPRETATION OF THE THEFT ACT

[8] The Theft Act represents an almost completely fresh start, and its words should be interpreted in their natural meaning to produce sensible results,[7] without harking back unnecessarily to the concepts of the common law.

> "It is expressed in simple language as used and understood by ordinary literate men and women. It avoids so far as possible those terms of art which have acquired a special meaning understood only by lawyers in which many of the penal enactments which it supersedes were couched."[8]

Very little attention seems to have been paid to the actual words of the Larceny Act 1916, for the courts constantly had recourse to the common law and assumed that the Act was intended to preserve it, even when the wording was somewhat difficult to reconcile with this view. The definition of larceny in the 1916 Act was a new statutory definition, but it did not purport to do more than codify the common law. There is therefore a fundamental difference between the Act of 1916 and that of 1968. The Theft Act enacts, for the most part, completely new law. Only in a limited number of cases will it be necessary or desirable to resort to earlier case law. When the bill was before the House of Lords, Lord Wilberforce introduced an amendment[9] to the effect that it should not be permissible "to refer to any decisions of any Courts prior to the passing of this Act, other than decisions in general terms dealing with the interpretation of Statutes." It is submitted that this amendment was wisely withdrawn. Such a rule might be workable in some statutes but only if they were drafted with such a rule of interpretation in mind, which the Theft Act was not. In this field, moreover, it would simply not be possible to dispense with the previous case-law altogether. The Theft Act assumes the existence of the whole law of property much of which is to be found only in decided cases; and any such Act must surely make a similar assumption. The Act includes expressions like "tenancy," "proprietary right or interest," "trust," and many other terms describing concepts of the civil law which it would be quite impracticable to spell out in an Act concerned with theft. The court can be informed as to the circumstances in which a person is "under an obligation to make restoration" of property, its proceeds or its value,[10] only by

---

[5] Yet this anomaly will arise in respect of many acts which will be both theft and handling under the new Act; but it is submitted that, while this is a little untidy, it is of no great importance.

[6] Below, para. [30].

[7] *Baxter*, [1971] 2 All E.R. 359 at 362, *per* Sachs, L.J.

[8] *Treacy* v. *D.P.P.*, [1971] A.C. 537 at 565; [1971] 1 All E.R. 110 at 124, *per* Lord Diplock.

[9] Parl. Debates, Official Report (H.L.), Vol. 290, col. 897.

[10] Section 5 (4), below, para [70].

reference to the law of contract and quasi-contract which is embodied in case-law.

[**9**] No doubt Lord Wilberforce had in mind, not the civil law, but the old cases on the criminal law of larceny and related offences with all their technicalities and absurdities. Only in rare instances should there be any ground for citing such cases. Generally they will be utterly irrelevant, because the criminal concepts in the Act are new ones. Where, however, the Act incorporates the substance of the provisions of earlier statutes—as, for example, with the amended version of taking motor vehicles[11]—it is surely undesirable that the courts should have to go back to square one and re-litigate points of construction previously settled, with perhaps different and not necessarily better results. Again, where terms with a well settled meaning under the Larceny Acts have been used in a similar context in the Theft Act, it would seem desirable—and certainly in accord with the intention of the framers of the Act—that those concepts should be given their well-settled meaning. Examples are the use of the word "menaces" in blackmail[12] and "receives" in handling stolen goods.[13]

[**10**] The old law is also relevant as an aid to construction insofar as its inadequacies illuminate the mischief at which the Act is aimed and in that it may persuade the court that Parliament could not have intended to legalise conduct which it thinks ought to be criminal and which was criminal under the old law.[14] Beyond such instances, however, it should be unnecessary and indeed, improper to cite cases on the old law of larceny and related offences. In the following pages, many of the old cases are referred to, but it will be noted that they are cited, not as authorities, but as illustrations of actual situations which have caused difficulty in the past, in order to demonstrate how the Act deals, or does not deal with those situations for the future.

[**11**] Lord Wilberforce's amendment would also have provided that the Act should be interpreted "according to the plain and natural meaning of the words used, read in the context of the Act as a whole, and given a fair, large and liberal construction." It is submitted that the Act should be interpreted according to the plain and natural meaning of the words used (if they have one) except where it appears that the word has a technical meaning which, in the context, it is intended to bear. Thus, if the word "menaces" were given its plain and natural meaning, it might be held to be confined to threats of violence and the like. This would result in a drastic narrowing of the offence of blackmail and would plainly defeat the intention of Parliament. The word should be given the extended meaning which, in this context, it has long borne in the law.

[**12**] No one could object to the words of the Act being given a "fair" construction but the other expressions used in the amendment, "large and liberal", are of much more doubtful import. They suggest that the Act should be given an extensive meaning, so as to prohibit acts not clearly within its terms. It is submitted that the Act should not be so interpreted. There is much to be said for ignoring the rule (only applied spasmodically and inconsistently) that

---

[11] Section 12, below, para. [**312**].
[12] Section 21, below, para. [**333**].
[13] Section 22, below, para. [**430**].
[14] *Treacy* v. *D.P.P.*, [1971] A.C. at 557-558; [1971] 1 All E.R. at 118, *per* Lord Hodson.

penal statutes should be strictly construed; but this is achieved by giving words their plain and natural meaning and adopting the "fair" interpretation—"fair", that is, to both sides. It is not desirable that the courts should go to the other extreme and extend the meaning of penal provisions by a "large and liberal" construction. The principle, *nulla poena sine lege*, is of as great importance today as ever it was.

2 THE LAW OF STEALING UNDER THE LARCENY ACTS

[13] A very brief résumé of the position before the Theft Act will assist the understanding of some of its provisions. There existed the following crimes:

A. SIMPLE LARCENY

(i) Simple larceny was most commonly committed where D by a trespass took possession of goods which were in the possession or custody of P without his consent. It was from this notion that the common law began. The concept of "taking" was expanded by the courts until, in the 1916 consolidation, it was defined to include:

> "obtaining the possession—
> (*a*) by any trick;
> (*b*) by intimidation;
> (*c*) under a mistake on the part of the owner with knowledge on the part of the taker that possession has been so obtained;
> (*d*) by finding, where at the time of the finding the finder believes that the owner can be discovered by taking reasonable steps".[15]

It was essential in all these forms of larceny that, as well as a taking there should be a "carrying away" and the Act provided:

> "the expression 'carries away' includes any removal of anything from the place which it occupies, but in the case of a thing attached, only if it has been completely detached."[16]

(ii) At common law a possessor could not steal but legislation from 1857 onwards made it larceny for a bailee to misappropriate the bailed goods and the 1916 Act provided:

> ". . . a person may be guilty of stealing any such thing notwithstanding that he has lawful possession thereof, if, being a bailee or part owner thereof, he fraudulently converts the same to his own use or the use of any person other than the owner."[17]

Here a physical "taking and carrying away" was unnecessary. It was enough, for example, that D should have contracted to sell goods bailed to him, without laying hands on them at all. Though larceny was commonly (and, in general, accurately) described as an offence against possession, larceny by a bailee was plainly an offence by a possessor against ownership.

---

[15] Larceny Act 1916, s. 1 (2) (i).
[16] *Ibid.*, s. 1 (2) (ii).
[17] *Ibid.*, s. 1 (1), proviso.

B

B. LARCENY BY A SERVANT

[**14**] Where a master entrusted his servant with goods it was held at an early stage in the development of the common law that possession remained in the master and the servant merely had custody so that a misappropriation of the goods by the servant amounted to larceny. This was an aggravated form of larceny under s. 17 (1) (*a*) of the 1916 Act.

C. EMBEZZLEMENT

[**15**] The position was different where the servant received goods from a third party to transmit to the possession of the master. Here the servant was held to acquire possession and therefore to be incapable of larceny at common law. He was, no doubt, a bailee; but, in 1799, before legislation dealt with bailees generally, Parliament created the offence of embezzlement to deal with the particular case here discussed. The distinction between embezzlement and larceny by a servant was a subtle one. If D received money for his master and put it straight into his pocket this was embezzlement; but if he put the money into his master's till and then took it out again this was larceny since putting the money into the till reduced it into the possession of the master. Like larceny by a servant, embezzlement was punishable with fourteen years imprisonment.[18]

D. FRAUDULENT CONVERSION

[**16**] By a series of statutes from 1812 onwards the offence known as fraudulent conversion was created and extended. By s. 20 of the 1916 Act it was provided that anyone who had been entrusted or become entrusted[19] with property for various purposes or had received property for or on account of another should be guilty of a misdemeanour, punishable with seven years' imprisonment. On the face of it, the definition of this offence comprehended within it larceny by a bailee, larceny by a clerk or servant and embezzlement. It also clearly applied to another category of persons—those who had been entrusted not merely with the possession but with the ownership of the property. It was argued by some[20] that fraudulent conversion was confined to this case and did not overlap the other offences. The controversy was never authoritatively settled and is now, happily, dead.

E. OBTAINING BY FALSE PRETENCES

[**17**] Where D by a false statement induced P to transfer to him possession of the goods with intent to appropriate them, this was larceny by a trick at common law. Where D by a false pretence induced P to transfer to him *ownership* of the goods with intent to appropriate them, this was no offence at common law but was made a misdemeanour by statute in 1757; and, by s. 32 of the 1916 Act, it was an offence punishable with five years' imprisonment. The distinction between larceny by a trick and obtaining by false pretences was a fine one and a fruitful source of difficulties. As an example, if D by false pretences induced P to let him have goods on hire purchase intending to appropriate them,

---

[18] *Ibid.*, s. 17 (1) (*b*).
[19] *Grubb*, [1915] 2 K.B. 683.
[20] See Russell, 1112 *et seq.*; Kenny, 334 *et seq.* For the other point of view see [1961] Crim. L.R. 741, 797.

this was larceny by a trick since the property did not pass; but if he induced him to let him have the same goods on credit-sale terms, this was obtaining by false pretences, since the property did pass.

CHAPTER II

STEALING UNDER THE THEFT ACT

[**18**] Section 1 (1) of the Theft Act 1968 provides:

"A person is guilty of theft if he dishonestly appropriates property belonging to another with the intention of permanently depriving the other of it; and 'thief' and 'steal' shall be construed accordingly."

1 THE ACTUS REUS OF THEFT

[**19**] The *actus reus*, then, consists simply in the *appropriation of property belonging to another*. The two questions which require detailed consideration are, What is an appropriation? and, When does property belong to another?

A. APPROPRIATION

[**20**] By s. 3 (1) of the Act,

"Any assumption by a person of the rights of an owner amounts to an appropriation, and this includes, where he has come by the property (innocently or not) without stealing it, any later assumption of a right to it by keeping or dealing with it as owner."

[**21**] This is a "partial definition . . . which is included partly to indicate that this is the familiar concept of conversion . . .".[1] "Conversion" is the name of a tort about which there is a great deal of complicated law; and conversion was the principal ingredient of the former offences of larceny by a bailee and fraudulent conversion. The Committee thought that "conversion" and "appropriation" had the same meaning, but preferred "appropriation" on the valid ground that, in ordinary usage, it more aptly describes the kind of acts it is intended to cover.[2] Though the civil and criminal cases on "conversion' may occasionally be useful in elucidating the meaning of "appropriation" it is clear that they are not binding. An act may amount to appropriation even though it does not constitute the tort of conversion.[3] There is no ground for incorporating the technicalities of the law of tort into the definition of theft and "appropriation" may be given its ordinary, natural meaning even if that conflicts with the meaning of "conversion" in the civil or the criminal law.

[**22**] The adoption of appropriation as the act constituting the offence gets rid of the necessity for both a trespassory "taking" and a "carrying away" as constituents of stealing. These elements were never necessary in larceny as a bailee or in fraudulent conversion but they (and more particularly the former) led to endless complication in simple larceny. The law is freed from its involvement with the difficult and controversial concept of possession since it is only

---

[1] The *Report*, Cmnd. 2977, para. 34.
[2] *Ibid.*, para. 35.
[3] *Bonner*, [1970] 2 All E.R. 97; below, para. [**64**].

in the rarest cases that it is now necessary to prove that infringement of the possession of another which was an essential constituent of all instances of larceny except larceny by a bailee.

(a) *Appropriation by taking and carrying away or attempting to do so*

[**23**] Though taking and carrying away are no longer necessary constituents of the offence it seems clear that all instances of taking and carrying away the property of another (with appropriate *mens rea*) amount to appropriations. If, for example, D picks a watch from P's pocket, removes a brief case from his car or takes money from his safe, he may aptly be said in each case to have appropriated P's property.

[**24**] Clearly the full crime may now be committed at an earlier stage than formerly. Acts which were only attempted larceny will constitute theft. If D only grasps the watch in P's pocket without succeeding in moving it, this seems clearly enough to amount to an assumption of ownership and therefore an appropriation. More doubtful is the case where D puts his hand into the pocket, or in the direction of the pocket with intent to steal the watch. This may be only an attempt, or, possibly an act of preparation.[4]

(b) *Appropriation by a bailee*

[**25**] If D is a bailee of P's car and, without P's authority, he enters into a contract to sell it to E, this would be an obvious act of appropriation. The crime would be complete even though the car was never moved or even touched. Even if D never got beyond the stage of an offer, it is reasonably clear that the theft would be complete. Thus in *Rogers* v. *Arnott*[5] the Divisional Court held that the offence of larceny by a bailee was complete on the making of an offer to sell a tape-recorder: "The reason is that the bailee in such a case has usurped the rights of the owner for his, the bailee's, benefit."[6] It was suggested by counsel[7] in that case that the crime was completed at an even earlier stage:

> "Once the defendant decided to keep the appointment to sell the tape recorder, and certainly once he had put it into the car, he committed an act of conversion."

It is submitted, however, that a mere decision in D's mind to sell the tape-recorder, not accompanied or followed by any act—even if such a decision could be proved—would amount neither to a conversion under the old law nor an appropriation under the new. Donovan, J., did not go so far, saying no more than that D is guilty when he proceeds to carry into effect his previously formed intention by making an offer to sell.

(c) *Appropriation by possessors other than bailees*

[**26**] "Appropriation" includes—

> ". . . where he has come by the property (innocently or not) without stealing it, any later assumption of a right to it by keeping or **dealing with it as owner**."[8]

---

[4] Below, para. [**49**].
[5] [1960] 2 Q.B. 244.
[6] *Per* Donovan, J., delivering the judgment of the court.
[7] Basil Wigoder at pp. 246–247.
[8] Section 3 (1).

This confirms what would probably have followed from the terms of s. 1 (1) anyway—that the former rule, that the intent to steal must be formed at the time of taking, is abolished. No rule gave rise to more difficulty in the law of larceny and a number of subtle distinctions are eliminated from the law. Of the following cases, (i) and (iii) were no offence under the old law and all presented difficulties; but it is submitted that theft is committed in all of them under the Theft Act. Cases (i) and (ii) are quite clear; but, as to the remainder, it may be argued that, since D intended to assume all the rights of an owner when he first took the thing, there is no room for any "later assumption of a right to it"; that one cannot assume what one has already assumed. It is submitted however that the words "*later* assumption" pre-suppose an earlier assumption; and that the later assumption envisaged may be an exercise of rights which have been assumed on "coming by" the thing in question. The contrary view would be disastrous for, it should be noted, s. 5 (4)[9] does no more than vest a fictitious property in the prosecutor and leaves open the necessity for an appropriation.

(i) D receives stolen property. He intends to restore it to the true owner or the police. Later he changes his mind and conceals the thing, intending to deprive the owner permanently of it.[10]

(ii) D, a carrier, receives a number of sacks of pig-meal into his lorry for carriage from A to B. When he arrives, D discovers that ten sacks too many have been loaded. He appropriates them.[11]

(iii) D finds a banknote in the highway. There appears to be no reasonable means of ascertaining the owner and D decides to keep it for himself. This is no offence—D has "come by the property . . . innocently." Two days later, being still in possession of it, he discovers that P is the owner and then uses the note for his own purposes.[12]

(iv) In the dark P hands a coin to D. Both believe it to be a shilling. In fact it is a sovereign. Some time later, D discovers it is a sovereign and spends it.[13] (It is assumed that the property in the sovereign does not pass in this situation. If this assumption is wrong, D will not escape liability, but it will then be necessary to rely on s. 5 (4)).[14]

(v) D is handed his workmate's pay packet by mistake. When he has been in possession of it for some hours he discovers that it contains more than he is entitled to and appropriates the money.[15]

[**27**] In the above cases the original possession was innocent. The same result follows where it is not:

D has left his flock of sheep for the night on P's farm. When he drives the flock away next morning it has been joined, without his knowledge, by one of P's sheep. When D discovers the additional sheep he appropriates it.[16]

---

[9] Below, para. [**70**].
[10] *Cf. Matthews* (1873), 28 L.T. 645.
[11] *Cf. Russell* v. *Smith*, [1958] 1 Q.B. 27.
[12] *Cf. Thurborn* (1849), 1 Den. 397; *Thompson* v. *Nixon*, [1965] 2 All E.R. 741.
[13] *Cf. Ashwell* (1885), 16 Q.B.D. 190.
[14] Below, para. [**70**].
[15] *Cf. Flowers* (1886), 16 Q.B.D. 643.
[16] *Cf. Riley* (1853), Dears. 149.

Whether D came by the sheep innocently or by the tort of trespass, he is guilty of theft at the moment of appropriation.

D, in a drunken frolic, takes P's bicycle. He has no intent to steal at that time. When he becomes sober he appropriates it.[17]

(d) Appropriation without taking by persons not in possession

[**28**] The Theft Act makes an important extension of criminal liability in that the rules which were previously applicable only in the case of bailees[18] are now of general application. The effect of this may be illustrated by the case of *Bloxham*.[19] There D not only offered, but actually contracted to sell and received the price for a refrigerator belonging to the Urban District Council which employed him; and yet was held to be not guilty of an attempt to commit larceny on the ground that he had never done any act which was sufficiently proximate to the complete crime—a striking contrast with the result in *Rogers* v. *Arnott*.[20] D was plainly not a bailee of the refrigerator nor, so far as appears, did he even have custody of it. It was presumably simply standing on the premises of his employer. He was not guilty of attempted larceny because:

> "The very essence of the offence of larceny is the asportation, and if the appellant had done anything which could amount to an attempt to take and carry away the refrigerator, he would of course have been guilty of the offence with which he was charged. But the fact is that he took no step whatever connected either immediately or remotely with taking and carrying away this refrigerator."[1]

[**29**] If Bloxham had in fact intended to deliver the refrigerator there is no doubt that under the new law he would be guilty, not merely of an attempt, but of the full offence of theft. The crime would be complete when he offered to sell. The absence of any attempt at asportation would be quite irrelevant and it would also be immaterial that there was little or no chance of his carrying the enterprise through to a successful conclusion.

Bloxham probably never had any intention of delivering the refrigerator. This appears, at first sight, to be fatal to a charge of theft since it negatives "the intention of permanently depriving." However, s. 6 (1) provides that this requirement is satisfied by an intention "to treat the thing as his own to dispose of", even where the rogue does not mean "the other permanently to lose the thing itself." Bloxham appears to have treated the refrigerator as his own to dispose of, and so to be guilty of theft. Griew[2] objects to this conclusion on two grounds: (i) that there is no appropriation. "D's reference to the property is a mere device to support the deception practised on the purchaser. If D and E are not in the presence of any property when they conclude their bargain, it would seem to be all one whether the property referred to is actual or fictitious." Mr. Griew does not shrink from the corollary to this argument, that a bailee "who uses his possession *merely* as a device to defraud a dupe

---

[17] *Ruse* v. *Read*, [1949] 1 K.B. 377; *cf. Kindon* (1957), 41 Cr. App. Rep. 208.
[18] And possibly servants in custody of their masters' goods—but this was doubtful: [1961] Crim. L.R. 448–451. Happily, controversy on the point is now irrelevant.
[19] (1943), 29 Cr. App. Rep. 37.
[20] Above, para. [**25**].
[1] *Per* Tucker, J., (1943), 29 Cr. App. Rep. at 39.
[2] Griew, 2–32 and 2–42.

will not appropriate—save in a rare case such as that where the victim acquires title by the transaction, as on a contract to sell specific goods in market overt.'' It is submitted, however, that there is no valid ground for a distinction based on the presence of the property—and the property *was* present in *Bloxham;* that the case of fictitious property is plainly distinguishable; and that theft never has and does not depend on whether the true owner has been deprived of his title. In such a case, D causes the buyer to have a *bona fide* claim of right to the true owner's property. That claim may be easy to resist or it may be difficult,[3] but, in either event, it seems not unreasonable to describe the creation of it as an appropriation. (ii) In the last resort, Mr. Griew would be prepared to argue that "to dispose of" in s. 6 (1) should be construed narrowly, so as not to apply in this situation. But that subsection is undoubtedly intended to apply to the case where D purports to sell P's own property to P. Is there any less "a disposition" when he purports to sell P another's property?

If the words of the Act appear, as they do, to make a person like Bloxham guilty of theft,[4] there is no reason to strain to exclude him from liability; but it would certainly be preferable to charge the accused with obtaining the money by deception and so avoid any of the difficulties discussed above. Cases are however conceivable where a charge of obtaining by deception will not lie; for example, D has a claim of right to the money which he obtains from E,[5] though not to the property of P which he purports to sell to E.

(e) Appropriation of property obtained by a trick

[30] There is unhappily a good deal of uncertainty as to the proper interpretation of s. 1 where property has been obtained from another by a trick or deception. This uncertainty need cause no practical difficulty, however, if the advice given below is followed.

The problem springs from the existence of the two following situations:

(i) D, by deception, causes P to transfer possession or custody of property to D, ownership remaining in P. D dishonestly intends to, and does, assume the rights of the owner, P, over the property.

(ii) D, by deception, causes P to transfer his entire interest in property to D. D dishonestly intends to, and does, assume those entire rights.

Case (i) was formerly the crime of larceny by a trick, case (ii) the crime of obtaining by false pretences. The distinction between the two was exceedingly troublesome and one of the objects of the Theft Act was to eliminate these difficulties. Consequently, s. 15, obtaining property by deception, is so drafted that it undoubtedly covers both situations and, if the charge is brought under that section, the distinction is quite immaterial. The golden rule for prosecutors, therefore is:

Whenever D has obtained property from P by any kind of trick or false pretence, he should be charged under s. 15 (1) and not under s. 1.

---

[3] In *Bloxham*, the buyer might have claimed that she had a title on the ground of D's ostensible authority to sell.

[4] There is one other, rather technical objection which might be valid. A stolen article ceases to be "stolen" on being restored to the true owner: s. 24 (3). How then can it be stolen if it never leaves his possession? It is submitted that s. 24 (3) applies only where the thing has in fact left the owner's possession.

[5] Below, para. [240].

There can be little doubt that it was the intention of the Committee that, while s. 15 should cover both cases (i) and (ii), s. 1 (1) should cover only case (i). They stated[6] that ("to the regret of some members") they gave up the idea of extending the offence of theft to cover cases of obtaining by false pretences under the Larceny Act 1916.

> "Obtaining by false pretences is ordinarily thought of as different from theft, because in the former the *owner in fact consents to part with his ownership*; a bogus beggar is regarded as a rogue but not as a thief, and so are his less petty counterparts. To create a new offence of theft to include conduct which ordinary people would find it difficult to regard as theft would be a mistake."

It may of course be perfectly proper for the court to put on the Act an interpretation different from that intended by the framers of it. The question is one of the proper interpretation of the words enacted by Parliament and it could be that the Act does what the Committee thought was not practicable and what they did not intend it to do. It is submitted, however, that the right interpretation of the Act is that intended by the Committee.

[31] The present uncertainty arises because it has been suggested that s. 1 (1) also covers both situations. Two separate grounds have been advanced for this view:

(i) That this is the natural meaning of the words of s. 1 (1).

(ii) That this is the effect of s. 5 (4). This argument is considered below, para. **[78]**.

The first argument is to be found in a judgment of the Court of Appeal in *Lawrence*.[7] The court took the view that the former distinction depended on the presence in the Larceny Act of the words, "without the consent of the owner," and, as these words do not appear in the definition of theft, the distinction is gone; all cases of obtaining by deception, contrary to s. 15, are also theft.[8] This argument, however, appears to give insufficient weight to the words, "property *belonging to another*." Suppose that D writes to P falsely representing that he urgently needs a bottle of brandy for the medical treatment of his sick mother. P calls at D's house in his absence and leaves the brandy. He intends to and does make P the entire owner of it. D is detained and does not get his hands on the brandy until a week later. Can it really be said that he has appropriated property *belonging to another*? Before he does anything which could be described as an appropriation he has acquired the entire proprietary interest in the bottle. The case is clearly covered by s. 15 but not by the natural meaning of the words of s. 1. More usually, the alleged appropriation will approximate more closely in time to P's act of divesting himself of his proprietary interest. D makes the false pretence in P's presence and P takes the bottle and hands it over to D. The gift is complete only on delivery so that D's alleged appropriation is coincident with his acquisition of the entire proprietary interest. It is much more arguable that this is covered

---

[6] The *Report*, Cmnd. 2977, para. 38.
[7] [1971] 1 Q.B. 373; [1970] 3 All E.R. 933 at 935. See comment at [1971] Crim L.R. 51.
[8] An exception to this would be an obtaining by deception of land, which cannot be the subject of theft.

by s. 1, but it is thought that a better view is that it is not really distinguishable from the case first put.

[**32**] The facts of *Lawrence* were that P, an Italian with very little English, on arriving in London on a first visit to England, went up to D, a taxi driver, and showed D an address to which he wished to be carried. D said it was very far and expensive. P got into the taxi and tendered £1. D said it was not enough. P's wallet was still open and D took from it a further £1 note and a £5 note. He drove P to the address and gave him no change. The correct fare was about 10s. 6d. D was convicted of stealing "the approximate sum of £6." The Court of Appeal thought that this was a case which might have been obtaining by false pretences, not larceny by a trick under the old law, but, for the reasons discussed above, upheld the conviction. Leave was given to appeal to the House of Lords, their Lordships being asked (i) whether s. 1 (1) should be construed as though it contained the words "without the consent of the owner" and (ii) whether s. 1 (1) and s. 15 (1) were mutually exclusive.[9] The answer to both these questions was obviously in the negative, and, understandably, Viscount Dilhorne expressed surprise that leave had been given.[10] It was in fact argued that D had not appropriated property belonging to another, but the House disposed of this contention shortly on the ground that "the money in the wallet which he appropriated belonged to another, to [P]." If this means that the ownership never passed to D then, of course, the problem under discussion did not arise. The House interpreted the facts differently from the Court of Appeal who, since they thought this crime would formerly have been false pretences and not larceny by a trick, must have assumed that the ownership did pass to D. The question thus remains open, though it should be noted that the House said that "there are cases which only come within s. 1 (1) and *some which are only within s. 15 (1)*".[11] It is unlikely that their lordships had in mind only cases such as obtaining *land* by deception, and this casts doubt on the view of the Court of Appeal.

[**33**] If the views of the Court of Appeal in *Lawrence* are correct, much of the discussion in the following pages of this chapter is affected. Where this is so it is pointed out that the propositions in the text are subject to "the *Lawrence* (C.A.) principle." This principle is assumed to be:

D appropriates property belonging to P when he assumes the rights of an owner over property in which P has transferred to him P's entire proprietary interest.

The following cases, which gave difficulty under the old law, are discussed subject to the *Lawrence* (C.A.) principle. If that principle is correct, there is little doubt that *all* the cases amount to theft.

[**34**] In the classic case[12] of larceny by a trick, D obtained the hire of a horse from P by saying that he wanted to ride it to Sutton. He then rode the horse

---

[9] *Lawrence v. Metropolis, Police Commissioner*, [1971] 2 All E.R. 1253.
[10] For a suggestion as to the questions which *ought* to have been asked, see [1971] Crim. L.R. 53.
[11] [1971] 2 All E.R. at 1256. Author's italics.
[12] *Pear* (1779), 1 Leach 212.

to Smithfield Market and sold it. He was held to be guilty of larceny as soon as he took possession. Clearly D would be guilty of theft under the Act at the latest when he actually sold the horse. There might be a question, however, whether there was an appropriation at the moment when he took possession of the horse, since he was entitled to do this under the terms of the bailment—which is only voidable and not void. It is likely, however, to be held that taking possession with the theftuous intention is a sufficient act of appropriation,—just as retaining possession with such an intention is.

[35] In the case just considered, if there was an appropriation, there was no doubt that it was the property of another that was appropriated. There were other cases under the old law, however, where it is very difficult to see how this could be so. A case in point is *Buckmaster*.[13] D, a bookmaker, took bets from P and, while the race was being run, left the course. The horse backed by P won the race. It was held that D was fraudulent from the start and therefore guilty of larceny by a trick. This case has often been validly and forcefully criticised on the ground that the property in the money must have passed to D.[14] Of course the criminal court held that it did not; but it is to be hoped that the construction of the new Act will not be marred by such strained decisions which are quite irreconcilable, not only with well-established civil law, but also, as the learned editor of Russell[15] says, with the experience of ordinary men. Of course the backer intends to part with his ownership in the money—he can have no complaint if he sees the bookmaker take the note handed to him and spend it on beer. Subject to the *Lawrence* (C.A.)[16] principle, the welshing bookmaker does not appropriate the property of another and is therefore not guilty of theft. He may, however, be guilty of criminal deception.[17]

All the observations here made on *Buckmaster* are equally applicable to *Russett*[18]—P agrees to buy a horse from D for £23, pays £8 and agrees to pay the balance on delivery of the horse. D, as he all along intended, absconds with the money and never delivers the horse.

[36] A modern problem which has not yet been the subject of any reported decision in a higher court[19] but which is known to have arisen on more than one occasion is as follows:

Two pieces of meat in a supermarket bear price tickets of £2 and £1 respectively. D takes the £2 ticket, puts it in his pocket and attaches the £1 ticket to the £2 piece of meat which he then tenders at the cash desk. It cannot be said that D has yet appropriated the property (except in the £2 ticket) for he has not assumed the rights of an owner. When he tenders the meat, he is offering to buy it[20] which is an act inconsistent with present ownership and thus not an appropriation. If the cashier were to ask D for £1 and, on receiving it, allow him to take away the meat, it is submitted that this would clearly

---

13 (1887), 20 Q.B.D.182.
14 Kenny, 264–265; Russell, 935–938; Smith and Hogan (1st ed.), 352, n. 15.
15 See footnote 14, above.
16 Above, para. [**33**].
17 This question is discussed, below, para. [**218**].
18 [1892] 2 Q.B. 312.
19 For a discussion of a case in a magistrates' court see (1961), 25 J. Cr. L. 168.
20 *Pharmaceutical Society* v. *Boots (Cash Chemists), Ltd.*, [1953] 1 Q.B. 401.

be obtaining by deception and not theft. D's offer to buy that particular piece of meat has been accepted and a contract (though voidable for fraud) has vested the property in the meat in D.[1] The position would be different if D had induced in P a mistake as to the identity of the subject-matter of the contract and not, as he did, merely as to the price of the subject-matter. In *Bramley*[2] D, having loaded his cart with coal in P's yard, covered it with slack and, on being asked by the weighing machine operator what he had in the cart, replied, "Slack" and was charged accordingly. It was held that he was guilty of larceny and he would now be guilty of theft of the coal as well as of obtaining it by deception since a contract is negatived—it is void, and not merely voidable—where the parties do not intend to contract for the same commercial commodity.[3]

(f) Appropriation of property obtained by intimidation

[37] The Larceny Act 1916 specifically[4] provided that obtaining possession of goods by intimidation was a sufficient taking. There is no corresponding provision in the Theft Act, but its absence must not be taken to show that such conduct was not intended to be covered.[5] The question in each case is then: Was this an appropriation by D of property belonging to another? If the effect of the intimidation is such that property does not pass from P to D then D is clearly guilty of theft. If property does pass, then it is submitted that he cannot be so guilty. This is so even though the transaction may be rendered voidable by the intimidation. If, however, the *Lawrence* (C.A.) principle is correct and D is guilty of theft when he receives the ownership in property under a transaction voidable for fraud, there is no reason why it should not equally be theft to receive the ownership in property under a transaction voidable for intimidation.

[38] To determine whether property passes we must turn to the civil law. The great weight of authority there is to the effect that transactions induced by duress are merely voidable and not void.[6]

[39] If D says to P "Your money or your life" and P hands over his money in order to preserve his life, no one will doubt that this is stealing and indeed robbery; and this can be technically justified by the fact that sparing P's life was no consideration for P's giving up his money. The "contract" was void for lack of consideration, even if it were not void for duress; and, plainly, no gift was intended. The decision in *McGrath*[7] could be similarly justified under the new law. D and his accomplices asserted that P had bid twenty-six shillings for some cloth at an auction sale and refused to let her leave the room until

---

1 It is submitted that D is not under an obligation to make restoration within s. 5 (4): below, paras. [78]-[80].
2 (1861), Le. & Ca. 21.
3 *Scriven Bros., Ltd.* v. *Hindley*, [1913] 3 K.B. 564 (hemp and tow).
4 Section 1 (2) (i), above, para. [13].
5 *Cf. Bonner*, below, para. [64].
6 *Whelpdale's Case* (1604), 5 Co. Rep. 119a; 2 Co. Inst. 583; *Halsbury's Laws of England* (3rd ed.), Vol. 8, 85, Vol. 14, 479; Leake on *Contract*, 63; Pollock, *Contracts* (12th ed.), 472; Chitty, *Contracts* § 341; Cheshire and Fifoot, *Law of Contract* (7th ed.), 262. Treitel, *Law of Contract* (3rd ed.), 344. See D. J. Lanham, "Duress and Void Contracts" (1966), 29 M.L.R. 615.
7 (1869), L.R. 1 C.C.R. 205.

she had paid. She paid because she was frightened. D was convicted of larceny. It is submitted that he would be guilty of theft. P had in fact made no bid and D's assertion that she had made a contract, when he knew she had not, clearly could not constitute a contract, even a voidable one, for there was not even the outward appearance of a contract. Similarly with *Lovell*.[8] D ground some knives for P. The ordinary charge would have been one shilling and three-pence. D demanded five shillings and sixpence and by threats induced P to pay. The threats did not induce a contract—the contract was already made—they induced the payment of a sum to which—as the jury's verdict of guilty of larceny showed—D knew very well he was not entitled. And, clearly, no gift was intended. He would be guilty of theft.

[**40**] Suppose, however, that D offers to buy P's car for an absurdly small sum and induces P to accept his offer by threatening to beat or imprison him if he does not do so. If the civil law authorities are correct in asserting that duress makes the contract voidable only, the car becomes D's as soon as it is delivered to him and, subject to the *Lawrence* (C.A.) principle,[9] it is difficult to see how he can be guilty of theft. But although the civil authorities are so nearly unanimous, they are not really strong; for the cases are few and far between and in the great majority of them the result would have been the same whether the transaction was void or voidable. It is, moreover, difficult to see how the term "voidable" can properly be applied to this situation. A transaction between A and B is voidable when it is liable to be set aside on A's bringing it to the notice of B that he wishes to avoid the transaction. But where D has got property from P by duress (unlike fraud), he knows very well from the start that P wishes to avoid the transaction. In the case put at the beginning of this paragraph, D would probably expect P to go to the police as soon as he was free from the threat. Yet a voidable transaction which is avoided *ab initio* is indistinguishable from one which is void. Such a case, it is submitted, is rightly treated as void. Moreover, the authorities on robbery and on s. 30 of the Larceny Act 1916[10] are difficult to support except on the basis that at least some sorts of duress and intimidation make transactions void.

It should finally be noted that these difficulties might be overcome by charging blackmail under s. 21, where it would seem to be immaterial whether the transaction be void or voidable provided only that the demand be "un-warranted".

(g) *Appropriation by a handler of stolen goods*

[**41**] The wide definition of theft seems to mean that every person who would have been a receiver of stolen goods under the old law and almost every-one who is a "handler" under the new law will be guilty of theft. One who dishonestly receives stolen goods is plainly appropriating the property of another; and the various other forms of handling would seem generally to amount either to an appropriation or the aiding and abetting of an appropri-ation.

---

[8] (1881), 8 Q.B.D. 185.
[9] Above, para. [**33**].
[10] *Cf.* A. Hooper, "Larceny by Intimidation", [1965] Crim. L.R. 532 and 592.

Theft could conveniently have swallowed the law of receiving stolen goods but the wider concept of handling is retained as a separate offence carrying a higher penalty. Where D's act constitutes both offences[11] presumably the appropriate charge is handling.

(h) Appropriation by a purchaser in good faith of stolen goods

[**42**] Section 3 (2) creates an exception to the general rule that appropriation of the property of another is theft. It provides:

"Where property or a right or interest in property is or purports to be transferred for value to a person acting in good faith, no later assumption by him of rights which he believed himself to be acquiring shall, by reason of any defect in the transferor's title, amount to theft of the property".

[**43**] This is designed to except from the law of theft the case where D purchases goods in good faith and for value and then later discovers that the seller had no title and that the goods still belong to a third party, P. P may simply have lost the goods or they may have been stolen from him. Having paid for the goods, D may well, in many cases, be innocent of any crime simply on the ground that he believes he has a right to keep them and is thus not dishonest. But suppose he is enough of a lawyer to appreciate that the goods are not his but P's: he is still not guilty—while he may have *mens rea*, the subsection makes it clear that there is no *actus reus*. The result is otherwise, however, if D has not given value—if the thief has made D a present of the property. If, for example, C purchases the property in good faith from the thief and gives it to D who later discovers the truth and decides to keep it, D is guilty.

The protection afforded by s. 3(2) is limited. D may with impunity keep the goods or give them away to an innocent donee. If, however, he sells the goods to an innocent buyer he will probably be guilty of obtaining the price by the implied deception that he is entitled to sell the goods. If he sells or gives the thing to one who knows it is the property of a third party, the recipient will be guilty of theft (and possibly of handling) and D, it seems, of abetting him. Section 3 (2) does not seem wide enough to exempt him from liability for abetting theft or handling by another of the property.[12]

If D assumes rights over and above those which he believed himself to be acquiring, he may be guilty of theft. If C finds goods in such circumstances that he reasonably believes the owner cannot be discovered by taking reasonable steps, and sells the goods to D who knows these facts, D is aware that he is acquiring only the rights of a finder. If, then, D subsequently discovers who the owner is, a later assumption of a right to keep the thing is the *actus reus* of theft.

[**44**] It should be noted that there is no similar exemption for the *handler* of stolen goods which have been bought in good faith. Suppose D enters into a contract to buy a picture hanging in a gallery, delivery to be made at the end

---

[11] The argument (which was advanced in connection with the Larceny Act 1916—see Russell, 1112 *et seq.*) that the statute must be so construed that the definitions of the offences be mutually exclusive, is clearly untenable in connection with the Theft Act.

[12] *Cf. Sockett* (1908), 1 Cr. App. Rep. 101; and see *Beasley*, [1971] Crim. L.R. 298.

of the exhibition. Unknown to D, the picture has been stolen. Before the end of the exhibition, he discovers the truth, but dishonestly takes delivery of the picture. He is not guilty of theft (s. 3 (2)) but is apparently guilty of handling the picture by receiving it knowing it to be stolen, contrary to s. 22.[13] Section 3 (2) would not exempt *Ashwell*.[14] He took the coin in good faith and for value (his promise to repay) and later (it is arguable) assumed rights of ownership which he believed himself to be acquiring when he received the coin; but his guilt would arise, not from any defect in the transferor's title, for there was none, but from a defect in his own title.

B. APPROPRIATION NOT A CONTINUING ACT

[**45**] "Appropriation" is somewhat similar to the *contrectatio* of the Roman Dutch law of theft, and South African courts have held that this makes theft a "continuing" crime:

> "... the theft continues so long as the stolen property is in the possession of the thief or of some person who was a party to the theft or of some person acting on behalf of or even, possibly, in the interests of the original thief or party to the theft."[15]

It is submitted, however, that appropriation does not "continue" in this way. Section 3 (1)[16] applies only where D has come by the property *without stealing it*. Where D has stolen the property, later exercise of proprietary rights over it, which he has already assumed and not abandoned, will not constitute theft. This view is also supported by s. 22 (1).[17] There the "course of the stealing" is distinguished from subsequent dishonest dealings with the property. It is different where rights are assumed, abandoned and resumed. Where D steals property but leaves it on the owner's premises because his van will not go, his later removal of it may amount to a second theft.[18]

What is the position if D steals property abroad, brings it to this country and exercises proprietary rights over it here? Mere possession in England of property stolen abroad is no longer an offence,[19] though handling it, contrary to s. 22, is. If D does nothing amounting to handling, he can be made liable only if he has committed theft in England. It is possibly arguable that "without stealing it" in s. 3 (1) means "without committing an offence under s. 1 (1) of the Theft Act," in which case there is no problem; D's subsequent appropriation is theft; but s. 24, though not directly applicable, suggests that the theft abroad is regarded by the English law as "stealing."

C. INTENTION AN ESSENTIAL ELEMENT OF APPROPRIATION

[**46**] "Appropriation" is being discussed as the principal constituent of the *actus reus* of theft; but the traditional (and useful) analysis of the crime into *actus reus* and *mens rea* must not be allowed to obscure the fact that, in many if

---

[13] Below, para. [**485**].
[14] Above, para. [**26**], and below, para. [**71**].
[15] *Attia*, [1937] T.P.D. 102 at 106. See Hunt, *South African Criminal Law and Procedure*, II, 603.
[16] Above, para. [**26**].
[17] Below, paras. [**430**] and [**478**]-[**479**].
[18] *Starling*, [1969] Crim. L.R. 556 (C.A.) (Larceny).
[19] Below, para. [**438**].

not all cases, it is impossible to determine whether there has been an appropriation without having regard to the intention with which an act was done. Even if there had been no express provision requiring an intent permanently to deprive, such an intent would probably have been implicit in the notion of appropriation. This may be illustrated by the case of *Holloway*.[20] D broke into the warehouse of his employer, P, and took a number of dressed skins. It was his intention to produce the skins to P's foreman and pretend that he had done the work of dressing them and thereby to get paid for them. He was acquitted of larceny on the ground that he had no intent permanently to deprive P of the skins. On the same ground he would not be guilty of theft; but he would surely also be innocent of the new crime on the more fundamental ground that he had never appropriated the goods since he did not assume the rights of an owner but intended to act only as the servant—which he was—handling his master's goods.

D. ACT OR OMISSION AN ESSENTIAL ELEMENT OF APPROPRIATION

[47] It seems probable that some act or omission is required to constitute an appropriation and that a mere decision in D's mind to assume the rights of an owner is not enough.[1] Appropriation can be performed by omission as well as by act. This seems to be implicit in the provision in s. 3 (1) that a person may appropriate by "keeping . . . as owner" property which he has come by innocently. "Keeping" would not seem necessarily to involve doing any act but to be satisfied by D's omission, with the appropriate intent, to divest himself of possession.

[48] If D's seven-year-old child brings home P's tricycle and D, knowing that the child has come by it unlawfully, does nothing about it,[2] intending that P shall be permanently deprived of the tricycle, it is submitted that this would be theft by D. This might be regarded as an assumption of ownership through the innocent agency of the child who, no doubt, would continue to act as owner. If D were to say to his wife, "Let Richard keep it," this, it is thought, would probably be sufficient assumption of ownership. Even where D does nothing at all, as where sheep stray from P's land on to D's and he simply allows them to remain there,[3] he ought to be guilty if it can be proved that he omitted to act with the appropriate intent. In such circumstances it may, however, be difficult or impossible to prove any such intention and the charge will then fail, not merely on the ground of lack of *mens rea*, but because there was no appropriation.

E. ATTEMPTED THEFT

[49] One result of the wide meaning of appropriation is that attempts to commit theft are likely to be extremely rare. It was argued[4] in *Rogers* v. *Arnott*:

> "One has not heard of attempted fraudulent conversion because if one attempts a fraudulent conversion, one commits the full offence."

It may well be that *any* act done with intent to assume the rights of an

---

[20] (1849), 1 Den. 370; below, para. [136].
[1] Above, para. [25].
[2] *Cf. Walters* v. *Lunt*, [1951] 2 All E.R. 645.
[3] *Cf. Thomas* (1953), 37 Cr. App. Rep. 169.
[4] By Basil Wigoder, [1960] 2 Q.B. at 246–247.

owner amounts to an actual assumption of such rights and, if so, there can be no attempt in the normal run of cases. For instance, an attempt to make an offer—D puts into the post an offer to sell P's tape-recorder which never arrives—appears to be no less an assumption of ownership than a complete offer. More doubtful, perhaps, is the case where D has merely written the letter making the offer and it is still lying on his desk. But if this is not an assumption of ownership it is probably not an attempt to assume ownership either, but a mere act of preparation.

[50] One instance of attempted theft which will certainly continue to exist however, is the celebrated empty pocket case.[5] D puts his hand into P's pocket with intent to steal the contents. The pocket is empty. It cannot now be established that D actually assumed the rights of an owner over any property, since there was no property—but he certainly attempted to do so. The attempt was complete (at the latest) when D's hand entered the pocket and groped for its contents.[6] If D were to find that the pocket contained only an article which he at once rejected—say a piece of string—this could not undo the completed attempt. An indictment for stealing or attempting to steal *the piece of string* however would fail. D never formed an intention to deprive P of the string, nor did he appropriate it or attempt to appropriate it. He examined it to decide whether it was worth appropriating and decided it was not. An indictment for attempting to steal from P, not specifying what was to be stolen, ought to succeed. In *Easom*,[7] D picked up a woman's handbag in a cinema, rummaged through the contents and put it back having taken nothing. The handbag was attached by a thread to a policewoman's wrist. D was convicted of stealing the handbag and the specified contents: tissues, cosmetics, etc. The conviction was quashed because there was no intention permanently to deprive; and, for the same reason, it was held that a conviction for an attempt could not be substituted. The court said "If a dishonest postal-sorter picks up a pile of letters intending to steal any which are registered, but, on finding that none of them are, replaces them, he has stolen nothing . . ." He is guilty of an *attempt* to steal the non-existent registered letters—just as the pickpocket is guilty of an attempt to steal the non-existent contents of the pocket—but he must be acquitted of stealing and of attempting to steal the actual, non-registered letters. Another possible instance of an attempt is indicated in the next paragraph.

F. THE EFFECT OF THE OWNER'S CONSENT TO THE APPROPRIATION

[51] If P consents to D's appropriating his property and D knows this when he appropriates, he does not commit theft because he is not acting dishonestly. Suppose, however, that P in fact consents but D does not know this. If he then appropriates, he does so dishonestly. Under the old law[8] D would not have been guilty of larceny because there was no taking "without the consent of the owner" as required by the Larceny Act 1916 and thus no *actus reus*. Whether D could have been convicted of attempted larceny has been disputed[9]

---

[5] *Cf. Ring* (1892), 17 Cox C.C. 491.
[6] In *Ring*, the evidence was merely that the accused were endeavouring to find the pockets in the dresses of unknown ladies.
[7] [1971] 2 Q.B. 315; [1971] 2 All E.R. 945 (C.A.). *Cf* commentary at [1971] Crim L.R. 488.
[8] *Turvey* (1946), 31 Cr. App. Rep. 154.
[9] [1962] Crim. L. R. 135, 212 and 300.

but in a recent case[10] (in which, with respect, the authorities and the issues were not fully considered) the Court of Criminal Appeal held that it was an attempt. The absence of the owner's consent is not a constituent of theft.[11] If the effect of P's consent was to vest the property in D before his act of appropriation took place, D (subject to the *Lawrence* (C.A.) principle[12]) would not be guilty of theft because he would not have appropriated property *belonging to another*. For example, D appropriates a fountain pen which he believes P has left on his desk by mistake. In fact, P put the pen there intending to make D a gift and thus constituted him the owner.[13] The question whether there is attempted theft would then arise, and according to *Miller and Page*,[14] it should be answered affirmatively. But if, as is more usual, consent was ineffective to pass the property (because there was no intention that it should pass) then D would have dishonestly appropriated the property of another and there seems no reason why he should not be convicted of the full offence. For example, as in *Miller and Page*, P's servant, O, with P's consent agrees to hand over and does hand over P's property to D in order to entrap D. No gift is intended, for P does not intend to part with ownership and D knows it, so D does not become the owner. He is guilty of theft as soon as he appropriates the property.

G. PROPERTY "BELONGING TO ANOTHER"

[52] Theft can be committed only in respect of a specific piece of property and it is essential that that property should belong to another. "Belonging to another" is however widely defined to include almost any legally recognised interest in property. By s. 5 (1) of the Act:

> "Property shall be regarded as belonging to any person having posses-
> sion or control of it, or having in it any proprietary right or interest (not
> being an equitable interest arising only from an agreement to transfer
> or grant an interest)."

[53] Almost anything can be owned, but one exception appears to be a human corpse. There could be no larceny of a corpse at common law.[15] This was not simply a rule of the criminal law (like the rule that dogs could not be stolen) which has died with larceny. It seems to be a rule of the law of property to which we must have recourse in interpreting s. 5 (1). Thus a civil action for detinue and conversion will not lie in respect of a human corpse.[16] No one can have any proprietary right or interest in it. But Kenny points out[17] that:

> "It is not entirely certain whether the rule must be taken to be 'once a
> corpse, always a corpse'; if so the protection of the criminal law would
> perhaps not extend even to skeletons and similar anatomical preparations
> on which great labour has been expended or to ethnological collections of
> skulls and mummies—a conclusion which does not seem reasonable."

---

[10] *Miller and Page* (1965), 49 Cr. App. Rep. 241; *cf. Curbishley* (1971) 55 Cr. App. 310.
[11] *Lawrence* v. *Metropolis Police Commissioner*, [1971] 2 All E.R. 1253 (H.L.); above, para. [32].
[12] Above, para. [33].
[13] *Standing* v. *Bowring* (1885), 31 Ch. D. 282.
[14] Above, footnote 10.
[15] *Handyside*, 2 East P.C. 652; *Sharpe* (1857), Dears. & B. 160.
[16] *Doodeward* v. *Spence* (1907), 9 S.R. (N.S.W.) 107.
[17] *Outlines of Criminal Law* (19th ed.), 294.

[54] As Kenny also points out, anything inserted into or attached to the corpse, such as the wiring of a skeleton or the wrappings of a mummy, could certainly be stolen. It would be unfortunate however, if we were driven to charge the theft of something entirely incidental to the real object of the appropriation—as happened before the Act when men, believed to have stolen a very valuable greyhound, were charged with stealing the coat it was wearing, since the taking of the dog would have been only a summary offence.

[55] It is probable that parts of the living body may be stolen from the living person. Thus, a magistrates' court has held a man guilty of larceny when he cut some hair from a girl's head without her consent[18]: and this seems entirely reasonable. It would be extraordinary if a woman did not own her own hair!

[56] If the property belongs to no one, it cannot be stolen. So if property is abandoned there can be no theft of it. Whether an owner has abandoned his property or not is a question of the intention evinced by him in disposing of his property. If he intends to exclude others from it, he does not abandon it, though it may be clear that he intends to make no further use of it himself. So it will be theft for D to appropriate diseased carcasses which P has buried on his land.[19] A householder does not abandon goods which he puts in his dustbin. *Prima facie*, he intends the goods for the local authority which collects the refuse, so that a dustman may be guilty of theft if he appropriates the goods knowing that he is not entitled to do so.[20] A person who loses property does not necessarily abandon it because he abandons the search for it.[1] The test is whether P has evinced an intention to relinquish his entire interest in the property, without conferring an interest on anyone else. Of course, if D mistakenly believes that P has abandoned his interest in the property, D's appropriation cannot be theft, whether his belief be reasonable or unreasonable, because he is not dishonest.[2]

(a) Ownership, possession and control

[57] Since the law protects all interests in property, it is clear that a person with a greater interest in a specific chattel can be guilty of theft from a person with a lesser interest in the same chattel. As was the case with larceny[3], an owner in the strict sense can be guilty of stealing his own property from one who has mere possession or custody of it. For example, D pledges his watch with P as security for a loan but takes it back again without repaying P and without his consent. This is an appropriation by D of property which belongs to P for the purposes of the section. The position is precisely the same where D bids for a car at an auction, it is knocked down to him and he then induces P, the auctioneer, by deception to let him have possession of the car.[4] The car became D's property on the fall of the hammer but P retained his seller's lien for the price and D has therefore appropriated P's property. As noted above,

---

[18] (1960), *The Times*, December 22.
[19] *Edwards* (1877), 13 Cox C.C. 384.
[20] *Williams* v. *Phillips* (1957), 41 Cr. App. Rep. 5.
[1] *Cf. Hibbert* v. *McKiernan*, [1948] 2 K.B. 142.
[2] Below, para. **[118]**.
[3] *Cf. Rose* v. *Matt*, [1951] 1 K.B. 810.
[4] *Dennant* v. *Skinner*, [1948] 2 K.B. 164.

however, it would be desirable in such a situation to charge deception under s. 15 (1) rather than theft.

[**58**] The owner may steal from his bailee at will. Though he has a right to terminate the bailment at any time, he will be guilty of theft if he simply dishonestly appropriates the bailed chattel. It is only in exceptional cases that the problem will arise, because it will usually be clear that the bailor had a claim of right to recover possession. In *Turner (No.* 2),[5] however, D, who had delivered his car to P to be repaired, took it back, dishonestly intending not to pay for the repairs which P had carried out. In truth, P probably was not a mere bailee at will, having a lien on the car. But the judge directed the jury that they were not concerned with liens and so the Court of Appeal had to decide the appeal on the basis that there was no lien. An argument that P's possession as a bailee at will was insufficient, was rejected. The court said there was no ground for qualifying the words "possession or control" in any way.

It looks a little odd that, where D has a better right to possession than P, he can nevertheless commit theft by the exercise (however dishonestly) of that "right." It might have been thought that a thing does *not* belong to a possessor, P, as against D who has an immediate right to take possession from him. Possibly *Turner (No.* 2) may be explained by holding that a bailor has no right, even in the civil law, to take back the chattel bailed, without notice to the bailee at will.

Suppose D's car is stolen by P, and D later finds the car standing outside P's house (or the house of a *bona fide* purchaser. P). D has, of course, a right to take it back. But suppose he does not know this, and thinks that a court order is necessary to enable him lawfully to resume possession. Believing that he has no right in law to do so (i.e. dishonestly), he takes the car. According to *Turner (No.* 2), he is guilty of theft. If he were convicted and the court asked to exercise its power to order the car to be restored to the person entitled to it,[6] the incongruous result would be that the car should be given to the convicted thief, who was and always had been the person entitled to it. Perhaps the decision in *Turner (No.* 2) would not be pressed so far.

[**59**] Similar problems arise where D retains possession as well as ownership and P has that lower interest which is described as "control" in the Act. D, an employer, entrusts his employee, P, with goods for use in the course of his employment. D continues both to own and to possess the goods; but, if he dishonestly deprives P of control, he may, to the same extent as the bailor at will, be guilty of theft. It was larceny at common law for a master who had entrusted money to his servant, to re-take it, intending to charge the hundred for an alleged theft. So if today an employer takes his own property from the custody of his servant, intending to claim against his insurers for its loss, he might be held to have stolen it. The more natural charge would be under s. 15; but he might not have reached the stage of an attempt to obtain by deception.

---

5 [1971] 2 All E.R. 441; [1971] Crim L.R. 373.
6 See s. 28(1), below, para. [**503**].

[60] Where the property belongs to more than one person, as may easily occur under s. 5 (1), and D appropriates it for himself, it follows that he may be convicted of stealing it from any one of the persons to whom it belongs. P lets a lawn-mower on hire to Q who hands it over to his servant, R, to mow the lawn. P remains the owner, Q remains in possession as bailee and R has control. If D now appropriates the lawn-mower for himself, he commits theft from all three of them. If, in order to appropriate the lawn-mower, he uses force on R, he commits robbery from P, Q and R.[7]

(b) Equitable interests

[61] It is clear that equitable as well as legal interests are protected. If T, a trustee, holds a painting on trust for P, and D appropriates it, this is theft not only from the legal owner, T, but also from the equitable owner, P. Equally, if T appropriates the picture it will be theft by him from P.

[62] Excluded from the protection of the law is "an equitable interest arising only from an agreement to transfer or grant an interest". If D, the owner of land, enters into a specifically enforceable contract to sell it to P, an equitable interest in the land passes to P, and D is, in some respects, a trustee of the property for P. If D were to sell the land to a third party, it might have been held, but for the provision under consideration, that this was theft of the land under s. 4 (2) (a).[8] If, after D has contracted to sell to P, a third party, E, enters on the land and appropriates something forming part of the land by severing it, this will be theft from D but, because of the provision under consideration, it will not be theft from P. An equitable interest similarly passes to the buyer under a specifically enforceable agreement to buy shares. The seller who dishonestly re-sells is protected.[9]

[63] A contract for the sale of goods may be a sale or an agreement to sell. If it is a sale, the legal interest passes to the buyer and a re-sale by the seller who remains in possession may thus constitute theft from the buyer.[10] If however, it is an *agreement* to sell, the buyer usually acquires neither a legal, nor (since contracts for the sale of goods are generally not specifically enforceable) an equitable interest,[11] so the provision will not generally be required in such cases. It may be, however, that in the exceptional case where a contract for the sale of goods is specifically enforceable, an equitable interest does pass to the buyer before the legal ownership does so. Again, it is clear that there can be no theft from the buyer. The reason for this provision probably is that an action for breach of contract is a sufficient sanction against a person who, having contracted to sell to X, re-sells in breach of contract to Y. Such conduct is, perhaps, not generally thought to be more reprehensible than other breaches of contract. It is probably incidental that an appropriation by a third party is not a theft from the buyer; but this is not serious since it is inevitably a theft from the seller.

---

[7] See s. 8 of the Act. At common law, it would have been robbery only from R, and similarly under the Larceny Acts. *Cf. Harding* (1929), 21 Cr. App. Rep. 166.

[8] Below, para. [84].

[9] Gower, *Modern Company Law* (3rd ed.), 349, n. 25.

[10] See below, paras. [113]—[115].

[11] *Re Wait*, [1927] 1 Ch. 606.

(c) Co-owners and partners

[**64**] D and P are co-owners of a car. D sells the car without P's consent. Since P has a proprietary right in the car, it belongs to him under s. 5 (1). The position is precisely the same where a partner dishonestly appropriates the partnership property. Whether or not his conduct constitutes the tort of conversion, it is theft.[12]

(d) Trustee and beneficiary

[**65**] Conversion by a trustee was a special offence under s. 21 of the Larceny Act 1916. Now it is ordinary theft. The beneficiary, by definition, has a proprietary interest in the trust property and any act of appropriation of it by the trustee is theft.

The restrictions on the prosecution of trustees which existed in the Larceny Act, have been repealed.

Section 5 (2) provides:

"Where property is subject to a trust, the persons to whom it belongs shall be regarded as including any person having a right to enforce the trust, and an intention to defeat the trust shall be regarded accordingly as an intention to deprive of the property any person having that right."

Where the trust is a charitable one, its object is to effect some purpose beneficial to the public, rather than to benefit particular individuals. Such trusts are enforceable by the Attorney-General, and an appropriation of the trust property by a charitable trustee will, accordingly, be regarded as theft from that officer.

[**66**] Trusts for the purpose of erecting or maintaining monuments[13] or maintaining animals[14] have been held valid, though unenforceable for lack of a human beneficiary or a charitable intent. If the trustee of such a trust were to appropriate the funds for himself it would seem clear that he would commit theft from anyone who was entitled to the residue. If the trustee were himself entitled to the residue, he could not commit theft, since he would be, in effect, the absolute and exclusive owner of the property.

(e) P's right that D shall retain and deal with property

[**67**] There are other cases which would have amounted to fraudulent conversion under the old law where D is an owner but where there is only doubtfully a proprietary right or interest in P. These are brought within the scope of theft by s. 5 (3):

"Where a person receives property from or on account of another, and is under an obligation to the other to retain and deal with that property or its proceeds in a particular way, the property or proceeds shall be regarded (as against him) as belonging to the other."

It will be noticed that the obligation must be to deal with *that property* in a particular way. Therefore the appropriation of an advance payment for

---

[12] *Bonner*, [1970] 2 All E.R. 97.
[13] *Trimmer* v. *Danby* (1856), 25 L.J. Ch. 424; *Re Hooper*, [1932] 1 Ch. 38.
[14] *Pettingall* v. *Pettingall* (1842), 11 L.J. Ch. 176; *Re Dean* (1889), 41 Ch. D. 552.

work to be done by D will be theft only if the money was given with an obligation to use it for a specific purpose. In this respect, the Act seems to reproduce the old law of fraudulent conversion.[15]

[68] Suppose, for example, D agrees to paint P's house for £50 and simply asks for "an advance payment of £10". If he appropriates the £10 to his own use this will not be theft for P has no proprietary right or interest in it nor is D under any obligation to deal with *that* property in any particular way.

The result should be different where D agrees to paint P's house and asks for £10 *to buy the paint* which he will use on the job. If he appropriates the £10, it is submitted that this now will be theft.[16] Similar situations arise where D employs P and requires him to deposit a sum of money as security for his honesty. If the terms of the arrangement are that D can do what he likes with the money then D cannot steal it[17] but if, as is more likely, D has agreed to retain the money, as by depositing it at a bank,[18] then it is capable of being stolen.

Similarly where D is a debt-collector who is required by the terms of his contract to hand over the money he collects, less a certain percentage, to the creditors: if he is under an obligation to keep in existence a separate fund, then the money he receives is capable of being stolen.[19] If however, the arrangement with the creditors is such that D is merely their debtor to the extent of the debts collected, less commission, the money he receives from the debtors is his and he is under no obligation to deal with *that* money in a particular way. It is a question of the construction of the contract between the debt-collector and the creditors.

[69] The following cases, however, do not amount to theft:

D, a bargee employed by P, uses P's barge without P's authority to carry O's goods and receives a fee from O which he keeps for himself.[20] D is under a duty to *account* to P for the sum so earned but in the meantime he owns it— he is P's debtor—he is under a duty to pay P a certain amount of money, but he is under no obligation to retain and deal with the particular notes received in any way.

D, who is P's agent, receives a bribe in return for acting in a certain manner in P's business. He is liable to account to P for the amount of the bribe but he does not commit theft by keeping the money for himself.[1]

(f) An obligation to make restoration of property

[70] Suppose that D acquires possession of property by another's mistake and is liable (a question of civil law) to account to P for the value of the property

---

[15] See [1961] Crim. L.R. 741, 797.

[16] *Cf. Jones* (1948), 33 Cr. App. Rep. 11; *Bryce* (1955), 40 Cr. App. Rep. 62; *Hughes,* [1956] Crim. L.R. 835.

[17] As in *Hotine* (1904), 68 J.P. 143.

[18] As in *Smith,* [1924] 2 K.B. 194.

[19] *Lord* (1905), 69 J.P. 467.

[20] *Cf. Cullum* (1873), L.R. 2 C.C.R. 28; the *Report,* Cmnd. 2977, para. 38; and (1956), 19 M.L.R. 39, but D may now be guilty of an offence under s. 12: below, para. **[312]**.

[1] P has no proprietary interest in the money: *Lister* v. *Stubbs* (1890), 45 Ch. D. 1; and O does not get the property by another's mistake under s. 5 (4), para. **[70]**, below.

so obtained. The ownership in the property may pass to D, or it may remain in P, depending on the character of the mistake. If the ownership remains in P, then, under the rules already discussed, D may steal the property: but if the ownership passes to D then P retains no proprietary right or interest and (subject to the *Lawrence* (C.A.) principle[2]) D can commit no offence under the provisions so far discussed. Such a case is, however, covered by s. 5 (4) which provides:

> "Where a person gets property by another's mistake, and is under an obligation to make restoration (in whole or in part) of the property or its proceeds or of the value thereof, then to the extent of that obligation the property or proceeds shall be regarded (as against him) as belonging to the person entitled to restoration, and an intention not to make restoration shall be regarded accordingly as an intention to deprive that person of the property or proceeds."

[71] This provision is obviously apt to cover such a case as *Ashwell*:[3]

P, in the dark, gave D a sovereign in mistake for a shilling. When, some time later, D discovered that he had a sovereign and not a shilling, he at once decided to keep it for himself. Likewise with the case of *Middleton*:[4]

P, a post office clerk, referred to the wrong letter of advice and handed to D, a depositor in the Post Office Savings Bank, a sum which ought to have gone to another depositor. D took it, knowing that it was a much larger sum than he was entitled to.

In neither of these cases, however, is s. 5 (4) strictly necessary. In *Ashwell*, it was implicit in the decision (and rightly so) that no property in the sovereign passed to D (a sovereign is necessarily a different coin from a shilling—it was a mistake of identity)—so D today would be guilty of appropriating property belonging to another under s. 1 (1) and s. 3 (1) of the Act.[5] The basis of *Middleton* too was that no property in the money passed to D because of a mistake as to the identity either of the deposit or of the depositor. If, however, *Ashwell* and *Middleton* should have been wrongly decided (because the property did pass)—and both have been criticised[6]—s. 5 (4) makes it quite clear that under the Act, persons who act as they did should nevertheless be convicted. Even if the property in the money did pass to D in each of those cases, it is clear that D would be under an obligation to make restoration, if not of the actual property or its proceeds, at least of its value; and therefore the property would be treated as belonging to P. The only slight distinction is this: Middleton received £8 16s. 10d. and was convicted of stealing that sum—rightly on the basis of mistake of identity. He was, however entitled to 10s. and, if the property had passed, he would under the Act be guilty of stealing only £8 6s. 10d.—the amount which he was bound to restore.

[72] The real object of s. 5 (4) however (or, at least of that part of it which deals with the value of the goods) is to get rid of the decision in *Moynes* v.

---

2 Above, para. [33].
3 (1885), 16 Q.B.D. 190.
4 (1873), L.R. 2 C.C.R. 38.
5 Above, paras. [18]–[20].
6 Russell, 970–974, 979–982, 1553–1574.

Coopper.[7] D, a labourer, had received most of his week's wages in advance from his employer. It was the employer's intention to tell the wages clerk to deduct the amount of the advance when paying D at the end of the week. He forgot to do so. The clerk therefore gave D a packet containing the full amount of his wages. D did not discover this until he arrived home when he opened the envelope and, knowing he was not entitled to it, decided to keep the whole sum. The divisional court dismissed the prosecutor's appeal on the ground that D had no larcenous intent at the time of taking as required by the Larceny Act 1916. This is no longer a problem: see s. 3 (1). The Court of Quarter Sessions (chairman, Mr. Thesiger, Q.C.), however, had acquitted Moynes on the more fundamental grounds that (*a*) D received ownership in the money and (*b*) D took the money with the consent of the owner. These were valid grounds.[8] The wages clerk, no doubt, had a general authority to pay each workman the weekly wage due to him. You do not revoke your agent's authority by deciding to do so and then forgetting about it. When the clerk handed the wages packet to D it seems clear that he transferred to him both ownership and possession in the money. In that case, it was quite impossible for D to be guilty of larceny of the money and it was really irrelevant (as Mr. Thesiger decided) whether D decided to keep the money for himself at the wages table, or later wnen he got home. No one else had any legal interest in the money—D was merely under a quasi-contractual obligation to repay to his employer an equivalent sum. He was in fact merely a particular kind of debtor. On such an analysis, there is a good deal to be said in favour of Moynes's acquittal; but few cases have attracted so much adverse criticism and it is hardly surprising that it was thought necessary to bring this case within the new law of theft; and s. 5 (4) (and particularly the words "or the value thereof") does so. Though the money would still be D's, a notional property in it would be vested in P for the purposes of this Act; and D's intention not to repay would be regarded as an intention to deprive P of the money.

[**73**] There remains the necessity for an appropriation—it will be noted that s. 5 (4) does not itself create any offence—and this must be an appropriation of the property which was given by mistake or its proceeds. Suppose that Moynes had given his pay packet to E without opening it and been informed later of how much it contained. His resolution not to make repayment would not make him guilty of any offence, for there would be no appropriation. It would be otherwise if E repaid him the sum by which the actual contents of the packet exceeded the supposed contents and D retained that. He would then have appropriated the proceeds. Suppose that D had opened the packet and, forgetting for the moment about his "sub.", bought a bicycle with the money. Since he was under an obligation to make restoration of the value, it would seem that the bicycle would be deemed to belong to his employer. Suppose D then realised the mistake had been made: any act of appropriation of the bicycle would seem to make him guilty of an *actus reus*—but dishonesty might be hard to establish in such a case.

---

[7] [1956] 1 Q.B. 439, criticised in [1956] Crim. L.R. 516.

[8] This is implicitly recognised by the Act which, by s. 5 (4), circumvents ground (*b*). Ground (*a*) has become irrelevant with the disappearance of trespass as a constituent of stealing.

[74] If Moynes, not appreciating the mistake, had spent the whole of the contents of the wages packet on beer which was consumed by himself and his workmates, he could not thereafter be guilty of any offence. After learning of the mistake, the intention not to restore would provide *mens rea* but there would be nothing which could be the subject of an appropriation. He would be simply a recalcitrant debtor.

[75] Plainly, s. 5 (4) extends the scope of stealing. Bringing Moynes within the net inevitably involves bringing in a number of others whose activities have not generally been thought of as criminal. For example, P pays money to D under the mistaken belief that the property of D has been lost through a peril insured against. D receives the money under the same belief.[9] Or P pays money to D under a contract for the sale of a fishery. In fact the fishery already belongs to P.[10] In both these cases, D discovers the truth and resolves not to make restoration. In legal analysis, D's situation is indistinguishable from that of Moynes: he has received money under a mistake and is under an obligation to make restoration of the value thereof. Plainly, then, the money (notionally) belongs to P in both these cases and (if D's resolution not to repay can be regarded as dishonest) D is guilty of theft if he appropriates the money or the proceeds (e.g. the Rolls Royce which he has bought with it). Only if the money cannot be traced into some property in his possession will he be exempt. Whether such cases are wisely brought within the net of theft is questionable but it is the inevitable result of covering the *Moynes* situation. The difficulty is, essentially, one of making a thief of a particular kind of debtor when debtors generally cannot steal. And it can involve the criminal law in some of the finest distinctions drawn in the civil law. Suppose that P wishes to terminate the employment of his servant, D. Both P and D believe that a binding contract of service exists between them and P pays D £30,000 to be released from his obligation to continue to employ D. The parties then discover that P could (and, had he known the truth, would) have dismissed D without paying him a penny, since D had committed breaches of contract which were unknown to P and not present to D's mind when he accepted the £30,000. D then appropriates the £30,000. If, as the Court of Appeal held,[11] D was under an obligation to restore the value of £30,000, this would be the *actus reus* of theft by D; but as the House of Lords held[12] that there was no such obligation, it is no offence. It may be that all of the cases discussed in this paragraph would founder from the inability to prove a dishonest intention; yet these recipients of money are, in law, in no different situation from Moynes himself.

(g) *The meaning of "obligation"*

[76] The word "obligation", in s. 5 (4) can hardly be supposed to mean anything other than a legal obligation. In an unreported case, D placed a bet for a small sum with a bookmaker, P. The horse backed won and D was entitled to receive 44s. Because of a mistaken calculation he was paid £26 4s. He

---

[9] *Cf. Norwich Union, Fire Insurance Society, Ltd.* v. *Price*, [1934] A.C. 455.
[10] *Cooper* v. *Phibbs* (1867), L.R. 2 H.L. 149. It is assumed for the purpose of this example that the contract was void.
[11] *Lever Bros., Ltd.* v. *Bell*, [1931] 1 K.B. 557. The Court of Appeal thought the contract was void.
[12] *Bell* v. *Lever Bros., Ltd.*, [1932] A.C. 161.

refused to repay the excess and was charged with theft of £24. The learned chairman of Quarter Sessions ruled that the facts did not amount to theft and directed an acquittal. No doubt this result followed because money paid in such circumstances is not recoverable in a civil court. In *Morgan* v. *Ashcroft*[13] the Court of Appeal held (i) that, since the Gaming Act 1845 makes wagering transactions void, the court could not examine the state of account between the parties and (ii) that money paid under a mistake is recoverable only if the mistake was as to a fact which, if true, would have made the payer legally liable to pay.

Thus there is no redress in civil or criminal law against a client who is accidentally overpaid by a bookmaker. The same principle no doubt governs other cases where the transaction is void or illegal by statute or at common law. If this is a defect in the law, the fault lies with the civil law and not with the Theft Act. If the civil law says that the defendant is the exclusive owner of the money and under no obligation to repay even an equivalent sum, it would be incongruous for the criminal law to say he had stolen it.

[**77**] It may be of interest to note that if the bet had been placed with the "Tote" the result would have been different. Such a bet is not a wager, since the Tote can neither win nor lose.[14] The bet is an enforceable contract. An overpaid invester no doubt is under an obligation to repay and his dishonest refusal to do so will amount to theft.

(h) A right to rescind is not property

[**78**] Where D gets property from P by deception he gets it "by another's mistake". If P is not deceived, the offence is not committed. All cases of obtaining by deception contrary to s. 15 (1)[15] are thus cases in which D gets property by another's mistake. This is the second ground on which it has been argued[16] that almost all cases falling within s. 15 are theft contrary to s. 1 (1). Even if the *Lawrence* (C.A.) principle[17] is invalid, the same result may follow through s. 5 (4). This was plainly not intended by the Committee, and, since it would have the effect of making s. 15 substantially redundant, it may be argued that it was not the intention of Parliament either. So it has been argued that "Reading the Act as a whole it is probably necessary to exclude most obtaining by deception from the sphere of theft, i.e. to treat the word 'mistake' in section 5 (4) as meaning 'mistake not induced by the dishonest deception of the accused'."[18] The difficulty about this view is that it involves reading into the Act words which are not there. It is submitted, however, that a proper construction of the words which are there excludes the typical case of a s. 15 offence from the operation of s. 5 (4) and so from theft.

[**79**] The question is whether D, having obtained property by deception, is under an obligation to make restoration of the property or its proceeds or its value. In most cases there will be a voidable contract between P and D.

---

[13] [1938] 1 K.B. 49.
[14] *Tote Investors, Ltd.* v. *Smoker*, [1968] 1 Q.B. 509; [1967] 3 All E.R. 242 (C.A.).
[15] Below, para. [**170**].
[16] See Roy Stuart, "Law Reform and Reform of the Law of Theft" (1967), 30 M.L.R. 609.
[17] Above, para. [**33**].
[18] Griew, 2-18.

A voidable contract has all the effects of a perfect contract until it is avoided by rescission. Generally, P can avoid only by giving notice to D of his intention to do so. When the right to rescind has lapsed, as it does if it is not exercised promptly, it is indistinguishable from a perfect contract. Until that occurs P certainly has the power to subject D to an obligation to make restoration, but that is not the same thing as a present obligation. The Act says "is", not "may be", under an obligation. D is under no obligation to repay until P does a positive act, which he may never do, or may not do until it is too late to be legally effective.[19]

Until the voidable contract is avoided it would seem that D is under no obligation to make restoration to P. If that is correct, D's retaining or dealing with the property cannot amount to theft. He is not appropriating property belonging to P since, under the voidable contract, the property has passed to D and it is his own property that he is retaining or dealing with; nor is the property to "be regarded as" belonging to P under s. 5 (4) since D is under no obligation to make restoration. Where a legal transaction other than a contract is induced by deception,—for example, a gift—it is presumably again voidable, and the same considerations apply.

[80] There are cases of obtaining by deception, however, where the deception induces a mere payment or transfer of property, unaccompanied by any new voidable transaction. This occurs where the payment is made supposedly in pursuance of an existing valid transaction. This is the situation in the example based on *Norwich Union* v. *Price*.[20] The mistake led to no new legal transaction but to a payment supposedly in pursuance of an existing insurance contract. It is thought that, in these circumstances, P has an immediate right to repayment; there is no transaction to be set aside.[21] Suppose then that P's mistake had been induced by D's deception. D would, of course, be guilty of an offence under s. 15, but he would also, it would seem, be guilty of theft by virtue of s. 5 (4).

Again if, for example, Moynes had induced the pay clerk's mistake by telling him that he had not received an advance payment, he would still be guilty of theft, as well as of obtaining by deception. Thus the question is not whether or not there was any deception. It is: Was the mistake (whether induced by deception or not) such that D was, there and then, under an obligation to repay? If so, it is theft. Otherwise, it is not.

[81] Where there is a voidable contract or other transaction and P has avoided it, the matter is entirely different. The property now does belong to P and D's keeping it or dealing with it as owner is an appropriation of property belonging to another. There is no need to rely on s. 5 (4) to vest a fictitious property in P since he is now once again the owner under the civil law.

---

[19] See the criticism of this argument by P. Glazebrook in 10 S.P.T.L.J. (N.S.) 299 at 300. Mr. Glazebrook argues that there is a quasi-contractual action to recover property obtained by fraud which is unaffected by the victim's ability to rescind the contract. *Sed. qu.?* A quasi-contractual action will not lie while there exists an inconsistent contract.

[20] [1934] A.C. 455., above, para. [75], footnote 9.

[21] The statute of limitations would begin to run against P immediately; whereas, in the case of the voidable transaction, it would run only from the time when the transaction was avoided.

[82] If, as will usually be the case, D has put it out of P's power to communicate his intention to rescind, P may rescind the contract by overt acts falling short of communication.[1] D may therefore commit the *actus reus* of theft by retaining or dealing with the property even though he does not know that the contract has been rescinded. Has he the necessary *mens rea* in such a case? Of course, he is dishonest throughout and undoubtedly intends to deprive P permanently of his property. The difficulty is that he does not know of the facts which, in law, give P property in the goods. It is submitted that D has a sufficient *mens rea*. Unless he happens to be a lawyer or a law student he will not appreciate the niceties of the problem discussed in this paragraph or the nature of P's interest. If he were asked to whom the property belonged, however, and he were to answer truthfully, he would probably say that it belonged to P. The fact probably is that D intends to deprive P of his interest in it, whatever that interest may be. This should be enough.

H. WHAT CAN BE STOLEN

[83] Stealing is the dishonest appropriation of property and, by s. 4 (1):
> " 'Property' includes money and all other property, real or personal, including things in action and other intangible property."

It should be noted at once that this definition is highly qualified, so far as land and wild creatures are concerned, by subsections (2), (3) and (4) of s. 4.[2] Under the old law, there could be no theft of land, things in action or other intangible property or wild creatures while at large. The point about the first two cases was that there could be no taking and carrying away. Land was regarded as an immovable and things in action had no physical existence. The difficulty with wild creatures at large was that they had no owner. Each of these items requires separate consideration.

(a) Land

[84] Now that the requirement of taking and carrying away has disappeared from the law, the technical obstacle to land being the subject of theft has disappeared. Land has always been a possible subject of fraudulent conversion and, since fraudulent conversion has now been swallowed by theft, it was essential that land should, in some circumstances at least, be stealable. It would have been possible to leave s. 4 (1) unqualified and a perfectly workable law would have resulted. The Committee, for reasons of policy, decided against this course. Section 4 (2) provides:
> "A person cannot steal land, or things forming part of land and severed from it by him or by his directions, except in the following cases, that is to say—
> (a) when he is a trustee or personal representative, or is authorised by power of attorney, or as liquidator of a company, or otherwise, to sell or dispose of land belonging to another, and he appropriates the land or anything forming part of it by dealing with it in breach of the confidence reposed in him; or

---

[1] *Car and Universal Finance Co., Ltd.* v. *Caldwell*, [1965] 1 Q.B. 525.
[2] Below, paras. [84], [94] and [99].

(*b*) when he is not in possession of the land and appropriates anything forming part of the land by severing it or causing it to be severed, or after it has been severed; or

(*c*) when, being in possession of the land under a tenancy, he appropriates the whole or part of any fixture or structure let to be used with the land.

For purposes of this subsection 'land' does not include incorporeal hereditaments; 'tenancy' means a tenancy for years or any less period and includes an agreement for such a tenancy, but a person who after the end of a tenancy remains in possession as statutory tenant or otherwise is to be treated as having possession under the tenancy, and 'let' shall be construed accordingly."

It may be helpful to spell out the possible liability of the various categories of persons in detail.

(*i*) *Trustees, personal representatives, and others authorised to dispose of land belonging to another*

[85] Any of these persons may steal the land or anything forming part of it by dealing with it in breach of the confidence reposed in him. So if he sells or gives away the land or any fixture or structure forming part of it, he commits theft.

(*ii*) *Other persons not in possession*

[86] Such a person may steal only by severing, or causing to be severed, or obtaining severance of the thing in question. A purported sale by such a person of the land would not be theft. An attempt to sever, as by starting to dig out a sapling, is an assumption of ownership which is not a sufficient appropriation, though no doubt an attempt to steal.

The rule formerly was that a person could not be convicted of stealing anything which he had severed from the realty (subject to specific statutory exceptions) unless he first abandoned and then re-took possession. Under the Act the general rule is that a person who is not in possession of land can steal fixtures, growing things and even the substance of the land itself, if, in each case, he first severs it from the realty. The following acts, which would not (or may not) have been larceny under the old law, are theft under the new:

D enters upon land in the possession of P and (i) demolishes a brick wall and carries away the bricks; (ii) removes a stone statue fixed in the land; (iii) digs sand from a sand pit and takes it away; (iv) cuts grass growing on the land[3] and at once loads it onto a cart to drive away; (v) takes away P's farm gate.[4]

Outside the law of theft remains the case where D appropriates land without severing it as where he moves his boundary fence so as to incorporate a strip of P's land into his own.[5]

---

[3] *Cf. Foley* (1889), 17 Cox C.C. 142.
[4] *Cf. Skujins*, [1956] Crim. L.R. 266.
[5] The arguments for and against making land the subject of theft are summarised in the *Report*, Cmnd. 2977 at pp. 21-22.

(iii) Other persons in possession as tenants

[87] If a tenant removes a fixture—for example a washbasin or fireplace—he may be guilty of stealing it. Likewise if he removes any structure—for example a shed or greenhouse which is fixed to the land. If the structure is resting on its own weight and not a fixture then it is, of course, stealable under the general rule and there is no need to rely on 4 (2) (c). But the tenant will not be guilty if he digs soil or sand from the land and appropriates that. This exemption applies only to the person in possession of the land. If his wife or a member of the family were to dig and sell sand, it would seem that s. 4 (2) (b) would be applicable and theft would be committed. In such a case, there is some authority for suggesting that the husband could be convicted as an aider and abettor.[6] If the husband were the principal in the act it is possible that anyone assisting him might be held liable as an aider and abettor, even though he could not himself be convicted.[7]

(iv) Other persons in possession otherwise than as tenants

[88] A person may be in possession of a land as a licensee.[8] Curiously, he is not within the terms of s. 4 (2) (c) and so is incapable of stealing the land or anything forming part of it. He thus commits no offence if he dishonestly appropriates fixtures or digs sand or ore from the land. This appears to be an oversight in the Act. He of course may be guilty of stealing structures not forming part of the land.

[89] It may still occasionally be important to determine whether a particular article forms part of the land. Generally appropriation will involve severance, so non-possessors will be caught by s. 4 (2) (b) while tenants are caught by s. 4 (2) (c). But if a licensee in possession appropriates a structure, it is vital to know whether it forms part of the land. This is a question of the law of land and the answer depends on the degree of annexation and the object of annexation. The chattel must be actually fixed to the land, not for its more convenient use as a chattel, but for the more convenient use of the land.

[90] Incorporeal hereditaments[9] are now stealable. The most important of these are easements, profits and rents. The main purpose of the provision would seem to be to cover the theft of a rent-charge. No doubt this was the subject of fraudulent conversion under the old law, and called for a provision of this kind. But instances of theft of the other interests can only be extremely rare. For example, P has a right of way over O's land—an easement. D executes a deed purporting to relieve O's land of the burden of the easement. Or D, a tenant of P's land, purporting to be the freeholder, allows O, the adjoining landowner to erect a building which will necessarily obstruct the flow of light to windows on P's land which have an easement of light. These acts seem to be appropriations of the easement which, if done with the necessary *mens rea* will amount to theft. The most obvious instances will be those where a trustee

6 *Sockett* (1908), 1 Cr. App. Rep. 101.
7 *Cf. Bourne* (1952), 36 Cr. App. Rep. 125; Smith and Hogan, 91–94.
8 *Errington* v. *Errington and Woods*, [1952] 1 K.B. 290; [1952] 1 All E.R. 149; See Cheshire, *Modern Law of Real Property* (10th ed.), 101; and Megarry and Wade (3rd ed.), 624-625.
9 See Cheshire, *Modern Law of Real Property* (10th ed.), 100.

or personal representative disposes of an easement, profit or rent for his own benefit. These cases are not covered by s. 4 (2) (*a*) but incorporeal hereditaments can be stolen by persons generally.

[**91**] It will be noted that these examples relate to existing incorporeal hereditaments. Dishonestly to purport to *create* an easement in the land of another would not seem to amount to an offence unless it is done by one of the persons mentioned in 4 (2) (*a*). In the latter case, such an act would seem to amount to "dealing with the land in breach of the confidence reposed in him".

[**92**] The fact that D's efforts to dispose of an interest in P's land in these cases would be ineffective to do so would not seem to affect the result in the criminal law. When a bailee of goods purports to sell the goods, he is unable (in general) to pass a good title; yet it cannot be doubted that his purporting to do so amounts to an appropriation of the goods. The same is now true of a person who has no proprietary or possessory interest of any sort in the goods. The position must be the same in the case of a purported disposal of an interest in land.[10]

It may be added that where the person purporting to dispose of the interest in land has done so for reward, the simpler and more appropriate course will be to charge him with obtaining or attempting to obtain by deception from the person from whom he seeks the reward. Where D purports to dispose of the interest as a gift, however, the only possible charge will be one of stealing the interest; but such cases are likely to be extremely rare.

[**93**] A rather strange anomaly resulting from the exception of incorporeal hereditaments is that if D, not being one of the persons mentioned in 4 (2) (*a*), purports to dispose of the whole of P's interest in the land (for example, the fee simple) he will not commit theft (though he might be guilty of obtaining the price of the land by deception); whereas if, as in the examples given, he purports to dispose of a comparatively small part of P's interest he will be guilty of theft.

(b) Exception of things growing wild

[**94**] Things growing wild on land undoubtedly fall within the definition of property in the Act and therefore could be stolen by a person not in possession of land if he severed and appropriated them. Section 4 (3), however, provides:

"A person who picks mushrooms growing wild on any land, or who picks flowers, fruit or foliage from a plant growing wild on any land, does not (although not in possession of the land) steal what he picks, unless he does it for reward or for sale or other commercial purpose.

For purposes of this subsection 'mushroom' includes any fungus, and 'plant' includes any shrub or tree."

[**95**] The effect is in general to exempt things growing wild from the law of theft. It will be theft however if:

(i) (Except in the case of a mushroom) D removes the whole plant. For example, he pulls out a primrose or a sapling by the roots. This is not picking *from a plant* and so is not within the exception.

---

[10] The problem of "intention permanently to deprive" is the same as that discussed in connection with *Bloxham*, above, para. [**28**].

(ii) D removes the plant or part of it by an act which cannot be described as "picking". For example, he saws off the top of a Christmas tree growing wild on P's land, or cuts the grass growing wild on P's land with a reaper or a scythe.

(iii) D picks mushrooms or wild flowers, fruit or foliage, for a commercial purpose—for example, mushrooms for sale in his shop or holly to sell from door to door at Christmas. The provision is no doubt intended to be used against depredation on a fairly large scale but it would seem to cover such cases as where D, a schoolboy, picks mushrooms intending to sell them to his mother or the neighbours. It is possible, however, that such a single isolated case might be held not to fall within the law as not being a "commercial" purpose—for it will be noted that the wording of the subsection requires that sale, as well as other purposes, be "commercial". It might be argued that this requires that D, to some extent, must be making a business of dealing in the things in question.

It will, of course, be theft to pick a single *cultivated* flower, wherever it is growing.

(c) *Wild creatures*

[96] The distinction between wild creatures (*ferae naturae*) and tame creatures (*mansuetae naturae*) is a matter of common law.[11] Some tame animals, like dogs and cats, could not be stolen at common law; but now, all tame animals may be stolen. Wild creatures could not, while at large, be stolen at common law or under the Larceny Acts because no one had any property in them until they were taken or killed. The owner of the land on which they happened to be had an exclusive right to take them which was protected by the criminal law relating to poaching but was not protected by the heavier guns of larceny.

[97] When the wild creature was killed or taken, the property in it vested in the owner of the land on which this was done,[12] but the thing was now in the possession of the taker who could not therefore steal it. If, however, he abandoned the thing on P's land, then possession of it vested in P and a subsequent removal of it by D was larceny. Difficult questions could arise whether D had abandoned the creature or not. If he put rabbits into bags or bundles and hid them in a ditch on P's land, he retained possession so that it was no larceny if he returned later and appropriated them;[13] whereas if he merely left the things lying on the surface of the land, this might well have constituted abandonment of the thing.[14]

[98] Though this result was rightly criticised, it was the logical consequence of the rule of the civil law which provided that the thing was owned by no one until it was taken. Had no special provisions been made in the Theft Act for wild animals they could probably have been stolen by virtue of s. 3 (1): though there would have been no appropriation at the instant of taking (because the

---

[11] See East, 2 P.C. 607; Russell, 2, 903.
[12] *Blades* v. *Higgs* (1865), 11 H.L. Cas. 621.
[13] *Townley* (1871), L.R. 1 C.C.R. 315; *Petch* (1878), 14 Cox C.C. 116.
[14] *Cf. Foley* (1889), 17 Cox C.C. 142.

thing was no one's property) any subsequent assumption of ownership (as by carrying the thing away) would have been theft from the owner of the land on which it was taken.

[**99**] For reasons of policy, it was decided that it was undesirable to turn poaching generally into theft; and accordingly, s. 4 (4) provides:

"Wild creatures, tamed or untamed, shall be regarded as property; but a person cannot steal a wild creature not tamed nor ordinarily kept in captivity, or the carcase of any such creature, unless either it has been reduced into possession by or on behalf of another person and possession of it has not since been lost or abandoned, or another person is in course of reducing it into possession."

The effect of s. 4 (4) is that wild creatures cannot be stolen, except in the following cases:

(i) The creature is tamed or ordinarily kept in captivity. For example, P's tame jackdaw, the mink which he keeps in cages, the animals in Whipsnade Zoo. The eagle which escaped some time ago from London Zoo could be stolen while at large, because it was *ordinarily* kept in capitivity. (This phrase seems clearly to refer to the specific animal and not to the species of animal.[15]) Animals, like bees or pigeons, which roam freely are sufficiently reduced into possession if they have acquired a habit of returning to their home (*animus revertendi*).[16] Possession is not lost because they are flying at a distance. If bees swarmed, the common law rule was that the owner retained his proprietary interest only so long as he kept them in sight. If failure to do so constitutes loss of possession, the swarm could be stolen only if the bees could be said to be "tamed" or "ordinarily kept in captivity"—which seems improbable.

(ii) The creature has been reduced into and remains in the possession of another person or is in the course of being so reduced.[17] For example, P, a poacher, takes or is in course of taking a rabbit on O's land. This is not an offence under the Act. D takes the rabbit from P. This is theft by D from both P and O.

Except in these two cases, wild creatures cannot be stolen; so it will not be theft to take mussels from a mussel bed on an area of the foreshore which belongs to P and which P has tended in order to maintain and improve it.[18]

[**100**] The effect is that the poacher who reduces game into possession, abandons it and later resumes possession (so that he was guilty, under the old law, of larceny from the owner of land) no longer commits any offence of theft. The creature has not been reduced into possession by or on behalf of another

---

[15] In *Nye* v. *Niblett*, [1918] 1 K.B. 23, it was held that the words of s. 41 of the Malicious Damage Act 1861 (now repealed, see Criminal Damage Act 1971) ". . . being ordinarily kept . . . for any domestic purpose" referred to the species of animal; but Darling, J. thought the section also protected a particular animal which was kept for a domestic purpose though the class to which it belonged was not ordinarily so kept. In the present section, however, the interpretation actually adopted in *Nye* v. *Niblett* is untenable. Even though the great majority of animals of a particular wild species are ordinarily kept in captivity, a particular wild animal of that species which is and always has been in fact at large, can hardly be stolen.

[16] Blackstone, *Commentaries*, 2, 392-3.

[17] Section 4 (4).

[18] *Howlett and Howlett*, [1968] Crim. L.R. 222.

person. The landowner may have acquired possession when the game was left on his land[19] but it can hardly be said that the reduction into possession was by him or on his behalf. Clearly, this slight narrowing of the law of stealing is of no great significance.

[**101**] If the creature, having been reduced into possession, escapes again (and it is not a creature ordinarily kept in captivity) it cannot be stolen since possession of it has been lost. A more difficult case is that where the possession of the *carcase* of the creature is lost. P, a housewife, buys a pheasant and loses it from her shopping basket on the way home. D picks it up and reads her name and address on the wrapping but determines to keep it for himself. If possession of the pheasant has been lost then D is not guilty and we have a curious case of a particular kind of chattel where there can be no stealing by finding. It is very arguable, however, that even in this case, theft is committed, for the old law of larceny by finding must have proceeded on the assumption that even the person who had lost goods retained possession of them—otherwise there would not have been that trespass which was an essential element of larceny at common law.[20] If that argument is correct, however, then there is another rather anomalous distinction between the loss of a dead wild creature and the loss of a live one—for the Act clearly contemplates that it is possible to lose possession of a wild creature and, even if this is inapplicable to the carcase, it must apply at least to the living animal. This is one of very few instances where possession is important under the Act and, significantly, it presents problems.

(i) Poaching

[**102**] Poaching may amount to an offence under a variety of enactments—the Night Poaching Act 1828, the Game Act 1831 as amended by the Game Laws Amendment Act 1960, and the Poaching Prevention Act 1862. In addition certain provisions relating to the poaching of deer and fish were dealt with in the Larceny Act 1861 and, in view of the decision to repeal the whole of that Act, these are reproduced in the Second Schedule to the Act (below) in a simplified form and with revised maximum penalties. These provisions have been put in the Schedule rather than in the body of the Act to avoid giving the impression that they are intended to be a permanent part of the law of theft.[1] The Criminal Law Revision Committee has suggested that there should be a review of the whole law of poaching followed by comprehensive legislation which would repeal the Second Schedule.[2]

(ii) Criminal Damage

[**103**] The Criminal Damage Act 1971 defines "property" in such a way as to exclude those wild creatures and those growing things which cannot be stolen; so the provisions of the Theft Act cannot be circumvented by a charge of criminal damage.

---

[19] *Hibbert* v. *McKiernan*, [1948] 2 K.B. 142; [1948] 1 All E.R. 860.
[20] "It appears clear on the old authorities that every person who takes a thing upon a finding is civilly a trespasser, except in the one case of a person who finding a thing when it is really lost takes it 'in charity to save it for its owner'": Pollock and Wright on *Possession in the Common Law*, 171.
[1] The *Report*, Cmnd. 2977, para. 53.
[2] *Ibid.*

(d) Things in action

[**104**] Like land, things in action could be the subject of fraudulent conversion, but not of larceny under the old law. Whereas the Act has confined the theft of land substantially though not completely to those cases where it was larcenable under the old law, no such restriction has been imposed in the case of things in action. In practice relatively small numbers of cases might be expected to arise and the great majority of these will be cases of misappropriation by trustees, personal representatives and others, which would have been fraudulent conversion under the old law. The following cases will amount to theft:

D purports to sell the copyright in a book owned by P to O. This is theft of the copyright from P.

D, being in possession of P's books of account which show a credit balance, purports to assign the debts to O. This is theft from P of the book debts.

D, knowing that P has a bank balance of £500, draws a cheque for £400 on the bank in P's name. This is theft from P of a debt of £400 owed by the bank to P.

D purports to sell the right to use a trade mark owned by P to O. This is theft from P of the trade mark.

[**105**] It might be objected that these cases will amount to theft only if D believes he has the power (but not the right) to dispose of the thing in action. Otherwise, it may be said, he has no intention permanently to deprive the owner of it. This is the same argument as that considered above in relation to *Bloxham*[3] and the same answers apply. In each of these cases—as in the examples put concerning land—it would generally be simpler and more appropriate to charge D with obtaining by deception from O. There will be cases where D obtains nothing and a charge of theft may be appropriate and useful. For example:

D, a company secretary, receives signed but otherwise blank cheques from his employers to pay the company's creditors. He uses them to pay debts of his own.[4] This is theft from the company not only of the cheque forms but of the amount by which the company's credit balance is diminished.[5]

[**106**] It is thought that theft would not be committed by a mere breach of copyright. If D, in writing a book, were to copy out large sections of another book in which P owned the copyright, this would be a breach of copyright but it would not be theft. It is submitted that it would not amount to an appropriation of the copyright; and, in any event, there would seem to be no evidence in such a case of an intent to deprive P permanently of his property. It would

---

[3] Above, para. [**28**].

[4] *Cf. Davenport*, [1954] 1 All E.R. 602.

[5] In *Davenport*, D was in fact convicted of larceny of the money which was the proceeds of the cheques. His conviction was quashed. Lord Goddard, C.J. said: "I think the fallacy that led to this charge of stealing money was this. It was thought that, because the master's account had been debited, that was enough to make a theft, but, although we talk about people having money in a bank, the only person who has money in a bank is the banker. If I pay money into my bank, either by paying cash or a cheque, the money at once becomes the property of the banker. The relationship between banker and customer is that of debtor and creditor." A conviction for theft could be upheld under the Theft Act since it is now possible to steal a debt.

be more analogous to making a merely temporary use of another's chattel. Similarly in the case of one who misuses another's trade-mark or trade secrets.

(e) *The necessity for specific property*

[**107**] The necessity for the existence of some specific property has been insisted upon more than once in the above pages. This necessity, while not expressed in the Act, is really self-evident since there can be no appropriation unless there exists some thing to be appropriated. A resolution by D not to repay a debt he owes to P cannot be regarded as an appropriation because there is nothing to appropriate.[6]

[**108**] It is not intended to assert that the property must be "specific" in the sense in which that term is used in Sale of Goods Act 1893.[7]   It would be enough under the Theft Act that D had appropriated an unascertained part of an ascertained whole though such property would not be "specific" for the purposes of the Sale of Goods Act.   In *Tideswell*[8] P's servant, E, weighed a quantity of ashes into trucks for D, but entered a less quantity in P's books and charged D for that less quantity.   It was held that D was guilty of larceny of the balance of the ashes over those for which he had paid.   D's contract with P was not to buy the whole bulk of the ashes at so much per ton, but only to buy such as he might want at that price.   The court took the view that E had no authority to pass the property except in those ashes for which he charged; that the balance therefore remained P's property, and it was immaterial that it was not distinguishable from the bulk.[9]   It is submitted that this would be theft under the Theft Act.   Indeed, it might be suggested that it might be more accurate in such a case to charge D with theft of the whole; for it is difficult to see how property passed in any of the ashes since "Where there is a contract for the sale of unascertained goods no property in the goods is transferred to the buyer unless and until the goods are ascertained."[10]   The goods appear never to have been ascertained in that case.[11]   On the other hand, it may be said that, while there is an appropriation of the whole quantity (an *actus reus*), D has a claim of right in respect of the quantity for which he has paid or agreed to pay.   Such reasoning was not, however, used in *Middleton*[12] where D was convicted of stealing the whole sum of money although he was entitled to a less sum.

[**109**] A more intractable problem than that of *Tideswell* is presented by *Tomlin*[13]. D was the manager of P's shoe shop.   Between stocktakings in March,

---

[6] It should be noted that this is not an appropriation of the debt—a thing in action—because it is not an assumption of ownership of it.   That would occur if E purported to assign P's debt to another.

[7] Section 62.

[8] [1905] 2 K.B. 273.

[9] In *Lacis* v. *Cashmarts*, [1969] 2 Q.B. 400 at 411, the divisional court thought it an unavoidable and apparently fatal difficulty on a larceny charge that it was impossible to distinguish the goods alleged to be stolen from other goods lawfully taken.   The court thought there would be no difficulty under the Theft Act.   It is thought that it is as much, or as little, a difficulty for theft as for larceny; and that it is not a real difficulty in either case. The court seems to have overlooked *Tideswell*.   Difficulties do arise, of course, if there is a charge of handling and the stolen goods cannot be identified.

[10] Sale of Goods Act 1893, s. 6.

[11] *Cf. Re Wait*, [1927] 1 Ch. 606.

[12] (1873), L.R. 2 C.C.R. 38.

[13] [1954] 2 Q.B. 274; [1954] 2 All E.R. 272.

1953 and September, 1953 goods to the value of £420 had gone from the shop without the proceeds of sale being accounted for. D's conviction for embezzlement of that sum was upheld. The court[14] rejected the argument that there could be no conviction for embezzling a general deficiency and that embezzlement of specific sums on specific dates must be proved. Clearly in cases of this kind it is virtually impossible to prove that D took the money for a particular pair of shoes and put it straight into his pocket; and it is submitted that the defence that there can be no theft of a general deficiency would fail under the Theft Act. D has not in fact appropriated "a deficiency"; he has appropriated a sum of money, no doubt on a number of different occasions, but between specific dates. Thus far *Tomlin* should present no problems; but a further point which was not argued is not easily solved. On the evidence it is very difficult to see how the jury could have been satisfied beyond reasonable doubt that D took money and not shoes.[15] If D has appropriated shoes, it is difficult to see how he can properly be convicted on an indictment alleging that he stole money, even to the same value. If the jury are satisfied that he took the shoes or the money it may well be that, in practice, they will convict him of stealing the money if that is what he is charged with and they think it the more likely event; but strictly speaking, they ought not to do so unless satisfied beyond reasonable doubt; and, if the defence is raised, it would seem that the judge would be bound to so direct the jury.

[**110**] There are other instances of dishonest profit-making which may be morally indistinguishable from theft but which are not punishable under the Act because of absence of an appropriation of any specific thing. Where, for example, an employer withholds part of his servant's wages as a contribution to a pension fund and dishonestly omits to make that contribution. In the particular case where an employer fails to pay any contribution which he is liable to pay under the National Insurance Act 1946, he commits an offence punishable on summary conviction with a fine not exceeding £10. Finally, there is the example discussed *obiter* in *Tideswell*:

> "Suppose the owner of a flock of sheep were to offer to sell, and a purchaser agreed to buy, the whole flock at so much a head, the owner leaving it to his bailiff to count the sheep and ascertain the exact number of the flock, and subsequently the purchaser were to fraudulently arrange with the bailiff that whereas there were in fact thirty sheep they should be counted as twenty-five and the purchaser should be charged with twenty-five only, there would be no larceny, because the property would have passed to the purchaser before the fraudulent agreement was entered into."[16]

[**111**] If the property in the whole flock had passed, then it might be argued that there was no appropriation of "property belonging to another". Apart from the *Lawrence* (C.A.) principle,[17] however, it might be answered that

---

[14] Following *Balls* (1871), L.R. 1 C.C.R. 328.

[15] Or that he took the money before he put it into the till (embezzlement) and not after (larceny). As both types of appropriation are now theft, this problem need not be pursued.

[16] *Per* Lord Alverstone, C.J., [1905] K.B. at 277; see to the same effect, Channell, J., *ibid.* at 279.

[17] Above, para. [**33**].

the owner retained his lien for the unpaid part of the true price, and that the bailiff appropriated it by delivering the sheep. In any case, the purchaser and the bailiff would be guilty of a conspiracy to defraud.[18] Whether the property would have passed before the appropriation is, however, less clear than the learned judges appear to have thought; for, under the Sale of Goods Act 1893, s. 18, rule 3, where

> "the seller is bound to weigh, measure, test, or *do some other act or thing* with reference to the goods for the purpose of ascertaining the price, the property does not pass until such thing be done, and the buyer has notice thereof."

If the bailiff agreed to deliver the whole flock of sheep before he counted them, the agreement would be a sufficient act of appropriation of P's property.[19]

I. APPROPRIATIONS OF THE PROPERTY OF ANOTHER PERMITTED BY THE CIVIL LAW

[112] There are many cases where the civil law authorises D to appropriate P's property with the intention of permanently depriving P of it.[20] If, in such a case, D is aware of the law, then it is obvious that he is not acting dishonestly and he commits no offence. Suppose, however, that D is unaware of the civil law which authorises him to act as he does and proceeds in a furtive manner evincing a dishonest intention. He now falls literally within the terms of the Act (for it contains no such expression as "unlawfully"[1]) and nothing is expressed which could save him from conviction from theft. It is submitted, however, that it would be ludicrous to convict P where the civil law gave him express authority to do what he did and that the Act should be interpreted so as to exclude such cases.

[113] A mere liberty or power must, however, be distinguished from an express authority or right in the strict sense. D has a liberty under the civil law to do an act if the performance of that act does not amount to a civil wrong. There is no reason why the criminal law should not curtail such liberties in appropriate cases, and the Theft Act has done so in the case of a co-owner who dishonestly appropriates the joint property;[2] and where D has the power to pass a good title, he may nevertheless in some cases be properly convicted of theft when he does so. For instance, the mercantile agent who is in possession of goods with the consent of the owner, passes a good title if he sells to a *bona fide* purchaser, even though he does so dishonestly and in breach of the arrangement made with the owner.[3] This is clearly theft by the mercantile agent. The distinction between power and right appears in s. 48 of the Sale of Goods Act 1893 and it is instructive to consider the effect of the Theft Act upon the situations there envisaged. By subsections (1) and (2):

---

[18] Smith and Hogan, 158.
[19] *Cf. Rogers* v. *Arnott*, above, para. [25].
[20] E.g., Disposal of Uncollected Goods Act 1952. See Crossley Vaines, *Personal Property* (4th ed.), 187–190.
[1] Rightly, because there are cases which are and must be crimes under the Theft Act which do not amount to civil wrongs. The dishonest receiver of goods obtained by deception gets a title (though a voidable one) and commits no civil wrong; yet none would deny that his act should be a crime.
[2] *Bonner*, above, para. [64], and *Turner* (*No.* 2), above, para. [58].
[3] Factors Act 1889, s. 2 (1).

"(1) Subject to the provisions of this section, a contract of sale is not rescinded by the mere exercise by an unpaid seller of his right of lien or retention or stoppage in transitu.

"(2) Where an unpaid seller who has exercised his right of lien or retention or stoppage in transitu re-sells the goods, the buyer acquires a good title thereto as against the original buyer."

[114] The unpaid seller who re-sells after the property has passed has clearly appropriated the property of another (the first buyer) and committed the *actus reus* of theft although, in doing so he has passed a good title to the second buyer. It is unlikely that he could be convicted in most cases, for it would be difficult to prove dishonesty where no part of the price had been paid. But a seller is unpaid[4] until he receives the *whole* price, and a seller would certainly be dishonest if, having received 90 per cent[5] of the price, he were to re-sell the goods, intending not to repay. This subsection gives the seller a mere power, not a right. The re-sale is a wrongful one and the first buyer, if he were to tender the price, could sue in detinue. There seems to be no reason why this should not be a crime. A quite different situation is created by subsection (3):

"Where the goods are of a perishable nature, or where the unpaid seller gives notice to the buyer of his intention to re-sell, and the buyer does not within a reasonable time pay or tender the price, the unpaid seller may re-sell the goods and recover from the original buyer damages for any loss occasioned by his breach of contract."

[115] According to the interpretation formerly put upon this subsection,[6] the seller's action did not rescind the contract. If this were so, the seller would have appropriated the property of another; but it would be intolerable that the law should say, at one and the same time, that "the unpaid seller may re-sell the goods" and that he is guilty of theft if he does this, not knowing that the law permits him to do so. Therefore, even if this interpretation had been correct, the unpaid seller's act could not have been theft, whatever his state of mind. It is now clear, in any event, that a seller who re-sells under s. 48 (3) rescinds the contract[7] and is, therefore, appropriating his own property and not that of another, and is incapable of committing theft. The position is the same under subsection (4):

"Where the seller expressly reserves the right of re-sale in case the buyer should make default, and on the buyer making default, re-sells the goods, the original contract of sale is thereby rescinded, but without prejudice to any claim the seller may have for damages."

2 THE MENS REA OF THEFT

[116] The changes made by the Act in the *mens rea* of theft are certainly much less significant than the fundamental reforms of the *actus reus*. The characteristics of the old law were:

---

[4] Sale of Goods Act 1893, s. 38.
[5] As a part payment and not a deposit: see *Gallagher* v. *Shilcock*, [1949] 2 K.B. 765, *per* Finnemore, J.
[6] In *Gallagher* v. *Shilcock*, [1949] 2 K.B. 765.
[7] *R. V. Ward, Ltd.* v. *Bignall*, [1967] 1 Q.B. 534; [1967] 2 All E.R. 449, (C.A.), overruling *Gallagher* v. *Shilcock* on this point.

(i) The stealing need not be done *lucri causa*, that is, it was unnecessary to prove that D intended to make any kind of profit for himself or another.

(ii) It must be done "fraudulently" and

(iii) without a claim of right made in good faith; and

(iv) with intent permanently to deprive the owner of his property.

[**117**] Each of these characteristics is preserved. By s. 1 (2):

"It is immaterial whether the appropriation is made with a view to gain, or is made for the thief's own benefit."

Thus if D takes P's letters and puts them down a lavatory[8] or backs P's horse down a mine shaft[9] he is guilty of theft notwithstanding the fact he intends only loss to P and no gain to himself or anyone else. It might be thought that these instances could safely and more appropriately have been left to other branches of the criminal law—that of criminal damage to property for instance. But there are possible cases where there is no such damage or destruction of the thing as would found a charge under another Act. For example, D takes P's diamond and flings it into a deep pond. The diamond lies unharmed in the pond and a prosecution for criminal damage would fail. It seems clearly right that D should be guilty of theft.

A. DISHONESTLY

[**118**] By s. 2 of the Act:

"(1) A person's appropriation of property belonging to another is not to be regarded as dishonest—

(*a*) if he appropriates the property in the belief that he has in law the right to deprive the other of it, on behalf of himself or of a third person; or

(*b*) if he appropriates the property in the belief that he would have the other's consent if the other knew of the appropriation and the circumstances of it; or

(*c*) (except where the property came to him as trustee or personal representative) if he appropriates the property in the belief that the person to whom the property belongs cannot be discovered by taking reasonable steps.

(2) A person's appropriation of property belonging to another may be dishonest notwithstanding that he is willing to pay for the property."

(*a*) *Belief in the right to deprive*

[**119**] It is submitted that D is not dishonest if he believes, whether reasonably or not, that he has the legal right[10] to do the act which is alleged to constitute an appropriation of the property of another. This would be in accordance with the old law of larceny. In spite of the court's general insistence on reasonableness when defences of "mistakes" are raised, it never seems to have

---

[8] *Cf. Wynn* (1887), 16 Cox C.C. 231.
[9] *Cf. Cabbage* (1815), Russ. & Ry. 292.
[10] It is irrelevant that no such right exists in law. A dictum to the contrary in *Gott* v. *Measures*, [1948] 1 K.B. 234, is irreconcilable with the decision in *Bernhard* (below).

been doubted that a claim of right afforded a defence, even though it was manifestly unreasonable.[11]

The onus is clearly on the Crown to prove a dishonest intention and, therefore, if the jury are of the opinion that it is reasonably possible that D believed that he had the right to do what he did, they should acquit.

[120] The Act refers specifically to a right *in law*. This does not necessarily exclude a belief in a merely moral right.[12] Clearly a belief in a moral right by one who knows he has no legal right is not enough—otherwise robbing the rich to give to the poor might be justified. Belief in a moral right by one who did not advert at all to the legal position might be enough—but such a case is difficult to envisage.

It is made clear that a belief in the legal right of another will negative dishonesty, just as it amounted to a claim of right under the law of larceny.[13] If D, acting for the benefit of E, were to take property from P, wrongly but honestly believing that E was entitled to it, he would clearly not be guilty of theft.

The defence consisting in D's belief that he would have had the other's consent, if the other knew of the appropriation and the circumstances of it, was not spelled out in the Larceny Act 1916 but was probably implicit in the requirement that the taking be done "fraudulently".[14]

(b) What does "dishonestly" add?

[121] It was accepted under the old law that the word "fraudulently" added something to the words "without a claim of right"[15] but what that additional element was, was never satisfactorily elucidated. The old law is not irrelevant here, for the word "dishonestly" seems to have been substituted for "fraudulently" because it is more easily understood by laymen rather than because any changes of substance were intended.[16] It is submitted that under the new law the beliefs set out in s. 2 (1) do not exhaust the concept "dishonestly", and that, apart from the instances given, there may be other cases where D will have to be acquitted on the grounds that he was not dishonest. While it would be a mistake to seek to draw up a closed list of cases which do, or do not, amount to dishonesty, the function of "fraudulently" and "dishonestly" certainly seems to be limited. The problem has been particularly discussed in the context of D's taking P's money with the intention of permanently depriving him of those notes and coins but of returning an equivalent sum at a later date. In *Williams*[17] D took the Postmaster General's money from the till in her sub-post office and used it for the purposes of the general shop which she carried on in the same premises. The jury found that she intended to repay the money she took and that, in respect of the money referred

---

[11] *Bernhard*, [1938] 2 K.B. 264; below, para. [**363**].

[12] A belief in a moral right was not a defence to larceny: *Harris* v. *Harrison*, [1963] Crim. L.R. 497, (D.C.). *Cf.* Williams, *C.L.G.P.*, 322.

[13] *Williams*, [1962] Crim. L.R. 111.

[14] A similar defence was expressly provided by the Road Traffic Act 1960, s. 217, where, however, the belief had to be reasonable. See below, para. [**323**].

[15] *Williams*, [1953] 1 Q.B. 660 at 662.

[16] The *Report*, Cmnd. 2977, para. 39.

[17] Above. For a general discussion of the case, see [1955] Crim. L.R. 18.

to in some of the counts, she honestly believed that she would be able to do so; in respect of the other sums, she had no such belief. The Court of Criminal Appeal upheld her conviction on all counts. This suggests a rule that an honest belief in ability to repay in the future is no defence; but it is submitted that this would be going too far. D knew that she was at least taking a risk with the Postmaster General's money. The general shop was doing badly and her honest belief was presumably based on her faith that business would improve. It was conceded, even in defending counsel's argument,[18] that an intention to take such a risk was fraudulent.

> "If a person intends either to induce someone else to risk his money or himself to put someone else's money to risk, in cases in which he knows that the owner would not agree if he were aware of the true facts, such person is intending to act to the detriment of the owner against the owner's wishes. It must be conceded that an honest intention to repay, coupled with an honest belief in ability to repay in the future, is not necessarily a defence to larceny or to any other charge involving fraud."

[122] If, however, D knows that there is no risk and that he will certainly be able to replace the money before P can suffer in any way from the lack of it, then it is arguable that this should not be treated as dishonesty. Indeed, Lord Goddard, C.J. seems to have accepted this at the time *Williams* was decided, for he said[19] (in a passage which was omitted in the *Law Report* and *Criminal Appeal Report*[20] of the case):

> "It is one thing if a person with good credit and with plenty of money uses somebody else's money which may be in his possession and which may have been entrusted to him or which he may have had the opportunity of taking, merely intending to use those coins instead of some of his own which he has only to go to his room or to his bank to obtain. No jury would then say that there was any intent to defraud or any fraudulent taking. It is quite another matter if the person who takes the money is not in a position to replace it at the time but only has a hope or expectation that he will be able to do so in the future . . ."

[123] In the more recent case of *Cockburn*[1] the Court of Appeal held that the manager of a shop was guilty of larceny when he took money from the till of the shop on a Saturday, intending to replace it with a cheque from his daughter on the following Monday. The court said that the passage from Lord Goddard's judgment quoted above is one

> "which this court sincerely hopes will for the future be disregarded entirely by the Bar and all others who have occasion from time to time to refer to *R. v. Williams*."[2]

---

[18] J. H. Buzzard as reported in 37 Cr. App. Rep. 71 at 73–74.
[19] [1953] 1 All E.R. 1068 at 1070; [1953] 2 W.L.R. 937 at 942.
[20] See [1953] 1 Q.B. 660; 37 Cr. App. Rep. 71.
[1] [1968] 1 All E.R. 466. *Cockburn* has now been followed by the Supreme Court of Hong Kong (Rigby, C.J. dissenting) in *Pang Hei Chung* v. *R.*, [1971] Crim. L.R. 440, interpreting a provision substantially re-enacting s.1 of the Theft Act.
[2] The court thought that Lord Goddard had probably omitted the passage because on reflection he felt it was "an extremely dangerous and misleading statement." But it may equally well have been omitted because it was realised that it did not accord with the meaning attributed to the word "fraudulently" by the Lord Chief Justice (below). If the word meant no more than this, there would be nothing in it to require an acquittal in the case of the person with good credit described in Lord Goddard's dictum.

No apology is made for reproducing the passage here, however, for the following reasons:

(i) The decision in *Cockburn* is unsatisfactory in that the court enumerated what it described as the "complete and total elements of larceny"—and omitted all reference to the word "fraudulently". The court thought there might be a taking which, "whilst technically larcenous, reveals no moral obloquy and does no harm at all". It is difficult to see how an act can, at one and the same time, be dishonest and bear no moral obloquy[3]. According to the *Cockburn* view, it would be larceny for D to take P's shilling without his consent, intending and being able to replace it with another shilling within the hour and before P has an opportunity to miss it. Could such an act really be said to be dishonest?

(ii) The effect of *Cockburn* and of the revised judgment in *Williams* is to deprive the word "fraudulently" of all meaning. Yet in both the original and the revised judgments in *Williams*, Lord Goddard accepted that it was intended to add something. His view of what the word means—"that the taking is done intentionally, under no mistake and with knowledge that the thing taken is the property of another person"[4]—does not seem to add anything—and the example given to illustrate the point seems to confirm this.[5]

(iii) Whatever be the true view about "fraudulently" it is submitted that there is no doubt that "dishonestly" *is* intended to add something in the definition of theft. The Criminal Law Revision Committee thought that "The word 'dishonestly' . . . is very important, as dishonesty is a vital element in the offence."[6]

(iv) One suggestion as to the meaning of "fraudulently" was that it excused the accused who took, knowing that he did not have P's consent, but believing that P would have consented had he known about it.[7] Since s. 2 (1) (*b*) of the Theft Act provides in express terms for this specific case, "dishonestly", if it means anything, must mean something more than this.

(v) The only remaining function for "dishonestly" seems to be that of excusing such a person as that described in Lord Goddard's dictum.

[**124**] It is submitted that a sound test was proposed by counsel in *Williams*:[8] that a person is not fraudulent (or dishonest) unless he intends "to act to the detriment of any person against that person's wishes". By such a test, the person with good credit was not dishonest but Williams was, because she intended to risk P's money. If the manager in *Cockburn* knew (or thought he knew) that the money he took would otherwise merely lie in the till over the weekend and that he could certainly replace it on Monday, he intended no detriment and should be acquitted of dishonesty.

---

[3] Yet what of the starving man who takes a loaf of bread from a millionaire? It was always said that necessity is no defence to a charge of larceny.
[4] [1953] 1 Q.B. at 666.
[5] See discussion at [1955] Crim. L.R. 23–24 and further argument at [1956] Crim. L.R. 238.
[6] The *Report*, Cmnd. 2977, para. 39.
[7] Wing-Commander Lowe in [1956] Crim. L.R. 78.
[8] [1953] 1 Q.B. at 662-663, basing himself on Buckley, J. in *Re London and Globe Finance Corporation*, [1903] 1 Ch. 728 at 732.

This would be in accordance with the view taken of "fraud" in other branches of the criminal law. Thus in forgery, it appears that a man is defrauded only if he is induced to act to his injury, if there is some detriment or prejudice and that there is an intent to defraud, therefore, only if there is an intent to cause detriment of some kind.[9] It is not enough that the accused intended to obtain a benefit for himself.

(c) Dishonesty—law or fact?

[125] The Criminal Law Revision Committee thought that

" 'Dishonesty' is something which laymen can easily recognise when they see it, whereas 'fraud' may seem to involve technicalities which have to be explained by a lawyer."[10]

If *Cockburn* is followed in construing the Theft Act, the jury will presumably be directed that such conduct as was admitted in that case is an offence and they will be denied the opportunity to exercise their laymen's intuition to recognise dishonesty when they see it.

It is submitted that it is right that the question should be decided by the court and not by the jury. The question is one of the meaning of a word in a statute and that is a question of law.[11] It is thought, with respect, that the committee was over-optimistic in its estimate of the facility with which laymen can recognise dishonesty, and that laymen no less than judges[12] can reasonably hold different views about it. Leaving such cases to juries as an open question may well result in inconsistent verdicts.[13] It is submitted then that *Cockburn* was right (in effect) in treating the question as one of law; but that the answer to that question under the Theft Act requires more consideration than it received in that case—certainly when the question arises under the Theft Act.

(d) Belief that the person to whom the property belongs cannot be discovered by taking reasonable steps

[126] Though the Act makes no reference to finding, this is obviously intended to preserve the substance of the common law rule[14] relating to finding. The finder who appropriates property commits the *actus reus* of theft (assuming that the property does belong to someone and has not been abandoned) but is not dishonest unless he believes the owner can be discovered by taking reasonable steps. Even if the finder knows who the owner is, he may not be dishonest if he believes that the property cannot be returned except by taking wholly unreasonable steps. P inadvertently leaves a cigar in D's house and flies to his home in New Zealand. D finds the cigar and smokes it. Even if D does not believe that P would have consented to his smoking the cigar, it is submitted that D is not dishonest.

Suppose that D and E see a chattel lying in the highway. E picks it up. D recognises it as the property of P, but there is no means by which E could

---

9 *Welham* v. *D.P.P.*, [1961] A.C. 103.
10 The *Report*, Cmnd. 2977, para. 39.
11 "*Cf. Kelly*, [1970] 2 All E.R. 198; *Pico*, [1971] Crim. L.R. 599.
12 *Cf. Sinclair* v. *Neighbour*, [1967] 2 Q.B. 279 (C.A.) (a civil case with facts similar to those of *Cockburn*) where the trial judge thought there was no dishonesty; Sellers, L.J. was inclined to share that view but Sachs, L.J. thought such conduct was dishonest.
13 See McKenna, J. at [1966] Crim. L.R. 550-553.
14 *Thurborn* (1849), 1 Den. 387.

discover the owner by taking reasonable steps. D urges E to keep it for himself instead of leaving it where he found it. It is submitted that D should be convicted of theft; he has brought about the *actus reus* of the crime with *mens rea*.[15]

[**127**] The important change in the law of finding made by the Act, has already been dealt with.[16] At common law, if D's finding were innocent (either because he did not believe that the owner could be discovered by taking reasonable steps or because he intended to return the thing to the owner when he took it) no subsequent dishonest appropriation of the thing could make him guilty of larceny; but now, in such a case, he will be guilty of theft by virtue of s. 3 (1).[17]

It should be stressed that the question is one of D s actual belief, not whether it is a reasonable belief. If D, wrongly and unreasonably, supposed that the only way in which he could locate the owner of property he had found, would be to insert a full page advertisement in *The Times*, he would have to be acquitted unless that course were a reasonable one to take, which would depend upon the value of the property and all the surrounding circumstances.

[**128**] While this provision is intended mainly for the case of finding it is not confined to that case and there are other instances where it would be useful. Suppose that P arranges with D that D shall gratuitously store P's furniture in D's house. P leaves the town and D loses touch with him. Some years later, D, needing the space in his house and being unable to locate P, sells the furniture.[18] This is undoubtedly an appropriation of the property of another and D is civilly liable to P in conversion; but he appears to be saved from any possibility of conviction of theft by s. 2 (1) (c).[19] Though the purchase money probably belongs in law to P,[20] D's immunity must extend to the proceeds of sale.

[**129**] Where the property came to D as a trustee or personal representative and he appropriates it, he *may* be dishonest even though be believes that the person to whom the property belongs cannot be discovered by taking reasonable steps. The point seems to be that the trustee or personal representative can never be personally entitled to the property (unless it is specifically so provided by the trust instrument or the will) for, if the beneficiaries are extinct or undiscoverable, the Crown will be entitled to the beneficial interest as *bona vacantia*. If the trustee or personal representative appropriates the property to his own use, honestly believing that he is entitled to do so, then it is submitted that he must be acquitted. But if he knows that he has no right to do this and that the property in the last resort belongs to the Crown, he commits theft, from the beneficiaries if they are in fact discoverable and, if not, from the Crown.

B. THE INTENTION OF PERMANENTLY DEPRIVING THE OTHER

[**130**] The Theft Act preserves the rule of the common law and of the Larceny Act 1916 that appropriating the property of another with the intention of

---

[15] See the argument in Smith and Hogan, 91-94.
[16] Above, para. [**26**].
[17] Above, para. [**20**].
[18] *Cf. Sachs* v. *Miklos*, [1948] 2 K.B. 23; *Munro* v. *Willmott*, [1949] 1 K.B. 295.
[19] The bailee who disposes of goods under the Disposal of Uncollected Goods Act 1952 will not usually be able to rely on this provision, for he will know where the owner is; but since he is "entitled . . . to sell the goods", it is submitted that there is no *actus reus*. See above, para. [**112**].
[20] *Taylor* v. *Plumer* (1815), 3 M. & S. 562.

depriving him only temporarily of it is not stealing.[1] English law, in general, recognises no *furtum usus*—the stealing of the use or enjoyment of a chattel or other property. This is subject to two exceptions which are considered below. The first exception concerns the removal of articles from places open to the public[2] and is an innovation. The second exception, in so far as it relates to motor vehicles, has existed in the Road Traffic Acts since 1935, but the extension to other "conveyances" is new.[3] Outside these cases the law seems to remain substantially unchanged; so that, if D takes P's horse without authority and rides it for an afternoon, a week or a month, he commits no offence under the Act and, probably, no offence against the criminal law (though a civil trespass) if he has an intention to return the horse at the end of this period.

(a) Deprivation of persons with limited interests

[**131**] Theft may be committed against a person having possession or control of property or having any proprietary right or interest in it.[4] The element of permanence relates to the deprivation of P, not to the proposed benefit to D. It would seem clear, therefore, that where P has an interest less than full ownership, an intention by D to deprive him of the whole of that interest, whatever it might be, is sufficient. If, as D knows, P has hired a car from Q for a month, and D takes it, intending to return it to Q after the month has expired, this must be theft from P, for he is permanently deprived of his whole interest in the property, but it is not theft from Q for he, plainly, is not permanently deprived. It should be stressed that the question is always one of intention; so if, in the above example, D, when he took the car, believed P to be the owner, he would apparently not commit theft even though P was, in fact, deprived of his whole interest.

This is capable of producing rather odd results where the interest of the person deprived is a very small one. O writes a letter and gives it to P to deliver by hand to Q. D intercepts P and takes the letter from him. Having read it, he delivers it (as he always intended) to Q. This appears to be theft of the letter from P (though not from O or Q) since P is permanently deprived of his possession or control of it. If the letter is taken by force or threat of force, it will be robbery from P.

(b) Disposition of property as one's own

[**132**] There is no comprehensive definition of "intention of permanently depriving" in the Act, but s. 6 "gives illustrations, as it were, of what can amount to the dishonest intention demanded by section 1 (1). But it is a misconception to interpret it as watering down section 1."[5] Section 6 (1) provides:

> "A person appropriating property belonging to another without meaning the other permanently to lose the thing itself is nevertheless to be regarded as having the intention of permanently depriving the other of it if his intention is to treat the thing as his own to dispose of regardless of the other's rights; and a borrowing or lending of it may amount to so treating

---

[1] *Warner* (1970), 55 Cr. App. Rep. 93.
[2] Section 11, below, para. [**296**].
[3] Section 12, below, para. [**312**].
[4] Section 5 (1), above, para. [**52**].
[5] *Warner* (above, footnote 1) at 97, *per* Edmund Davies, L.J.

it if, but only if, the borrowing or lending is for a period and in circumstances making it equivalent to an outright taking or disposal."

[133] It seems clear that this is intended to affirm the common law rule that where D appropriates P's property with the intention that P shall have it back again only by paying for it, D has a sufficient intent permanently to deprive. For example, D takes P's £1 note and tenders it to P, asking if he can give change for it. Where D, the servant of P, a tallow-chandler, with an accomplice who purported to be E's servant, took fat from P's store room and offered it to P for sale as the property of E, D was guilty of larceny of the fat.[6] If D had alleged that the property was his own, he would have come squarely within the words of the s. 6 (1)—his intention would have been to treat the thing *as his own* to dispose of regardless of the other's rights. On the actual facts, D and his accomplice treated the thing as the property of another which they had power to dispose of regardless of P's rights. Since s. 6 does not lay down an exclusive definition of the intention required, it is submitted that this would undoubtedly be theft within the Act; it is not distinguishable in principle from the case which is specifically dealt with in s. 6 (1).

[134] Another type of case which would be covered by s. 6 (1) is that where D appropriates P's property, sells it to O, and then tells P where his property is to be found, knowing that P will be able to assert his proprietary rights against O and recover the property.

[135] In all of these examples D has probably committed an offence of obtaining property (the price) by deception contrary to s. 15 (1) and the simplest course might be to charge that offence. If, however, D were to appropriate P's property and offer it to P in return for something other than property or a pecuniary advantage—for example, an office or appointment of some kind— theft would be the only charge (unless the offer amounted to an offence of corruption). There might seem to be no difference in principle if D offered P P's own property as a gift. D, by purporting to be the owner, treats the thing as his own to dispose of regardless of P's rights; and to deceive P into supposing that he is receiving a gift is evidently dishonest. It would, however, be remarkable that one should evince an intention to deprive another permanently of his property by giving that property back to him; and it may be that the courts will think it proper to draw the line at the case where D asks for consideration for the return to P of P's own property. In this case, it may be said that there is a real conditional intention to deprive—P may refuse to pay the price—which is lacking in the case of an outright gift.

[136] It has been submitted above[7] that on the facts of *Holloway*[8] there would be no theft under the Act, because there is no appropriation. Even if this is wrong, it would seem that a prosecution would fail because of the lack of evidence of intent permanently to deprive. Holloway did not intend to treat the skins as his own, or as the property of P to be disposed of regardless of P's rights; he intended to treat them as P's property and he did not intend to "dispose" of them.

---

[6] *Hall* (1849), 1 Den. 381.
[7] See para. [46].
[8] (1848), 1 Den. 370.

(c) *Conditional intention to deprive*

[**137**] In *Easom*,[9] the Court of Appeal said that "a conditional appropriation will not do." In that case, however, the chattels were rejected as soon as identified, so it may be better to say that there was no appropriation, not even a conditional one. The difficulty of supporting this proposition is that all intention is conditional, even though the condition be unexpressed and not present to the mind of the person at that time. It is submitted that the better view is that an assumption of ownership, which is conditional because there is an intent to deprive only in a certain event, is theft. For example, D takes P's ring intending to keep it if the stone is a diamond, but otherwise to return it. He takes it to a jeweller who says the stone is paste. D returns the ring to P. It is submitted that he committed theft when he took the ring. The fact that he returned it is relevant only to sentence.

A similar problem may arise where D takes the property of P, intending to claim a reward from P for finding it. If he intends to return the property in any event and hopes to receive the reward, he is not guilty of stealing though he is attempting to obtain property by deception, contrary to s. 15 (1). But if he intends to retain the property *unless* he receives the reward, he seems to be in substantially the same situation as the taker who *sells* the property back to the owner. It might be said, however, that in this example, the taker is not treating the property *as his own*. There are two possible answers to this; the assertion of a better right to possession might be regarded as treating the property as one's own; or, s. 6 not providing an exclusive definition, this might be regarded as an analogous case falling within the same general principle.

[**138**] It is submitted that, on a similar basis, there is no reason why there should not be a conviction for theft in a case like that of the taker of the Goya from the National Gallery: "I will return the picture when £X is paid to charity". Substantially, the taker is offering to sell the thing back and his case is, in principle, the same as those contemplated by s. 6 (1). Nor should it make any difference that the price demanded is something other than money. "I will return the picture when E (who is imprisoned) is given a free pardon"—this should be sufficient evidence of an intent permanently to deprive.

The general principle might be that it is sufficient that there is an intention that P shall not have the property back unless some consideration is supplied by him or another; or, more generally still, unless some condition is satisfied.

(d) *Borrowing or lending*

[**139**] Unlawful borrowing is generally not theft because the borrower, by definition, intends to return the thing. If the borrowing "is for a period and in circumstances making it equivalent to an outright taking . . .", however, the borrower may be regarded as having the intention of depriving the owner permanently. This is a rather puzzling provision, because it would seem, *prima facie*, that borrowing cannot be an "outright taking". Clearly, however, this part of the subsection is intended to do something and, therefore, certain borrowings are to be treated as the equivalent of outright takings. Once this is accepted, it is not difficult to divine the kind of borrowings which are intended

---

[9] [1971] 2 Q.B. 315 at 319; [1971] 2 All E.R. 945 at 947; above, para. [**50**].

to be covered: they are those where the taker intends not to return the thing until the virtue is gone out of it. D takes P's dry battery, intending to return it to P when it is exhausted; or P's season ticket, intending to return it to P when the season is over. Similar in principle are those cases where D intends to return the thing only when it is completely changed in substance; D, being employed by P to melt pig iron, takes an axle belonging to P and melts it down in order to increase his output and, consequently, his earnings;[10] or D wrongfully feeds his employer's oats to his employer's horses.[11] Likewise where D takes possession of P's horse, intending to kill it and leave him the carcase[12]—though, plainly, theft is not the most appropriate charge.

[140] The difficulty has sometimes been raised in connection with the theft of cheques that, if they are cashed as the thief presumably intends, they will be returned in due course to the bank of the drawer. How can the thief be said to intend to deprive him permanently of the cheque? The case might be regarded as one where D is treating the cheque as his own to dispose of, because the drawer is only to have it back when he has paid for it through his bank— the case is thus indistinguishable in principle from *Hall*—or it might be put on the ground that the cancelled cheque which the drawer receives back is a thing as different in substance from what he parted with as is the carcase from the living horse, or the axle from the pig-iron to which it is reduced. From whichever angle it is approached, D should be guilty of stealing the cheque. The same arguments apply to the case where D appropriates a ticket belonging to British Rail. He intends that British Rail shall have it back only by paying for it, through services rendered; or, he intends to return only a cancelled ticket, a substantially different thing.

[141] The cases considered above are examples of situations where the property has been entirely deprived of an essential characteristic, which has been described as its "virtue". But what if the virtue has not been entirely eliminated—but very nearly. D takes P's season ticket for Nottingham Forest's matches intending to return it to him in time for the last match of the season. Is this an "outright taking" so as to amount to theft of the ticket? If it is, is it theft if D intends to return the ticket in time for two matches?—or three, four, five or six—where should the line be drawn? The difficulty of drawing a line suggests that it should not be theft of the ticket unless D intends to keep it until it has lost *all* its virtue.[13] This means, of course, that if D takes P's car and keeps it for ten years, he will not be guilty of theft if, when, as he intended all along, he returns it to P, it is still a roadworthy vehicle, though the proportion of its original value which it retains is very small. If it can no longer be described as a car, but is scrap metal, then, if D intended to return it in this state, he has stolen it.

[142] The provision regarding lending appears to contemplate the situation where D is in possession or control of the property and he lends it to another.

---

[10] *Richards* (1844), 1 Car. & Kir. 532.
[11] *Morfit* (1816). Russ. & Ry. 307.
[12] *Cf. Cabbage* (1815), Russ. & Ry. 292; in that case he may in fact have been deprived of the carcase.
[13] The difficulty might satisfactorily be overcome in this particular case by holding that the right to see each match is a separate thing in action, of which P is permanently deprived once that match is over.

If D knows that the effect is that P will never get the property back again, he clearly has an intent permanently to deprive. Similarly if D knows that, when P gets the property back again, the virtue will have gone out of it, this is equivalent to an outright disposal. The examples of the dry battery, season ticket, etc.[14] are applicable here, though they seem less likely to arise in the context of lending than of borrowing.

(e) Parting with property under a condition as to its return

[143] Section 6 (2) provides:

"Without prejudice to the generality of subsection (1) above, where a person, having possession or control (lawfully or not) of property belonging to another, parts with the property under a condition as to its return which he may not be able to perform, this (if done tor purposes ot his own and without the other's authority) amounts to treating the property as his own to dispose of regardless of the other's rights."

[144] This is clearly intended to deal with the kind of case which gave difficulty under the old law, where D, being in possession or control of P's goods, pawns them. If D had no intention of ever redeeming the goods, there was no problem—he was guilty of larceny and he would now clearly be guilty of theft, apart from s. 6 (2). But what if D does intend to redeem? The answer now is that if he knows that he may not be able to do so, he is guilty of theft. The subsection does not seem to permit of a distinction between the case where D knows that the chances of his being able to redeem are slight and the case where he believes the chances are high; in either case, the condition is one which he knows he *may not* be able to perform.

[145] The common law cases suggested that it was theft, notwithstanding an intention to redeem, if the pawner had no reasonable prospects of being able to do so.[15] It is submitted, however, that the question under the Theft Act is a purely subjective one: D must *intend* to dispose of the property regardless of the other's rights, and s. 6 (2) merely describes what he must intend. If then D is in fact *convinced*, however unreasonably, that he will be able to redeem the property, he does not come within the terms of s. 6 (2) because he does not intend *to dispose of it under a condition which he may not be able to perform.*

[146] This is not necessarily conclusive, however, for subsection (2) is without prejudice to the generality of subsection (1); and it might reasonably be argued that even the pawner who is convinced of his power to redeem intends to treat the thing as his own to dispose of, regardless of the other's rights. This would be equally true if the pawner in fact had power to redeem; and, since pawning is not "lending", there is no need to prove that it was equivalent to an outright disposal. The difficulty about this interpretation is that it makes it very difficult to see why s. 6 (2) is there at all; if D's disposition of property under a condition which he *is* able to perform is theft under sub-

---

[14] Above, para. [139].
[15] *Phetheon* (1840), 9 C. & P. 552; *Medland* (1851), 5 Cox C.C. 292. *Trebilcock* (1858), Dears. & B. 453 and *Wynn* (1887), 16 Cox C.C. 231 are inconclusive.

section (1), why refer specifically to the case of a condition which he may not be able to perform? On the whole it would seem that the better approach is to hold that one who is certain of his ability to redeem does not have an intent permanently to deprive. Such a person, in some circumstances, may not be dishonest if the views expressed above[16] are followed. For example D, a tenant for a year of a furnished house, being temporarily short of money, pawns the landlord's clock, knowing that he will certainly be able and intending to redeem it before the year expires. A prosecution for theft of the clock should fail on the grounds both that he is not dishonest and that he has no intent permanently to deprive. The case may be adequately dealt with as one of unlawful pawning.[17]

(f) Abandonment of property

[147] Early nineteenth century cases on the taking of horses decided that there was no intent permanently to deprive, although D turned the horse loose some considerable distance from the place where he took it.[18] In the conditions of those times it might be supposed that D must have known that there was a substantial risk that P would not get his property back. This lenient attitude may be contrasted with that adopted in the pawning cases[19] and the right course would seem to be to attach no importance to these old decisions in the interpretation of the Theft Act.

[148] The case where the property is abandoned is not within s. 6 (2) for D does not part with the property under a condition. He might, however, be regarded as having an intention to treat the thing as his own to dispose of regardless of the other's rights. If D borrows the thing and then leaves it where he knows the owner or someone on his behalf will certainly find it, he clearly does not have an intent permanently to deprive. But if he abandons the thing in circumstances such that he knows that it is quite uncertain whether the owner will ever get it back or not, then it would not be unreasonable to hold that he has an intention to treat the thing as his own to dispose of regardless of the other's rights. By analogy to the pawning case discussed above, it would seem that it should be immaterial whether D believes that the chances of P's getting the property back are large or small; it is sufficient that he intends to risk the loss of P's property. Suppose, for example, that D, being caught in the rain when leaving a restaurant in London, takes an umbrella to shelter him on his way to the station and abandons it in the train on his arrival at Nottingham. He should be guilty of theft.

C. DISHONEST APPROPRIATION, NOTWITHSTANDING PAYMENT

[149] Section 2 (2) is intended to deal with the kind of situation where D takes bottles of milk from P's doorstep but leaves the full price there. Certainly D has no claim of right and he intends to deprive P permanently of his property. Doubts had, however, arisen as to whether this was dishonest.[20] This subsection

---

16 See paras. [121]–[124].
17 Pawnbrokers Act 1872, s. 33.
18 *Phillips and Strong* (1801), 2 East P.C. 662; *Crump* (1825), 1 C. & P. 658; *Addis* (1844), 1 Cox C.C. 78.
19 Above, para. [145].
20 *Cf.* Hawkins, 1 P.C. c. 34, s. 7; Blackstone, *Commentaries*, IV, 243; Russell, 855–856.

resolves them. If there is nothing more, the mere fact of payment will be no defence, though it will, no doubt be a mitigating factor to be taken into account in assessing the sentence. The fact of payment may be important evidence, in some circumstances, that there was no dishonesty. D takes milk bottles from P's unattended milk-cart and leaves the price. He says that he assumed that P would have been very happy to sell him the milk had he been there, but that he had not time to wait for P to return. If D is believed—and the fact of re-payment would be persuasive evidence—it would seem that he has no dishonest intent.[1]

---

[1] Section 2 (1) (*b*), above, para. **[118]**.

CHAPTER III

ROBBERY

[**150**] Robbery was a common law offence and was never defined in the Larceny Acts. A definition is now contained in s. 8 (1) of the Theft Act:

"A person is guilty of robbery if he steals, and immediately before or at the time of doing so, and in order to do so, he uses force on any person or puts or seeks to put any person in fear of being then and there subjected to force."

A. ROBBERY NOW A SINGLE OFFENCE

[**151**] Under the Larceny Act 1916, s. 23, there was a distinction between simple robbery, punishable with a maximum sentence of fourteen years, and robbery with violence and aggravated robbery, punishable with life imprisonment. No such distinction is drawn in the Theft Act. There is a single offence, punishable under s. 8 (2) with life imprisonment. This is in accordance with the general policy of the Act against creating separate offences depending on a single aggravating factor. The fact that force has actually been used as distinct from merely threatened may be a reason for imposing an increased punishment; but this fact alone could hardly justify a difference in the maximum between fourteen years and life. The threat may actually be the more serious factor—a threat to murder being, surely, a factor of greater aggravation than the use of a small amount of force.

[**152**] Assault with intent to rob formerly carried a maximum of only five years but now, under s. 8 (2) of the Theft Act, it is equated with actual robbery and carries life imprisonment. Assault with intent to rob will usually amount to an attempt to rob which would have been punishable with imprisonment at the discretion of the court at common law, so this is a less far-reaching change than might appear; and it is not unreasonable that the maximum should be the same, for the fact that the offence was never consummated may not detract in any way from its seriousness.

B. ROBBERY AN AGGRAVATED FORM OF THEFT

[**153**] Robbery under the Theft Act is essentially an aggravated form of stealing—the only one of many aggravated thefts to survive the repeal of the Larceny Acts. Proof of the commission of theft is essential to secure a conviction for robbery just as, at common law, the commission of larceny had to be proved. So it is not robbery if D has a claim of right to the property which he takes by force even if he knew he had no right to use force.[1] The extended definition of theft makes robbery a potentially wider crime than at common

---

[1] *Skivington*, [1968] 1 Q.B. 166.

law, but in practice this is likely to be of small importance since the occasions on which force is used or threatened in committing acts which amounted to the old crimes of embezzlement and fraudulent conversion must be very few indeed.

[154] Under the old law, it was necessary to prove that there had been a taking and carrying away—that the robber had got possession of the property stolen and moved it[2]. This is no longer necessary. It is sufficient to show that there has been an appropriation[3] of the property of another by force or threat of force. Taking hold of the property with the intention of appropriating it would be enough, whereas under the old law this might have constituted only an attempt. If D by threats of force induced P to lay down property with the intention of taking it up;[4] or if he snatched at a lady's earring but failed to detach it from her ear[5] the robbery, it is thought, would be complete. If D were pursuing P with intent to take his purse by force and P were to throw away the purse in order to escape,[6] this would not be theft until D did some act to appropriate the purse; but, even before he did so, he would be guilty of attempted robbery, for his pursuit of P would be a sufficiently proximate act; and he might also be guilty of an assault with intent to rob.

C. USE OR THREAT OF FORCE

[155] The aggravating factor is the use, or the threat of the use, of force against the person. The term "force" has been preferred to "violence" which was used in the Larceny Act 1916 to designate an aggravated form of robbery. Though the difference, if any, between the words is an elusive one, it is probable that "force" is a slightly wider term. Thus it might be argued that simply to hold a person down is not violence but it certainly involves the use of force against the person. Force denotes any exercise of physical strength against another whereas violence seems to signify a dynamic exercise of strength as by striking a blow.

[156] The force must be used or threatened *in order to steal*[7]. So, if D is attempting to commit rape on P and she offers him money to desist, which he takes, he is not guilty of robbery (even assuming that there is theft of the money) whether he in fact desists, or continues and completes the rape.[8] Similarly if D knocks P down out of revenge or spite and, having done so, decides to take, and does take, P's watch, he does not commit robbery. Such cases can, however, be adequately dealt with by charging rape or an offence under the Offences against the Person Act 1861, as well as theft.

[157] It is now clear that only force or threats of force *to the person* will suffice. This narrows the common law offence in some respects. Threats to

---

[2] *Cf.* Hale, 1 P.C. 533.
[3] See above, para. **[20]**.
[4] *Cf. Farrell* (1787), 1 Leach 322 n. (robbery held not complete).
[5] *Cf. Lapier* (1784), 1 Leach 320 (held robbery, because the earring *was* detached).
[6] *Cf.* Hale, 1 P.C. 533.
[7] *Shendley*, [1970] Crim. L.R. 49 (C.A.). If the jury are satisfied that D stole, but not satisfied that he used force for the purpose of stealing, they should acquit of robbery and convict of theft.
[8] *Cf. Blackham* (1787), 2 East P.C. 711.

damage property[9] or to accuse P of an unnatural offence[10] which would found an indictment for robbery at common law are no longer enough. Such cases are, however, properly dealt with as blackmail under s. 21.

[**158**] Force directed purely to gaining possession of the property stolen is probably not sufficient unless D knows that the use of such force must affect P's person or cause P to fear that his person will be affected. Thus force used to detach P's watch chain from his waistcoat pocket is not, in itself, sufficient. The force is directed at the watch chain not at D's person.[11] The bag-snatcher is not necessarily or even usually guilty of robbery. If, however, P retains or recovers a grasp on his property and D overcomes this by the use of force then, it is submitted, the crime has become robbery.[12] Likewise where, though P makes no resistance, D realises he must cause injury to P if he is to secure the property, and continues to do so; as where he drags on P's earring knowing that this will tear her pierced ear.[13]

[**159**] Though the Act omits the word "wilfully", which was included in the draft bill proposed by the Criminal Law Revision Committee,[14] it is submitted that the force or threat must be used intentionally or at least recklessly; so that for D accidentally to cause P to fall and injure himself while picking his pocket or accidentally to cut him while slitting his pocket to get his money would not be robbery.

D. IMMEDIATELY BEFORE OR AT THE TIME OF STEALING

[**160**] The force or threat must be used immediately before or at the time of stealing, and, in the case of a threat, it must be of force "then and there". Thus there can be no robbery or attempted robbery by letter or telephone, except in the most unlikely circumstances—for example, D telephones P that if P does not hand over certain property to E (Ds' innocent agent who has called at P's house) D will detonate an explosive charge under P's house. Where the threats seek to secure a transfer of property at some time in the future the proper charge would be blackmail, contrary to s. 21.

[**161**] To use force after a theft is complete, for example in order to escape, does not constitute robbery. There may be difficult questions, however, as to when a theft is complete. Larceny was held to be, in effect, a continuing act, so that D was still in the course of larceny some time after he had done enough to be successfully indicted. This appears both in cases[15] which were concerned with the question whether E, who had received goods from D, was a principal in the theft, on the one hand, or a receiver of stolen goods or accessory after the fact, on the other; and in cases[16] under the Homicide Act concerned with the question whether D was "in the course or furtherance of theft".

---

[9] *Simons* (1773), 2 East P.C. 731; *Astley* (1792), 2 East P.C. 729.
[10] *Donnally* (1779), 2 East P.C. 715; *Pollock and Divers*, [1966] 2 All E.R. 97.
[11] *Cf. Gnosil* (1824), 1 C. & P. 304.
[12] But see below, para. [**163**].
[13] *Lapier* (1784), 1 Leach 320.
[14] The *Report*, Cmnd. 2977, at p. 102.
[15] *Kelly* (1847), 2 Cox C.C. 171; *cf. King* (1817), Russ. & Ry. 332; below, para. [**478**].
[16] *Jones*, [1959] 1 Q.B. 291; *H.M. Advocate* v. *Graham*, [1958] S.L.T. 167.

[162] The common law rule relating to robbery seems to have been the same as that under the Theft Act. Where D picked a purse from P's pocket without his knowledge but P almost immediately afterwards saw it in D's possession and D thereupon uttered threats, this was held not to be robbery as the threats came after the taking.[17] Authority on when the theft was complete for the purposes of robbery at common law was slender and, if the rule were that the force or threat had to be used before the *taking*, then the authorities referred to in the preceding paragraph were not relevant. Under the Act, however, it is enough if the force or threat is used *at the time* of committing the theft—it does not necessarily have to occur *before* the theft is committed—and it is certainly arguable that force used *in the course of* a theft is used at the time of the theft and that the Homicide Act cases are applicable.

[163] A possible answer to this argument may be found in the new definition of theft. Larceny consisted in taking and carrying away and it was not unreasonable that the larceny should be held to be "in course" while D was, for example, in the process of removing the goods from the premises—he was still carrying them away. Now, however, theft consists simply in an act of appropriation, and it is arguable that once there has been such an act, the theft is over and it is not possible thereafter to turn it into robbery.[18] Such an interpretation might, however, have an unduly narrowing effect on the scope of the crime.[19] Suppose D puts his hand into P's pocket, takes hold of his wallet and lifts it to the edge of P's pocket. Quite clearly he has committed an appropriation, for this was even enough to constitute a taking and carrying away in simple larceny.[20] P then discovers what is going on and a struggle for the wallet takes place before D carries it off. It is submitted that this ought to be robbery. It can be held to be such only if appropriation is regarded, to some extent and in some circumstances at least, as a continuing act. This does involve some uncertainty as to when the appropriation terminates—just as there was a difficult question when a man came to the end of the course or furtherance of larceny.[1]

[164] Where an act of force has occurred after the theft is over, it would, of course, be proper to charge D both with theft and with the appropriate crime under the Offences against the Person Act 1861.[2] Where a mere threat has been used after the theft is over this will generally not constitute a separate offence for even a threat to murder is not an offence unless it is in writing.

E. FORCE OR THREAT AGAINST A THIRD PERSON

[165] It is clear that under the Theft Act, force used against *any person* will constitute robbery only if it is used in order to commit theft. Similarly a threat to use force against any person aimed at putting that person in fear of being then and there subjected to force is enough. So if D, being about to commit theft from P, is interrupted by a passer-by, Q, and repels Q's attempt

---

[17] *Harman* (1620), 1 Hale P.C. 534.
[18] *Shendley*, [1970] Crim. L.R. 49.
[19] And see below, para. **[478]**.
[20] *Taylor*, [1911] 1 K.B. 674.
[1] Smith and Hogan (1st ed.), 200-202.
[2] Offences against the Person Act 1861, s. 16.

to interfere, either by actual force or the threat to use force, he is guilty of robbery if he completes the theft. It is immaterial that no force or threat is used against P from whom the theft is committed. It would seem that in such a case the indictment would properly allege robbery from P, for clearly there was no robbery from Q.

[**166**] The case put above may be an extension of the common law of robbery; but there is another respect in which the Act may have narrowed the law. Suppose that D threatens P that, if P will not hand over certain property to D, D will use force on Q. This was probably robbery at common law.[3] It is difficult if not impossible, however, to bring such a case within the words of the Act since D does not seek to put any person in fear of being then and there subjected to force in order to commit theft. He does not put P in such fear because the threat is to use force on Q. He does not put Q in fear because the threat is not addressed to him. Such cases should again be treated as blackmail contrary to s. 21.

[**167**] It might be different in the example put in the previous paragraph if the threat were addressed to Q as well as to P or overheard by Q. If it were D's object to cause Q to intercede with P to hand over the property, so as to save himself from D's threatened force, this would be robbery.

[**168**] At common law, the theft had to be from the person or in the presence of the victim. In *Smith* v. *Desmond and Hall*[4] the House of Lords, reversing the Court of Criminal Appeal,[5] put a wide interpretation upon this rule, holding that it was satisfied if the force or threat of force was used on a person who had the property to be stolen in his immediate personal care and protection. D was therefore guilty of robbery when he overpowered a nightwatchman and a maintenance engineer in a bakery and then broke into a cash office some distance away and stole from a safe. Though the victims did not have the key to the office or the safe they were in the building to guard its contents which were, therefore, in their immediate personal care and protection.

[**169**] Such a case is obviously within the terms of the Theft Act. Indeed, it follows from what has been said above that there is no longer any necessity to prove that the property was in the care and protection of the victim of the force or threat. It is enough that that the force or threat was directed against any person so that, if in *Smith* v. *Desmond* the persons overpowered had been mere passers-by who happened to have interfered with D's plans, this would be enough under the Theft Act, though not at common law.

---

[3] *Reane* (1794), 2 East P.C. 734 at 735–736, *per* Eyre, C.B., *obiter*.
[4] [1965] 1 All E.R. 976.
[5] [1964] 3 All E.R. 587.

CHAPTER IV

CRIMINAL DECEPTION

[**170**] Section 15 of the Act creates an offence of obtaining property by deception, and s. 16 an offence of obtaining a pecuniary advantage by deception. Some elements are common to the definition of both offences, but they require separate consideration.

1 OBTAINING PROPERTY BY DECEPTION

[**171**] By s. 15 of the Act:

"(1) A person who by any deception dishonestly obtains property belonging to another, with the intention of permanently depriving the other of it, shall on conviction on indictment be liable to imprisonment for a term not exceeding ten years.

(2) For purposes of this section a person is to be treated as obtaining property if he obtains ownership, possession or control of it, and 'obtain' includes obtaining for another or enabling another to obtain or to retain."

These subsections replace the old crime of obtaining by false pretences contrary to s. 32 of the Larceny Act 1916. Their scope is, however, considerably wider than that of the old provision. The most important change is that the new offence embraces cases which were formerly larceny by a trick as well as false pretences[1] but it also extends the law to cover some cases which were previously not criminal at all. The various constituents of the offence are examined below.

A. THE OBTAINING

(a) *For one's self*

[**172**] There is a sufficient obtaining if D obtains ownership, possession or control. Under the old law it was doubtful whether obtaining ownership without also getting possession amounted to an offence.[2] It seems now to be clear that it does. So if D, by deception, induces P to enter into an unconditional contract to sell to D specific goods which are in a deliverable state, the offence is complete although the goods never leave P's possession. The ownership in the goods passes as soon as the contract is made and it is immaterial that the time of payment and of delivery is postponed.[3] Similarly if D, by deception, induces P to transfer to him a bill of lading in respect of goods which are at sea[4], he will be guilty of obtaining not merely the bill of lading but also the goods which it represents, for title to them passes on indorsement and

---

[1] Above, para. [**30**].
[2] Kenny thought it did not: *Outlines* (5th ed.), 243.
[3] Sale of Goods Act 1893, s. 18, rule 1.
[4] *Cf*. Kenny, footnote 2, above.

delivery of the bill. It may be that, in these cases, P will suffer no loss; but it is right that such conduct should be criminal since it puts P's property at risk. D has probably obtained a voidable title to it and, if he can re-sell to a *bona fide* purchaser before P succeeds in avoiding the contract, the *bona fide* purchaser will get an unimpeachable title to the property and P will be permanently deprived of it.

[173] It follows that if D, being in a foreign country, say France, sends a etter to England deceiving P into selling him goods which are in England, D is guilty of obtaining by deception in England as soon as the property passes to him. It is immaterial that he never sets foot within the jurisdiction. If the letter arrives within the jurisdiction but does not deceive P, (or, it is submitted, is lost before it reaches him) D is liable in England for an attempt:[5]

> "... he who despatches a missile or a missive, arranges for its transport and delivery (essential parts of the attempt), and is thus committing part of the crime within the jurisdiction by the means which he has arranged".

[174] Even if the "missile or missive" never reaches the jurisdiction (for example, the ship containing the missive sinks outside territorial waters) it is thought that D should be convicted. Though nothing has actually happened in England, it is the consequences here that the accused has in view, and it is to the consequences *intended* that we have regard when dealing with attempts (and conspiracy or incitement).

[175] The position regarding the converse case is less certain. D, in England, sends a letter to France, deceiving P into transferring property in goods to D in France. According to *Harden*[6], a case decided under the Larceny Act 1916, the English courts have no jurisdiction, but Lord Diplock has said[7] that that case should be reconsidered. According to his Lordship's view of jurisdiction under the Theft Act,[8] D would clearly be liable to conviction here. Not all the members of the House of Lords appear to take the same view; but even if Lord Diplock's approach is not upheld, it may well be held that obtaining by deception, like blackmail, is a continuing offence, committed both in the country from which, and in the country to which, a letter is despatched.

Even if *Harden* is right, so that no offence is committed in England when the property passes abroad, it may be that there will be an offence if the goods are subsequently delivered in England. Possession of the goods has now been obtained within the jurisdiction by the deception which is still operating (the seller would not have despatched the goods had he known the truth). It might be argued that this is not obtaining the property "of another", since D is now the owner, But it is clear that an offence would be committed if, *after* the contract of sale, D had by a fresh deception induced P to part with possession of the goods before payment of the price, P being deprived of his lien

---

[5] *Baxter*, [1971] 2 All E.R. 359 at 362, *per* Sachs, L.J.
[6] [1963] 1 Q.B. 8.
[7] *Treacy* v. *D.P.P.*, [1971] A.C. 537 at 563; [1971] 1 All E.R. 110 at 123.
[8] Below, para. **[496]**.

over the goods;[9] and it is submitted that the position is the same where an earlier deception which induced the transference of the property is still operative.[10] Where, however, both ownership and possession are transferred to D (perhaps through D's agent) abroad, no offence is committed within the jurisdiction, unless *Harden* is to be regarded as overruled.[11]

[176] If D merely obtains possession, his offence under the old law would have been larceny by a trick. Such conduct continues to be theft[12] but it is now also obtaining by deception and should always be indicted as such and not as theft. It is an offence under s. 15 (1) where D, by deception, induces P to let him have goods on hire, or hire-purchase, or on loan, with the appropriate *mens rea*. All sorts of difficult questions about whether the property passed or not, which had to be decided by criminal courts under the old law, are now irrelevant—provided the charge is brought under this section and not under section 1.

[177] It is enough that D obtains control. So if D, a servant, by deception induces his master, P, to entrust goods to D for use in the course of D's employment, D may be guilty of the offence though he has obtained not possession of the goods but control or "custody" as this particular relation to goods is sometimes called.

(b) Enabling another to obtain or retain

[178] " 'Obtain' includes obtaining for another or enabling another to obtain or retain".[13] So if D, by deception, induces P to make a gift of goods to E, D is guilty. That would be a case where D obtained for another. An instance of D's enabling another to obtain would be where E is negotiating with P for the sale of goods by E to P and D deceives P as to the quality of the goods so as to induce him to enter into the contract with and pay the price to E. Of course E, in these examples, would also be guilty if he was a party to D's fraud.

[179] The meaning of "enabling another . . . to retain" presents more difficulties. If E is in possession of P's goods and D, by deception, induces P to agree to transfer the ownership in the goods to E, this would be "obtaining for another" and not "enabling another to retain". The latter provision must be intended to apply to the situation where D induces P to allow E to retain some interest which E already has, for, if P is induced to transfer any new interest, this is obtaining for another.

---

[9] Below, para. **[198]**.

[10] It must be conceded that it appears to follow from this argument that *two* offences are committed when D, by a single deception, causes P (i) to sell and (ii) subsequently to deliver goods to him. But if there are two deceptions, one causing the property to pass, another causing delivery, it is inescapable that this must be so. And it is thought the position is exactly the same, in the case where there is only one deception. Of course, it would be improper to indict for both offences except where it is doubtful whether one count will lie because, e.g., of the jurisdictional difficulties referred to above.

[11] *Harden*, [1963] 1 Q.B. 8; *cf.* commentary at [1962] Crim. L.R. 250; and see Williams, "Venue and the Ambit of the Criminal Law" (1965), 81 L.Q.R. at 521–522.

[12] See above, para. **[30]**.

[13] Section 15 (1).

[**180**] There seem to be three possible cases:

(i) E is P's bailee at will and D, by deception and with the appropriate intent, induces P not to terminate E's possession.

(ii) E is P's servant and has custody of P's goods. D, by deception induces P not to terminate that custody, again with the appropriate intent.

(iii) E has obtained the ownership of property from P under the terms of a contract voidable by P. P is proposing to rescind that contract. D, by deception, induces him to refrain from doing so. It is clear that D has enabled E to retain ownership and therefore he is to be "treated as" obtaining property.

[**181**] It might be argued in the third case, however, that D is not guilty because he is not enabling E to retain property *"belonging to another"*. It has been seen that this expression must have a wide meaning but in this example P has neither ownership, possession nor control. The question is whether property can be said to "belong to" a person for the purpose of the section when he has nothing more than the right, by rescinding a contract, to resume ownership of it. *Prima facie*, one would have thought that the answer to this question would be in the negative; P has no proprietary right or interest in the property.[14] It is true that s. 15 (2) gives an extended meaning to the words "obtains property"—D is, in the specified circumstances, to be "treated as obtaining property", whether he does so or not—but it does not, in terms, extend the meaning of the equally important phrase, "belonging to another". Case (iii) can be brought within the section only by holding that the extended meaning of "obtains property" extends by implication the meaning of "belonging to another".[15] D is probably not guilty of obtaining by deception in that case.

[**182**] It will be noticed that the Act makes no provision for the case where D by deception retains goods for himself. In most cases this will clearly fall under theft contrary to s. 1 so there will be no problem. (Of course in examples (i) and (ii) in the previous paragraph, E, if he has *mens rea*, will be guilty of theft by "keeping [the property] as owner,"[16] and D of aiding and abetting him: whereas if E has no *mens rea*, D might well be thought to be guilty of theft through an innocent agent. But it is very doubtful if D or E would be guilty of theft in example (iii)).[17]

[**183**] If D is in possession or custody of P's property and, by deception, he induces P to allow him to retain that possession or custody as the case may be, with the intention of permanently depriving P of the property, D will be guilty of theft. If, however, D has acquired ownership and possession of the property from P before deception, it is difficult to see how he can be said to have appropriated the property of another. Suppose that D has acquired ownership and

---

[14] *Cf.* s. 5 (1), above, para. [**52**].
[15] The meaning given to this phrase by s. 5 applies only for the purposes of s. 1 (theft); above, para. [**52**].
[16] Section 3 (1), above, para. [**26**].
[17] Above, paras. [**78**]–[**80**].

possession of P's property under a contract voidable by P for an innocent misrepresentation committed by D. P is about to rescind the contract and thus regain his ownership in the goods. D, by deception induces him to refrain from doing so, intending to keep the goods permanently for himself. D can hardly be said to have appropriated the property of another since P has no interest, legal or equitable, in the property at this time;[18] nor is this obtaining under s. 15 (1). As has been seen, in the corresponding case where D enables E to retain his ownership and possession of property, it is just arguable that D is guilty of an offence. If so, this is a curious anomaly for the argument is inapplicable where D enables himself to retain; but such cases are likely to be extremely rare.

(c) *Necessity for specific property*

[184] It should be emphasised that, for D to be guilty of enabling E to retain, there must be some specific property which is the subject of the retention. So if D, E's accountant, deceives the Inland Revenue Inspector whereby E's liability to tax is reduced by £50, no offence is committed under this section. In a sense, of course, D has, by deception, enabled E to retain property; but it is not the property *of another*. It is submitted that the provision cannot have been intended to apply to the mere non-payment of a debt which is all that this is. D would, however, be guilty of obtaining a pecuniary advantage for E, contrary to s. 16.

(d) *Deception must be effective*

[185] As under the old law it seems that the deception must be the cause of the obtaining. So if P knows that the statement is false,[19] or if he does not rely on the false statement but arrives at the same erroneous conclusion from his own observation or some other source,[20] or, of course, if he does not read or hear the false statement, D is not guilty of obtaining. In each of these cases, however, D may be convicted of an *attempt* to obtain by deception.[1]

[186] A case that is difficult to reconcile with these principles is *Sullivan*.[2] D represented that he was the "actual maker" of dartboards. The representation was untrue and it was held that he was guilty of obtaining by false pretences from customers who sent him the price of a board although they said in evidence that they parted with their money "because I wanted a dartboard." No one said that he paid because he thought D was the "actual maker." The court apparently thought that there could be no other conceivable reason for their doing so. This seems doubtful. As Sullivan was unknown to them, it probably mattered not at all whether he was the actual maker, so long as he supplied a dartboard. It is not surprising then that the Court of Appeal should recently have stated that the principle in *Sullivan* should not be extended.

---

[18] It is submitted above, para. [79], that s. 5 (4) is inapplicable to this situation.

[19] *Ady* (1835), 7 C. & P. 140; *Mills* (1857), Dears. & B. 205; *Hensler* (1870), 11 Cox C.C. 570; *Light* (1915), 11 Cr. App. Rep. 111.

[20] *Roebuck* (1856), Dears. & B. 24. *Cf.* the similar principle which applies to misrepresentation in relation to the law of contract: *Attwood* v. *Small* (1838), 6 Cl. & Fin. 232; *Smith* v. *Chadwick* (1884), 9 App. Cas. 187.

[1] *Hensler* (1870), 11 Cox C.C. 570; Smith and Hogan, 173-174.

[2] (1945), 30 Cr. App. Rep. 132.

In *Laverty*[3], a case under s. 15, D changed the registration number-plates and chassis number-plate of a car and sold it to P. It was held that this constituted a representation by conduct that the car was the original car to which these numbers had been assigned; but D's conviction for obtaining the price of the car by deception from P was quashed on the ground that it was not proved that the deception operated on P's mind. There was no direct evidence to that effect and it was not a necessary inference. If the only flaw in the prosecution's case was that the representation did not influence P, it would have been in order for the court to substitute a conviction for an attempt. They did not do so, possibly because there was also insufficient evidence that D intended by this representation to deceive P into buying the car. The purpose of changing the plates may well have been, not to deceive the buyer, but to deceive the police, the true owner and anyone else who might identify the vehicle. It would seem that the prosecution would have been on stronger ground had they alleged that D had made a representation by conduct that he had a right to sell the car.

[187] The same problems of remoteness will arise as under the old law of false pretences. If D induces P to accept bets on credit by falsely representing that he is acting on behalf of a number of other persons, money paid by P to D on D's bet proving successful is not obtained by deception; the effective cause of D's receiving the money is not the deception, but the fact of having backed a winning horse.[4] It is an offence under s. 16 of the Theft Act.[5] An offence is committed under s. 15 (1) where D, an athlete, by deception procures a longer start in a race than he is entitled to and, consequently, wins the prize. Here the start is an effective cause of his winning the race and so the prize.[6] If, however, the deception merely gains D admission to the race, without any start or other advantage, it may well be that there is no offence under this section.[7]

[188] Another case where D's deception is too remote is that that where he obtains an appointment by deception and then receives wages or a salary; the money is held to be paid in respect of services rendered and not because of the misrepresentation.[8] This case, however, is specifically dealt with by s. 16.[9] A possible exception to this, however, is where D procures a higher salary because of some special qualification which he falsely pretends he has. Suppose that a higher salary scale is payable to a person with a second class honours

---

3 [1970] 3 All E.R. 432.

4 *Clucas*, [1949] 2 K.B. 226; [1949] 2 All E.R. 40. As there were two accused in that case, they were convicted of a conspiracy to defraud. If there were only one, it would be necessary to rely on s. 16.

5 Below, paras. [252] and [277].

6 *Button*, [1900] 2 Q.B. 597; *Dickenson*, Russell, 1186; *contra*, *Larner* (1880), 14 Cox C.C. 497. But suppose D's deception procures him an additional two yards start and he wins by five yards? It may be said that the deception was not an effective cause because he would have won anyway. It might be answered that the psychological effect of the long start was a contributory factor; but this could hardly be proved beyond reasonable doubt.

7 A start was obtained in each of the cases cited in footnote 6 above.

8 *Lewis* (1922), Somerset Assizes, *per* Rowlatt, J.; Russell, at 1186n. In such a case, the nature of the scheme is such that the deception can never be sufficiently proximate. Contrast the cases where D is interrupted or desists before a scheme which would constitute the complete crime if carried out, but has been advanced beyond the steps of preparation and became an attempt: *Robinson*, [1915] 2 K.B. 342; *Comer* v. *Bloomfield*, [1971] Crim. L.R. 230.

9 Below, paras. [252] and [275].

degree. D, who got a third, says he got a second and is paid accordingly. Here it is arguable that the deception is the direct and effective cause of his obtaining the additional money, and that an offence against s. 15 (1) is, therefore, committed.

B. PROPERTY

[189] The limitations put upon the meaning of "property" for the purposes of theft by s. 4 are inapplicable to deception. It seems clear, then, that the new crime extends far beyond the "chattel, money or valuable security" which could be the subject of obtaining by false pretences under the Larceny Act 1916, s. 32. Non-larcenable chattels, which were not the subject of false pretences[10] may be obtained by deception. Other cases require more detailed consideration.

(a) Land

[190] Land presents peculiarly difficult problems because of the nature of interests in land and the fact that the terminology of the Theft Act is geared to the traditional subject-matter of obtaining by false pretences, goods.[11] Under English law, ownership subsists not in the land itself but in an abstract entity called "an estate." The freeholder owns not the land but the fee simple estate in the land, and the leaseholder has a leasehold estate. The land itself may however be possessed. The offence may be committed therefore by obtaining the ownership of an estate in the land or by obtaining possession or control of the land, provided that there is an intention to deprive the victim permanently of his interest, whatever it is.

[191] (i) *Where P parts with his estate.*—There is little difficulty where the owner is induced to convey his whole estate to the rogue. For example, P, the owner of the freehold, is induced to convey the fee simple to D; or a lessee is induced to assign his whole leasehold interest to D. An obvious case is where an imposter procures the transference to himself of trust property or a deceased person's estate. But there are other cases. Suppose D induces P to sell him land for use as a coach-station, by agreeing that he will purchase all the petrol he needs for his coach-business from P. D never has any intention of honouring his promise. If the legal estate in the land is conveyed to D, or if D is given possession before conveyance, it seems clear that the offence is complete. It may be thought, however, that the offence is complete at an earlier stage. The general rule is that when A *contracts* to sell land to B, an equitable interest in the land passes at once to B. This arises from the fact that a decree of specific performance will normally be granted for a contract for the sale of land and "Equity looks on as done that which ought to be done". If the contract is not specifically enforceable, no interest passes.[12] Where there has been deception, it seems inevitably to follow that the contract is voidable for fraud by the vendor and thus not specifically enforceable against him.[13] If the transaction has got no further than the contract, it seems, then, that D could not be convicted of the full offence, though he might be convicted of an attempt.

---

[10] *Robinson* (1859), Bell C.C. 34.
[11] See Griew, 6-25.
[12] Megarry and Wade, *Law of Real Property* (4th ed.), 582.
[13] *Ibid.*, 585.

D

[192] (ii) *Where P creates a smaller estate.*—The main difficulty arises out of the necessity for an intention permanently to deprive the owner of the property. Such an intent may be difficult or impossible to discover where the owner is induced not to part with his whole estate, but to carve some smaller estate out of it. Suppose that D, by deception, induces P, the owner of the freehold, to grant him a lease of the land for two years. Clearly D does not intend to deprive P permanently, or indeed at all, of the property which belongs to him— i.e., his freehold interest. Nor, if he intends to vacate the property after two years, does he intend to deprive P permanently of possession of the land. The position would be the same if P were himself a lessee whose lease had three years to run and he granted D a sub-lease for two years. The position looks much the same as that of the owner of a ship who charters it for two years. If the charterer has induced the charter by deception but intends to comply with its terms, he does not commit an offence, because of his lack of intention permanently to deprive. There is a possible answer to this analogy. A lease of land differs from the letting of a chattel in that an estate in land is created by the granting of the lease. That estate is regarded in law as a separate piece of property; and D intends that P shall never have that particular piece of property. The snag about this is that it is impossible to say that the leasehold estate ever "belonged to", or could belong to P, the owner of the freehold. If it were surrendered to P it would cease to exist as a separate piece of property and merge in P's larger interest. The leasehold interest does not exist until the lease is granted—and then it belongs to D.

[193] (iii) *Where P retains his estate but D obtains possession.*—What is the effect of obtaining possession of land by deception? If P's only interest in the land is his possession of it, then, clearly the offence may be committed. For example, P is a squatter on the land with no title to it other than his actual possession. Even where P has a good title to the land which he does not lose through the deception, it is thought that the offence will be committed if he is to be deprived of possession for a period coincident with this interest. For example, D deceives P, who is a lessee of land for two years, to allow him into possession as a licensee for those two years. P's leasehold estate continues unimpaired. What then of the case where D obtains from P, the freeholder, a lease of the land for 99— or 999—years? P has not been deprived of his freehold interest but, fairly clearly, D has an intention to deprive him of possession of the land for the rest of his natural life. Is it an answer that the land will some day revert to some remote successor in title? It is submitted that when the Act speaks of permanently depriving "another", it means the living person whose property is taken or obtained; so that if he is never to have it back in his lifetime, this element of the offence is made out. (So it would be theft if D were to take P's property, intending to restore it to P's executor after his death.) Even if this argument is correct, it provides no answer to the case of the man who obtains a short lease by deception and there is an awkward question as to where the line is to be drawn.

[194] (iv) *Where P parts with a portion of his estate.*—The position is thought to be different where P is induced to transfer to D parts of his fee simple or other interest. For example, to convey to D the fee simple in the shooting-rights, or the minerals or to grant D an easement or profit *à prendre*. Here there is evidence that D *does* intend to deprive P permanently of a portion of his freehold interest.

If D is granted only a lease of the mineral rights, then there is the same difficulty as with grants of other leasehold interests; but may he be convicted of obtaining the actual minerals which he removes from the land? He certainly intends to deprive P permanently of these. The difficulty here might be that he is entitled by virtue of the estate which he holds, albeit an estate voidable for fraud, to take the minerals. The problem is essentially one of remoteness, and the authorities[14] rather suggest that the obtaining of the minerals is too remote from the deception. It might well be otherwise, however, in a case where D by deception obtains not a lease but a mere contractual licence to take the minerals. This would not differ in principle from the common case of obtaining by deception, where D obtains the property in pursuance of a contract voidable for fraud.

[**195**] (v) *Where the freeholder obtains from the lessee.*—It has been seen that the offence is committed if a lessee is induced to assign his lease. What if he is induced to surrender it to his landlord? P is permanently deprived of his interest, so there is no difficulty on that score. But is it possible to say that D has *obtained* property, when P's estate has simply ceased to exist? It certainly looks very odd, however, that D, the landlord, should commit no offence when anyone else in the world who persuaded P to transfer his estate would be so guilty. Perhaps the answer is that D has obtained possession of the land with intent that P shall have it no more and that that is enough.

(b) *Things in action*

[**196**] Things in action are clearly property so that D will be guilty of an offence under s. 15 (1) if, by deception, he causes P to transfer his book debts, his copyright or patent to him.

An equitable assignment of a thing in action requires no formality.

"Where there is a contract between the owner of a chose in action and another person which shows a clear intention that such a person is to have the benefit of the chose, there is without more a sufficient assignment in the eye of equity".[15]

[**197**] As in the case of a contract for the sale of land, this result is said to arise from the principle that equity looks on as done that which ought to be done.[16] It might therefore be argued by analogy that the assignment will not be complete where it has been induced by fraud. It is not clear that this result follows. The difference is that while the transference of the equitable interest in the land depends on the availability of specific performance, this does not seem to be true of the equitable assignment of an existing chose in action. Here it appears that the assignment may be regarded as complete, even though no consideration be given by the assignee.[17] In such a case, there is no question

---

[14] See above, para. [**185**].
[15] Cheshire and Fifoot, *Law of Contract* (7th ed.), 461.
[16] *Ibid.*, 434.
[17] *Ibid.*, 440–443.

of a decree of specific performance being given. If the equitable ownership of the thing in action passes where there is no contract at all, it would seem that, *a fortiori*, it must pass where there is a voidable contract. A purported assignment of a future chose in action can operate only as a contract to assign. One who, by deception, induces such an "assignment" will be guilty of an attempt to obtain by deception. If he gave consideration then, on the thing coming into existence, the full offence will be complete.

C. BELONGING TO ANOTHER

[**198**] Property "belongs to another" for the purposes of this section if the other has possession or control of it or any proprietary right or interest in it except an equitable interest arising only from an agreement to transfer or grant an interest.[18] Thus, the *owner* may be guilty of obtaining his own property by deception where, by deception, he dishonestly induces another to give up his lawful possession or control of that property. Suppose that D has pledged his clock with P as security for a loan and, by deception, he induces P to let him have the clock back again, intending neither to restore it nor to repay the loan.[19] Or D, by deception, induces his servant, P, to surrender his custody of D's goods, intending, for example, to charge P with having stolen them.[20] Both these cases seem to fall within the section and both, incidentally, probably amount to theft contrary to section 1. In both cases, P is entitled to retain his interest until it is properly terminated.

[**199**] If D is entitled under the civil law to have his property back again, but P declines to deliver it, it is submitted that D commits no offence by recovering possession by deception. Suppose D has made P a bailee at will. He terminates the bailment by demanding the return of the property. On P's refusal to restore it, D obtains it by deception. In most cases, of course, D will have a claim of right which will negative dishonesty; but, even if he does not, it is submitted that it ought to be held that there is no *actus reus* in such a case. It would generally be incongruous that a man should be guilty of an offence under the criminal law in obtaining property which, by the civil law, he is entitled to have. It is true that the manner of exercising such a right may be such that it justifies the intervention of the criminal law, as in the case of the statutes of forcible entry,[1] blackmail[2] and demanding property on a forged instrument contrary to s. 7 of the Forgery Act 1913.[3] Though the attempt to recover property is an essential part of these offences, it is evidently the use of the force, of the menace and of the forged instrument which is the gist of the offence. It might be argued that deception should fall into the same category. Deception, however, is less socially dangerous than force and does not attract that revulsion which nowadays attaches to blackmail. Demanding on forged instruments is less easily distinguishable; but, like blackmail, it is an offence the gist of which is the demand. In the present case, the gist of the offence is the obtaining of property *belonging to another*: and, as against D, it ought not

---

[18] The definition of "belonging to another" in s. 5 (1) (above, para. [**52**]) applies to s. 15: see s. 34 (1), below, page 215.

[19] *Cf. Rose* v. *Matt*, [1951] 1 K.B. 810.

[20] *Cf.* East 2 P.C. 558; *Smith* (1852), 2 Den. 449.

[1] Forcible Entry Acts 1381–1623; *Taunton* v. *Costar* (1797), 7 Term. Rep. 431.

[2] Below, para. [**350**].

[3] Below, para. [**240**].

to be said that property belongs to P merely because P is in possession of it, if D is entitled to recover possession from him.

If, in the example given above, D had not terminated the bailment, the answer might be different. If he were then to recover possession by deception and with a dishonest intent—for example, intending to charge P with having lost the property—he should be guilty.[4]

D. THE DECEPTION

[**200**] By s. 15 (4):

"For purposes of this section 'deception' means any deception (whether deliberate or reckless) by words or conduct as to fact or as to law, including a deception as to the present intentions of the person using the deception or any other person."

This gets rid of some, though by no means all, of the difficulties which arose under the old law because of the limited meaning of "false pretences".

(a) Deliberate or reckless

[**201**] It was never finally settled whether the making of a false pretence, being reckless whether it was true or false, was sufficient to amount to an offence under s. 32 of the Larceny Act 1916. In principle, it seems clear that it ought to have been an offence and the new provision puts the matter beyond doubt by enacting in express terms that the deception may be deliberate or reckless.

If then D says to P, "This watch chain is solid gold", not knowing whether it is solid gold or not and, either not caring a jot whether the statement is true or false or hoping that the statement will turn out to be true, he is guilty of an offence under s. 15 (1) if the statement turns out to be untrue and, in consequence, P is induced to pay money for the chain. As in the civil law relating to the tort of deceit, it is sufficient that D makes a statement which he knows to be false or does not believe to be true.[5]

[**202**] The next question is whether the provision does not go even further and make punishable the man who makes a statement which he believes to be true but which he most certainly ought to know is false. It is submitted at the outset and with some confidence, that the section is not intended to apply to this situation.[6] To hold that it did so apply would be contrary to the whole spirit of the Act which, throughout, emphasises the requirement of a subjective *mens rea.*[7]

[**203**] In particular, the section requires as well as a deliberate or reckless false pretence that the obtaining be dishonest; and negligence, however gross, is not dishonesty. This is one of those areas where it is of vital importance to distinguish carefully between evidence and law. That the statement was one which any reasonable person would certainly have known was false is evidence,

---

[4] *Cf.* the corresponding case in theft, above, para. [**59**]; and *Turner (No. 2)*, above, para. [**58**].

[5] *Derry* v. *Peek* (1889), 14 App. Cas. 337.

[6] See the *Report*, Cmnd. 2977, para. 101 (i) and *cf. Waterfall*, [1970] 1 Q.B. 148; [1969] 3 All E.R. 1048; below, para. [**265**].

[7] In one instance at least expressly overruling a decision under the Larceny Act 1916, which imposed an objective test. See s. 21 below and the discussion of *Dymond*, [1920] 2 K.B. 260.

and good evidence, that D knew it was false. It is not, however, conclusive; and if the jury, having heard D's story, think that he in fact believed it to be true or even that it is reasonably possible that he believed it to be true, then, it is submitted, D is entitled to be acquitted and the jury should be directed accordingly.

[**204**] The only reason why it is thought necessary to discuss this matter at all is the objective interpretation put by some judges on the word "reckless" in the Prevention of Fraud (Investments) Act 1958, s. 13.[8] This interpretation, however, was based on the view that recklessness did not necessarily connote dishonesty. The express requirement of dishonesty in the Theft Act seems to preclude any such interpretation.

(b)   By words or conduct

[**205**] These words make it clear that all the cases within the old law of false pretences are covered. Though reported examples of false pretences by conduct were far from numerous, it was universally accepted that such a pretence was enough. The stock example is the case of *Barnard*[9] where D went into an Oxford shop wearing a fellow-commoner's cap and gown. He induced the shop-keeper to sell him goods on credit by an express representation that he was a fellow-commoner; but Bolland, B. said, *obiter*, that he would still have been guilty even if he had said nothing. In an Australian case, the wearing of a badge was held to be a false pretence when it indicated that the wearer was entitled to take bets on a racecourse.[10]

[**206**] Positive steps taken by a seller to conceal from a buyer defects in the goods may amount to fraud in the civil law and would seem to be capable of being deception under the Theft Act. If P inspected the goods and, because of the concealment, failed to detect the fault, the offence would be complete. If P omitted to inspect the goods and so was not deceived,[11] D would be guilty of an attempt. The vendor of a house who papers over the cracks would seem to be in exactly the same position and a strict application of the law might interfere with some well-established practices which perhaps ought to be discouraged. It is thought that these cases were, in any event, within the old law relating to false pretences.

[**207**] To display a picture with a collection belonging to a particular seller may amount to fraud and seems to be capable of being a deception, if it is known that the price will be enhanced by the fact that the picture appears to belong to that collection.[12] The contestant in a beauty competition who, in breach of the rules, wears padding so as to enhance her feminine pulchritude, appears to be guilty of attempting to obtain the prize by deception.

---

[8] *Bates*, [1952] 2 All E.R. 842 (Donovan, J.) approved *obiter*, by the Court of Criminal Appeal in *Russell*, [1953] 1 W.L.R. 77. *Contra, Mackinnon*, [1959] 1 Q.B. 150 (Salmon, J.); and see *Grunwald*, [1960] 3 All E.R. 380 at 384 (Paull, J.).

[9] (1837), 7 C. & P. 784.

[10] *Robinson* (1884), 10 V.L.R. (L) 131.

[11] *Cf. Horsfall* v. *Thomas* (1862), 1 H. & C. 90. D, being employed by P to make a steel gun, drove a metal plug into the breach end of the chamber to conceal the fact that the metal was all soft and spongy. It was held that the concealment did not invalidate the contract, since it did not affect the mind of the buyer.

[12] *Cf. Hill* v. *Gray* (1816), 1 Stark. 434, a doubtful decision, since it is not clear that the seller induced the buyer's mistake.

[**208**] It has been held to be fraud in the civil law for the seller of a ship to remove her from the ways where she lay dry and where it might be seen that the bottom was eaten and her keel broken, and to keep her afloat so that these defects were concealed by the water.[13] This would seem to amount to deception. Suppose, however, that the ship was already in the water before any sale was in prospect. Would it be an offence for the seller to leave her there when viewed by the buyer and say nothing about the defects? It would seem not; there are no "words or conduct" here and presumably the seller would not even be civilly liable in such a case.

[**209**] (i) *Deception by implied statement.*—The most difficult question is as to how far statements should be held to be implied in words or conduct. Under the old law the court was unwilling to hold that one who ordered a meal in a restaurant impliedly represented that he had the money to pay; though it evidently thought that there was a *promise* to pay since D was held to be guilty of fraud[14]. On the other hand the court has said in a recent case[15] that one who takes a taxi impliedly states that he has the money to pay. This seems an inconsistent and better view. A well known instance of conduct which is held to contain implicit representations, for the purposes of the criminal law, is the signing of a cheque. In *Hazelton*,[16] it was held that this act implies statements (i) that drawer has authority to draw on the bank for that sum; (ii) that the cheque is a good and valid order for its amount and (iii) that the drawer has a banking account with the bank upon which his cheque is drawn. That case may be taken to be a well-established instance of deception by implied statement and it has been followed under the Theft Act. But in what other circumstances will statements be held to be implied? The principle was well stated by Lord Coleridge, C.J. in *Cooper*[17]:

"If the words can reasonably convey that which is charged as the false pretence in the indictment, and if they were meant by the prisoner to convey that which is so charged, the offence is as complete as though the false pretence had been made in express words".

[**210**] In that case D had ordered two trucks of potatoes "as samples" stating, "Let them be of good quality, then I am sure a good trade will be done for both of us". It was held that this amounted to a pretence that D was a substantial dealer, in such a large way of business as to be able to take this large quantity of potatoes, merely as a sample. In fact, he was a stall-holder in a market with dealings on a very small scale. This case perhaps goes to the limit and Denman, J. and Pollock, B. concurred with some hesitation. Compare the case put by Bramwell, L.J. in *Ward* v. *Hobbs*:[18]

"Suppose that an extravagant person, for the sake of display, wears handsome rings and drives a brilliant equipage; he purchases of a tailor a coat—the tailor draws the conclusion that he is a man of wealth, for he might reasonably argue that no man in his senses would dress so extravagantly or drive such an equipage unless he were a rich man. The tailor

---

[13] *Schneider* v. *Heath* (1813), 3 Camp. 506, approved by the Court of Appeal in *Ward* v. *Hobbs* (1877), 3 Q.B.D. 150 at 162.
[14] *Jones*, [1898] 1 Q.B. 119.
[15] *Waterfall*, [1970] 1 Q.B. 148; [1969] 3 All E.R. 1048.
[16] (1874), L.R. 2 C.C.R. 134 (C.C.R.). Principle applied in *Page*, [1971] 2 Q.B. 330 at 333. *Cf. Christou*, [1971] Crim. L.R. 653.
[17] (1877), 2 Q.B.D. 510 at 513.   [18] (1877), 3 Q.B.D. 150 at 158.

readily supplies his customer on the strength of the appearance that he represents. Afterwards the man does not pay, then the tailor alleges that the man by his conduct has made representations that are wholly false and fraudulent. . . . I do not think any person has a right to draw a conclusion from conduct which is not directed to him either as an individual, or as one of a class, or as one of the public for the purpose of acting on it".

Suppose, however, that D did intend his extravagant display to induce P to give credit; is this a sufficient deception? The adoption of a general air of affluence is much less specific than Cooper's implicit representation that he was a large dealer in potatoes and may not be enough.

[211] The owner of pigs who sends them to market for sale "with all faults" does not, in the civil law, thereby represent that they are free from infectious diseases: *Ward* v. *Hobbs*[19]—*a fortiori* he does not deceive for the purposes of the Theft Act.[20] Would the seller have been guilty of fraud and deception if he had not used the words "with all faults", or similar words? Blackburn, J. once expressed the opinion that there would, in those circumstances, be a representation that the seller believes that the animals are free from disease;[1] but Lord Cairns subsequently declined to commit himself on that issue. In *Ward* v. *Hobbs* the fraud alleged was that the seller impliedly represented that he believed, or had reason to believe, that the pigs were free from disease and it was recognised that such a representation would be quite consistent with the express exclusion, by the quoted words, of liability for any warranty; yet the representation was not implied. It seems likely, therefore, that the result would have been the same, even if the words of exclusion had not been used.

[212] It is certainly not enough to establish an implied deception that there is an implied term for the purposes of the law of contract and that the party bound by the term knows that it is unfulfilled; suppose, for example, that the seller of goods, in circumstances in which the law implies an undertaking on his part that the goods are of merchantable quality, knows that this is not the case, but says nothing. It will be necessary to prove that the seller knew that he was being taken by the buyer to be making a particular assertion and that he knew the assertion to be false or that he did not believe it to be true. An obvious example of a sufficient deception is where the seller induces a sale of an inferior article by producing a sample of superior quality.[2] Though he does not say so in terms, the seller inevitably knows[3] that the buyer understands him to assert that the bulk corresponds with the sample in quality.

[213] An apparently innocent act may constitute deception when considered in the light of a previous course of conduct. D laid before P a number of bars of metal of little value, saying "Eight ounces at four shillings an ounce". The fact that he had previously pledged ingots of silver, which were similar in appearance to the bars now produced, established fraud.[4]

---

[19] (1878), 4 App. Cas. 13.

[20] It could hardly be the law that the seller is entitled to sue for the price under a valid contract and yet is guilty of obtaining it by deception; below, para. [219].

[1] *Bodger* v. *Nichols* (1873), 28 L.T. 441 at 445.

[2] *Goss* (1860), Bell C.C. 208.

[3] The question must still be left to the jury—"Did *this* seller know?" Criminal Justice Act 1967, s. 8.

[4] *Stevens* (1844), 1 Cox C.C. 83.

[**214**] A decision which probably went too far in discerning an implied false pretence is *Berg* v. *Sadler and Moore*.[5] D, a tobacconist, was unable to obtain supplies because he had been put upon the stop-list by the Tobacco Trade Association. He procured E to buy cigarettes, ostensibly on E's own behalf, from P. E and P were members of the Association and P would not have sold the cigarettes had be known they were for D. The Court of Appeal decided that, because D was guilty of an attempt to obtain by false pretences, he could not recover the money he had paid to P, although P, having discovered the truth, never delivered the cigarettes. The false pretence found to have been practised by E would seem to be an implied representation that the tobacco was not intended for any person to whom P would have been unwilling to sell it. As C. K. Allen wrote:[6]

> "Our criminal law is wide and searching, and the way of the transgressor is hard; but if an act of this kind really amounts to false pretences within the meaning of the Larceny Act, the arm of the law is longer and more prehensile than seems quite necessary for the security of society".

[**215**] Equally, it seems to go farther than is called for in the interpretation of "deception". The consequences of such an interpretation are pointed out by the same critic:[7]

> "If X buys from Y cigarettes with the intention of selling **or giving** them to a small boy to whom Y would not be willing to sell them; or if he buys a bottle of whisky with the intention, unknown to the seller, of giving it or selling it to a drunken man to whom the publican would not be willing to sell it, or indeed, if he buys weed-killer with the concealed intention of killing not weeds but his wife; can it be said that he is guilty of obtaining the goods by false pretences? Whatever the morality of the matter may be, it is submitted that this would be a new and dangerous interpretation of the contract of sale of goods."

[**216**] It is submitted that the fallacy in *Berg* v. *Sadler and Moore* lies in the fact that there was no evidence (i) that the question of the ultimate destination of the goods was actually present to P's mind at the time when he made the sale; nor (ii) that E knew that that consideration was present to P's mind when he made the purchase. It is submitted that both these features are essential to a deception. If P had said, "You are not on the stop-list, are you?" and E had replied, "No," the case would have been a much stronger one.

There is one further objection to the decision, which is that the facts do not seem to be distinguishable from civil cases in which the person in the position of D has been held able to enforce the contract of sale made by E on the ground that D was an undisclosed principal.[8] It would be intolerable that the civil division of the Court of Appeal should find itself holding a transaction to be enforceable by a plaintiff, while the criminal division was sending him to prison for entering into it.

---

[5] [1937] 2 K.B. 158.
[6] "Fraud, Quasi-Contract and False Pretences", 54 L.Q.R. 200 at 213.
[7] *Ibid.*, at 210–211.
[8] *Dyster* v. *Randall & Sons*, [1926] Ch. 932 (*per* Lawrence, J.); *Nash* v. *Dix* (1898), 78 L.T. 445 (*per* North, J.). See C. K. Allen, above, footnote 6.

[**217**] (ii) *Deception by implied promise.*—In many of the old cases the prosecutor was driven to look for some implied representation of fact, because the real dishonesty of the accused consisted in an express promise which he did not intend to fulfil.[9] So where D induced P to sign a promissory note for £100 by promising to lend him £100, the court found that there was a false pretence as to an existing fact—that the money was ready for P on his signing the paper.[10] Where D induced P to pay her money on a promise to have intercourse with him, the conviction could be upheld only on the ground that there was a representation that there was a bedroom available for prostitution.[11] There is no need to go through this exercise any more. It would be enough in both cases to prove that D made the promise not intending to fulfil it.[12]

[**218**] An implied promise may be a sufficient deception. Obvious cases are where D orders a meal in a restaurant, or petrol for his car.[13] Though he makes no express promise to pay, he will be guilty of obtaining by deception if it can be established that he had no intention of paying when he made the request. It seems clear that the crime is committed when P makes a bet with a bookmaker, D, who does not intend to pay if the horse backed by P wins.[14] In such a case D may make no express statement whatever when he accepts P's bet but there is clearly an implied promise to pay money in a certain event. Having placed his bet, P leaves D, supposing that this is D's intention and it is fair to say that he has been deceived by D, and that D knows it. It is submitted that D is therefore guilty of obtaining by deception. Similarly where D, having agreed to sell a horse to P for £23 and received £8, absconds with the horse and the money as he all along intended.[15] There was a promise, implied if not express, to hand over the horse on payment of the balance, a promise which D never intended to fulfil. This is not to say that, whenever a promise on D's part is to be implied in the law of contract, D is guilty of deception if he does not intend to fulfil that promise. It must appear that P actually took D to be promising (not always, by any means, the case where promises are implied) and that D knew that P took him to be promising. It is submitted that, on the facts of *Buckmaster* and of *Russett* there would be evidence to satisfy these conditions.

[**219**] (iii) *Passive acquiescence in self-deception.*—There are other cases in which D may be thought to be to some extent dishonest, in which it is thought that the court will probably be unwilling—and, it is submitted, rightly so—to hold that D has deceived P. These are cases in which there is no implied representation in the civil law. For example:

> (a) D contracts to sell a specific parcel or part of a specific parcel of oats to P. P wants old oats. D knows this and he also knows that the oats are in fact new oats.[16]

---

[9] *Cf. Hazelton*, above, para. [**209**], where Pollock, B. said ((1874), L.R. 2 C.C.R. at 140) "I think the real representation made is that the cheque will be paid."
[10] *Gordon* (1889), 23 Q.B.D. 354.
[11] *Caslin*, [1961] 1 All E.R. 246.
[12] Below, para. [**218**].
[13] *Cf. Jones*, [1898] 1 Q.B. 119; *Collis-Smith*, [1971] Crim. L.R. 716.
[14] *Buckmaster* (1887), 20 Q.B.D. 182.
[15] *Russett*, [1892] 2 Q.B. 312.
[16] *Smith* v. *Hughes* (1871), L.R. 6 Q.B. 597.

Provided that D has done and said nothing to lead P to suppose that the oats are old, it is submitted that he is guilty of no offence. A contrary holding would be quite incongruous since, under the civil law, there is a valid contract, enforceable by D against P.[17] It would be absurd if D were to be held guilty of obtaining by the crime of deception money which he could recover by action in a civil court. Indeed to hold that an offence was committed in these circumstances might have the effect of altering the civil law; for the civil court could hardly be seen to lend its aid to enable D to recover the fruits of his crime. In the absence of any expression of Parliament's intention to alter the civil law, it would be wrong to attribute such an effect to the Theft Act.

[220] Supposing that, after an undoubted obtaining by deception by D from P, P, having discovered the deception, chooses to affirm the contract. In such a case D *may* sue upon the transaction which amounts in law to a crime. For instance, D obtains the deposit on a sale of goods to P, by deception. P affirms the contract. D may recover the balance of the price. This might have occurred under the old law and may be distinguished on the ground that D's right arises from P's conduct after the crime has been committed. D remains guilty of obtaining by deception; P's action cannot absolve him from criminal responsibility.

[221] The situation might conceivably be otherwise in only slightly different circumstances:

> (*b*) P believes, not merely that the oats are old, but that D is *contracting to sell the oats as old oats*. D knows that P so believes but has done and said nothing to induce such a belief.

Here the position in the civil law is different. Though the matter is not entirely free from doubt, the better view is probably that there is a contract for the sale of oats, guaranteed by D to be old oats.[18] Here D probably has no right to recover the price for P may rescind the contract for breach of condition.[19] It would be no more incongruous to hold this to be an obtaining by deception than so to hold in many other cases where contracts for the sale of property have been induced by fraud. The two questions are: (i) is D dishonest? and (ii) has there been any deception? It is certainly arguable that the first question should be answered in the affirmative. Even in 1871 the court evidently thought that the seller's conduct was not that of a "man of scrupulous morality or nice honour" and that in such circumstances "a man of tender conscience or high honour would be unwilling to take advantage of the ignorance of the seller".[20] Today the view might be taken that these standards should be required of everyone and not merely exceptional people. The second question poses greater difficulties for the prosecution. The fact is that this is an instance of "passive acquiescence of the seller in the self-deception of the buyer".[1] However, it is just arguable that D's remaining silent is conduct which deceives

---

[17] This assumes *Smith* v. *Hughes* still represents the law. *Cf.*, however, *Solle* v. *Butcher*, [1950] 1 K.B. 671; *Grist* v. *Bailey*, [1967] Ch. 532.
[18] *Cf. Roberts (A) & Co.* v. *Leicestershire County Council*, [1961] Ch. 555.
[19] Rescission is no longer barred by the fact that the contract has been performed: Misrepresentation Act 1967, s.1; see Atiyah, *Sale of Goods* (4th ed.), 289.
[20] (1871), L.R. 6 Q.B. at 604, *per* Cockburn, C.J.
[1] *Ibid.*

P into continuing to think that D acquiesces in his view of the contract. Thus, it is fairly clear that there would be a deception in the following case:

> (*c*) D and P are discussing the sale of a car by D to P under the terms of a standard form contract produced by D. C, an officious bystander, says, "Of course, the contract gives you an unconditional guarantee". D who knows that this is far from the case, says nothing. P, who knows that D overheard C's remark, then signs the contract believing that it gives an unconditional guarantee.

[**222**] It might be answered that this is a different case because D has adopted C's remark and so deceived P. It would, however, be an even clearer case of deception if P himself had said "Of course, the contract gives me an unconditional guarantee" and D had remained silent. This would have been passive acquiescence by the seller in the self-deception of the buyer; yet the buyer is hardly less deceived by the seller than if D had himself misrepresented the nature of the contract. And the only difference between this case and case (*b*)[2] is that in this case the buyer expressly states his misconception of the terms of contract whereas in case (*b*) the seller learns of the misconception of the terms of the contract in some other way. It is clearly not possible to give a confident answer to this problem.

[**223**] (iv) *Omission to correct a deception.*—Suppose that D, the seller of a business, makes a statement to P, the buyer, as to the turnover of the business. The statement is false, but P believes it to be true. Later, D discovers the truth but says nothing. P then enters into a contract to buy the business relying on the statement. Here D has, by words, deceived P and thereby obtained property—there is an *actus reus*. The difficulty is that, at the time of the deception, D had no *mens rea*.[3] D is guilty of a misrepresentation for the purposes of the law of contract[4] and of deceit in the law of tort.[5] *Prima facie*, however, there would seem to be no offence under s. 15.[6] There are, however, two ways in which it might be possible to obtain a conviction.

[**224**] The first way lies in giving a wide interpretation to the word "conduct" "Conduct" means "manner of conducting oneself . . . behaviour"[7] and this might be interpreted to cover omissions as well as acts. It is true that, in some of the cases discussed above, it has been considered that the mere omission of a seller to undeceive the buyer as to the nature of the thing bought will not amount to an offence. The present case may be thought to be different. The buyer's error arises from an express mis-statement by the seller and his moral responsibility is clearly greater. There is a duty imposed on him by the civil law to make a disclosure. The Criminal Law Revision Committee thought that:

---

[2] Above, para. [**221**].
[3] But he did have *mens rea* before the *actus reus* was complete.
[4] *With* v. *O'Flanagan*, [1936] Ch. 575.
[5] *Incledon* v. *Watson* (1862), 2 F. & F. 841.
[6] The Criminal Law Revision Committee considered this and the other cases considered in this paragraph and decided against making any express provision to cover them: the *Report*, Cmnd. 2977, p. 50.
[7] *Shorter Oxford Dictionary.*

" To provide expressly that concealment should be criminal only when there is a duty in the civil law to make disclosure would be unwelcome to criminal lawyers, who quite properly object to legislation by reference to the civil law". [8]

As has been seen, however, [9] it is both impracticable and undesirable to separate the civil and criminal law completely in this field. [10] The very fact that the civil courts are prepared to hold that there is fraud in the situation under discussion while they are not prepared to hold that the seller is even in breach of contract in the *Smith* v. *Hughes* [11] situation strongly suggests that there is a real difference of substance between them. It is submitted that there is no reason why the courts should not hold that there has been a dishonest deception by conduct.

[**225**] The second way of dealing with the matter is suggested by an analogy in the law of murder. Both *actus reus* and *mens rea* are present in this problem, but they do not coincide in point of time. It has been held that if D does an act with intent to kill P and fails to do so and then, as part of the same trans-action, does an act without intent to kill which does kill P, he is guilty of murder. [12] In the present problem, D uses words which deceive without intent to deceive and then intends to deceive without using any words. If D in the murder case may be said to have killed with intent to kill there is no reason why, in the present problem, he should not be said to have used words with intent to deceive; the only difference between the cases is that in the one the *mens rea* precedes the *actus reus*; in the other the relevant part of the *actus* precedes the *mens*. The present case may, indeed, be thought to be stronger for *mens rea* is present at the moment the *actus reus* is complete.

[**226**] Another situation to which the same arguments are applicable is that where D makes a statement to P which is true but a subsequent change of circumstances, known to D but not to P, renders it untrue and D allows P to transfer property to him under the misapprehension that his statement is still true.

[**227**] This is not to argue that criminal liability should be imposed in all cases where the civil law imposes a duty to speak. This is a highly technical matter and there are instances where it would not be obvious to the layman that to remain silent would be tantamount to deception. Such cases may be unsuit-able for the imposition of criminal sanctions. The point is that criminal liability should not be imposed where the civil law imposes no duty to speak. Where it does impose such a duty then the act may reasonably be held criminal if the words of the Act may fairly be said to cover the case.

In all cases, of course, there must be evidence of dishonesty and a jury must say whether the defendant was in fact dishonest. This does not absolve the court from its duty to decide whether the cases discussed above fall within the words of the Act.

---

[8] The *Report*, Cmnd, 2977, p. 51.
[9] Above, para. [**30**].
[10] Above, para. [**4**]. It is thought that an antithesis between "criminal lawyers" and "civil lawyers" is unfortunate. No one can have a proper understanding of this branch of the criminal law without some grasp of the principles of the civil law.
[11] Above, para. [**219**].
[12] *Thabo Meli* v. *R.*, [1954] 1 All E.R. 373; *Church*, [1965] 2 All E.R. 72.

(c) *As to fact or law*

[228] In the old law of false pretences the books unanimously stated that the misrepresentation must be as to a matter of fact.[13] They then went on to contrast representation of fact with representation of opinion or intention. No discussion is to be found of representations of law and no authority is cited to show that a misrepresentation of law would not have been a sufficient false pretence. Indeed there appears to be no authority to that effect. On the other hand there is no authority to show that a misrepresentation of law was enough. It is thus uncertain to what extent the express inclusion of deception as to a matter of law extends the law. Certainly it seems desirable that misrepresentations of law should be within the terms of the Act. Consider the following cases:

(i) D and P are reading a legal document and D deliberately misrepresents its legal effect. This would seem to be a misrepresentation of law since the construction of documents is a question of law. If D does so with the object of leading P to believe that D has some right over P's land so as to induce P to pay money for the release of that right, this would seem to amount to obtaining by deception.

(ii) P and his wife, D, have entered into a separation agreement whereby P covenanted to pay D an annual sum "free of any deduction whatever". D, knowing that the true legal construction of the document is to the contrary,[14] represents to P that this prevents P from deducting income tax. This is a misrepresentation of law and it would seem that D is guilty of obtaining the money (or at least that portion of it which represents the tax which ought to have been deducted) by deception.

[229] There are other cases which might fall within the Act, however, which some might regard as legitimate stratagems.

(i) D has entered into an oral agreement to purchase P's land. P now wishes to escape from the bargain. D, knowing that the contract is unenforceable for lack of a memorandum in writing,[15] writes to P pointing out that they have entered into a legally binding agreement and offering to release P from his liability on payment of £200.

(ii) P owes D a debt which, as D knows but P does not, is statute-barred. D writes to P stating that the money is recoverable by action and that he will sue unless it is paid.

Difficult questions might arise here since the contract in (i) is valid and only unenforceable by action; and the debt in (ii) remains due—the effect of the Limitation Act is to extinguish only the remedy and not the right. It is only the representation that an action will lie which may be false; and there are difficulties even about this, for an action *will* lie in both cases unless the Law of Property Act in the one case and the Limitation Act in the other is expressly pleaded.

There is the further point that D may well have a claim of right to the money which will negative dishonesty. Indeed since he may have an actual

---

[13] Archbold, 1945; Russell, 1171; Smith and Hogan (1st ed.), 408; Kenny, 358.
[14] *Ord* v. *Ord*, [1923] 2 K.B. 432.
[15] Law of Property Act 1925, s. 40.

right to keep the money in both cases if it is paid, it might be thought to be incongruous that the obtaining of it should amount to an offence.[16]

[230] A slightly different case arises where the right to recover land or a chattel is barred by the Limitation Act for in these cases the owner's title is extinguished.[17] In these instances a claim that the chattel or land was due in law to the claimant would be a misrepresentation, a belief in the existence of a moral right would probably not be enough to negative dishonesty[18] and if the land or chattel were handed over to D he would not be entitled to retain it.

It would appear therefore that to recover land or a chattel by misrepresenting the effect of the Limitation Act would amount to an offence under s. 15 (1). To recover a debt by a similar misrepresentation would probably not do so.

[231] In the cases just considered, it has been assumed that the law is quite clear and definite and D knows what it is. Many legal disputes arise, of course, where the law is uncertain. In these instances it is most unlikely that an offence could be committed under the Act. It must often happen that counsel make submissions as to the law in court which do not accord with, or are in direct opposition to the propositions which the same counsel would formulate if he were writing a text-book on the matter. The nature of his submission where the law is uncertain is governed by the interests of his client. A solicitor making similar submissions so as to exact money by way of compromise could not be said to be committing an offence because it is impossible to prove that the statement is (or was at the time) false—the law, *ex hypothesi*, being uncertain.

[232] The following proposition formulated by Street[19] for the law of the tort of deceit is probably equally true of deception under s. 15:

"If the representations refer to legal principles as distinct from the facts on which those principles operate and the parties are on an equal footing, those representations are only expressions of belief and of the same effect as expressions of opinion between parties on an equal footing. In other cases where the defendant professes legal information beyond that of the plaintiff the ordinary rules of liability for deceit apply".

(d) Deception as to intention

[233] Deception includes a deception as to the present intentions of the person using the deception or any other person.

This is an important and valuable extension of the law. It was held in *Dent*[20] that deceptions as to present intention did not amount to false pretences. Paradoxically, however, they did amount to fraud for the purposes of the Debtors Act 1869 so, if they resulted in an obtaining of credit, an offence under that Act was committed. If the deception as to intention did not result in an obtaining of credit—and "credit" was narrowly interpreted[1]—no offence whatever was committed.

---

16 See above, para. [76].
17 Sections 16 (land) and 3 (2) (chattels).
18 Above, para. [120].
19 *Torts* (4th ed.), 383.
20 [1955] 2 Q.B. 590.
1 *Fisher* v. *Raven*, [1964] A.C. 210; below, para. [269], footnote 3.

[**234**] An offence is committed under s. 15 (1):

(i) Where D induces P to advance money to him by promising to destroy the vermin on P's farm over a period of a year. D has no intention of carrying out his promise.[2]

(ii) Where D promises to make a painting for P from a photograph and receives a deposit from P. D has no intention of carrying out his promise.[3]

It should be emphasised that it must be clearly proved in these cases that D had no intention of carrying out his promise at the time he made it. If he intended to carry out his promise at that time but later changed his mind he is guilty of a breach of contract but of no criminal offence. It has long been recognised that a misrepresentation as to present state of mind will found a civil action for deceit and this is no more difficult to prove in the criminal than in the civil case—though the standard of proof is, of course, higher. Evidence as to the circumstances in which the promise was made, or as to a systematic course of conduct by D or, of course, as to a confession are examples of ways in which a jury might be convinced beyond reasonable doubt that D was deceiving P as to his present intentions.

[**235**] Deceptions as to the present intentions of another person are likely to be rare. The most likely case is that where an agent obtains property for his principal by representing that the principal intends to render services or supply goods, well knowing that the principal has no such intention. There are other possible cases as where an estate agent says that a particular building society is willing to advance half the purchase price of a house, knowing that this is not so, and thus induces a purchaser to pay a deposit.

(e) Statements of opinion

[**236**] A statement of opinion was not a sufficient false pretence under s. 32 of the Larceny Act 1916. The leading case, *Bryan*,[4] carried this doctrine to extreme lengths. There D obtained money from P by representing that certain spoons were of the best quality, equal to Elkington's A, and having as much silver on them as Elkington's A. These statements were false to D's knowledge.[5] Nevertheless ten out of twelve judges[6] held that his conviction must be quashed on the ground that this was mere exaggerated praise by a seller of his goods to which the statute was not intended to apply. Erle, J. said "Whether these spoons . . . were equal to Elkington's A or not, cannot be, as far as I know, decidedly affirmed or denied in the same way as a past fact can be affirmed or denied, but it is in the nature of a matter of opinion". This can hardly be true, however, of the statement that the spoons had as much silver on them as Elkington's A. This seems to be no less a misrepresentation of fact than that a six-carat gold chain is of fifteen carat gold which has subsequently been held to be a sufficient false pretence.[7] Recently it has been

---

[2] *Dent*, above, para. [**233**].
[3] *Fisher* v. *Raven*, above, footnote 1.
[4] (1857), Dears. & B. 265.
[5] D's counsel said: "I cannot contend that the prisoner did not tell a wilful lie . . .".
[6] Willes, J. *dissentiente* and Bramwell, B. *dubitante*.
[7] *Ardley* (1871), L.R. 1 C.C.R. 301.

held[8] that it is a misrepresentation of fact for the accused to state "that they [had] effected necessary repairs to a roof [which repairs were specified] that they had done the work in a proper and workmanlike manner and that [a specified sum] was a fair and reasonable sum to charge for the work involved". The evidence showed that nothing needed to be done to the roof, what had been done served no useful purpose and it could have been done for £5, whereas £35 was charged.

[**237**] The Theft Act gives no guidance as to whether a misrepresentation of opinion is capable of being a deception. In principle there is no reason why it should not be, where the opinion is not honestly held. A vendor's description of his tenant as "a most desirable tenant" when the rent was in arrears and, in the past, had only been paid under pressure was held by the Court of Appeal to be a sufficient misrepresentation to found an action in deceit.[9]

> "In a case where the facts are equally well-known to both parties, what one of them says to the other is frequently nothing but an expression of opinion. . . . But if the facts are not equally well-known to both sides, then a statement of opinion by one who knows the facts best involves very often a statement of a material fact, for he impliedly states that he knows facts which justify his opinion".[10]

[**238**] The way seems open to the courts, if they so wish, to hold that "deception" extends to this kind of case. The use of that term frees them from the fetters of false pretences. A view of commercial morality very different from that of the majority of the judges in *Bryan* now prevails and deliberate mis-statements of opinion would today be generally condemned as dishonest, no less dishonest, indeed, than mis-statements of other facts—for whether an opinion is held or not is a fact—and the law should follow the changed attitude. It may, moreover, be a significant fact that at the time *Bryan* was decided, it was not possible for the prisoner to give evidence in his own defence.[11]

Against this view, it might be argued that, since the Act has expressly removed one limitation on false pretences (representations as to intention) and has said nothing about this limitation, Parliament's intention is to allow it to continue. It is submitted that this would be quite an unjustifiable assumption. Parliament, in fact, has left it to the judges and, by the use of new terminology, given them a more or less free hand. The question now ought to be not "Is it a matter of opinion?" but, "If it is a matter of opinion, was it D's real opinion?" If the opinion is not honestly held there is, in truth, a misrepresentation of fact for the accused's state of mind is a question of fact. The Act indeed recognises this by holding false promises to be deception. If "I intend . . ." (not intending) is a deception, is not "I believe . . ." (not believing) equally a deception?

---

[8] *Jeff and Bassett* (1966), 51 Cr. App. Rep. 29.
[9] *Smith* v. *Land and House Property Corporation* (1884), 28 Ch. D. 7.
[10] *Ibid.*, at p. 15, *per* Bowen, L.J.
[11] In *Ragg* (1860), Bell 214 at 219, Erle, C.J., referring to *Bryan*, said ". . . if suchs tate-ments are indictable a purchaser who wishes to get out of a bad bargain made by his own negligence, might have recourse to an indictment, on the trial of which the vendor's statement on oath would be excluded, instead of being obliged to bring an action where each party would be heard on equal terms."

E. THE MENS REA

(a) *Deliberate or reckless*

[239] The deception must be " deliberate or reckless " and the meaning of these words has already been sufficiently discussed in connection with the meaning of deception.

(b) *Dishonesty*

[240] The deception must also be done "dishonestly". Section 32 of the Larceny Act 1916 required an "intent to defraud" and the Court of Criminal Appeal said repeatedly that this meant "dishonestly"[12] so the law would appear to be unchanged. The Court of Appeal has said,[13] however, that "dishonestly" has a wider ambit without indicating the respects in which it is wider. D may deceive deliberately or recklessly, yet not obtain dishonestly.[14] "Dishonestly" is a separate element in the *mens rea*. The jury should *always* be directed that they must be satisfied that the deception was done dishonestly; though the absence of direction on this point may not be fatal where dishonesty is, in the particular circumstances, an inevitable inference from a deliberate deception.[15] There is no definition of dishonesty for the purposes of this section and the partial definition in s. 2 (1) applies only for the purposes of section 1 of the Act. Obviously the provisions of s. 2 (1) (b) (finder who believes that owner cannot be discovered by taking reasonable steps) are inapplicable to the offence now under discussion. In other respects, however, it is likely that the meaning is the same. Thus it is reasonable to assume that one who obtains property by deception but under a claim of right made in good faith is not guilty.

Against this view might be cited (i) the case of *Parker*[16] and (ii) the provisions regarding blackmail[17] in the Theft Act. In *Parker*, Ridley, J. held that D, a moneylender, was guilty of demanding money upon a forged document, *with intent to defraud*, where he sent to his debtor, P, a letter which purported to come from P's superior officer and demanded that P repay the debt to D.[18] Ridley, J. said:

> ". . . if a man insists upon payment of debt which is due to him, or recovery of a chattel to which he is entitled, and for this purpose resorts to a forged instrument, that would afford evidence of an intent to defraud".

[241] It is clear, furthermore, that D may be guilty of blackmail under the Theft Act though he has not only a claim of right, but also an actual right to the property demanded.[19] It appears then that, if D believes he is entitled to a sum of money (and even if he *is* entitled to it):

---

[12] *Wright*, [1960] Crim. L.R. 366.
[13] *Potger* (1971), 55 Cr. App. Rep. 42 at 46.
[14] See *Wright* (above) and *Griffiths*, [1966] 1 Q.B. 589.
[15] *Potger* (above), footnote 13.
[16] (1910), 74 J.P. 208.
[17] Below, para. [350].
[18] According to the *Justice of the Peace* report, counsel argued that intent to defraud might be inferred from the fact that the sum demanded was more than P agreed to pay. But P did not allege that he was overcharged and the judge directed that there was evidence of an intent to defraud even if the debt was due. See 152 C.C.C. Sess. Pap. 321.
[19] Below, paras. [350]–[352].

    (i) he is guilty of forgery if he demands it with a forged instrument;

    (ii) he is guilty of blackmail if he demands it with menaces; but

    (iii) he is *not* guilty of theft if he appropriates it.

Should the "obtaining" offences be grouped with forgery and blackmail or with theft?[20] It is submitted that they belong with theft. Obtaining and blackmail are grouped together in the Act but (i) the definition of blackmail does not contain the word "dishonestly", and (ii) the relationship between theft and obtaining property is in fact closer than that between blackmail and obtaining property. Even if the *Lawrence* (C.A.) principle[1] is wrong and theft does not embrace virtually the whole of obtaining property, it is certain that theft and obtaining property overlap and are intended to overlap. If D induces P to let him have a horse on hire, dishonestly intending to sell it, D is *prima facie* guilty of offences contrary to both s. 1 and s. 15. If D believes the horse to be his, it would be unfortunate that he should have a defence under s. 1 but not under s. 15. The two offences should be in harmony on this fundamental point.

[242] If this be correct, D would have a defence in the following case:

D's car has been obtained from him by X who gave a cheque drawn on a bank where he had no account and who never paid the price. X has sold the car to a *bona fide* purchaser, P. P refuses to give up the car to D. D, believing that he is entitled to have the car back, recovers possession by pretending to be a mechanic from P's garage collecting the car for servicing.

Here D has no actual right to recover possession of the car; he is certainly guilty of a deliberate deception; but if he genuinely believes he is entitled to possession of the car, it is submitted he is not "dishonest" for the purposes of the section.

[243] Probably the same result must follow where D's belief relates not to any specific property but to the repayment of a debt:

D, a Hungarian woman, has been P's mistress. On the termination of the relationship, P promises to pay D £100. Later he declines to do so. D is advised by a Hungarian lawyer that she is entitled to the money. By a deliberate deception she causes P to pay her £100.[2]

In such a case there was, and no doubt is, a sufficient claim of right to negative an "intent to steal"; and, if so, there should equally be a defence to obtaining by deception.

[244] A more difficult case is that where D obtains something other than the thing to which he has a claim of right.

D's employer, E, cannot pay D's wages because he cannot obtain payment of a debt owed by P to E. D, by deception, obtains some of P's property and delivers it to E, hoping thereby to enable E to procure the payment of the debt—and the means to pay D's wages.

---

[20] If, as submitted above there is no *actus reus* where D is entitled to have the property which he obtains by deception, the question of *mens rea* does not arise. It deserves consideration, however, in case that view is wrong.

[1] Above, para. **[33]**.

[2] *Cf. Bernhard*, [1938] 2 K.B. 264, above, para. **[119]**; below, para. **[363]**.

[245] In such a case[3] Coleridge, J. thought that the facts negatived an intent to defraud; and in a subsequent case[4] Pollock, C. B. put this on the ground that D must have thought he had some right to obtain the property which he did obtain. Of course, he had no right in law so to do, in which case the decision on these facts must depend on the state of D's mind in the particular case. Did he, or did he not, believe he had, or that E had, a legal right to act in this way? Looked at in this way, it would seem rather unlikely that a claim of right could often be made out. D had a claim of right to his wages; E had a claim of right to payment by P of the debt (both being actual rights) but the question is whether D had a claim of right to the particular property he obtained by the deception. Few people would suppose today that they have a right to take the property of a debtor to compel him to pay his creditor.

[246] D may be dishonest even though it is his intention that P shall ultimately suffer no financial loss;[5] as where, by deception, he obtains a loan which he intends one day to repay;[6] or he induces P to invest money in a brickfield which he believes would have been a profitable investment had he been allowed to proceed;[7] or where by deception he obtains goods on credit for which he intends to pay when it is in his power to do so;[8] or where he procures by deception the deposit of money which he intends to repay.[9] In all of these cases P is induced to act to his detriment because he is induced to risk his property when, if he had known the true circumstances, he may well not have done so. There is clear evidence that D knows this—otherwise he would not need to deceive; and it is submitted that an intention to cause P to act to his detriment is enough, even if there is no intention to cause any ultimate economic loss. If D induces P to subscribe for magazines by a false representation that he is a student taking part in a points competition, it is no answer that magazines worth the money would have been delivered in due course.[10]

(c) Intent permanently to deprive

[247] Though it was not expressed in the Act, such an intent was always held to be an essential element in the former crime of false pretences.[11] D is not guilty of an offence under s. 15 if, by deception, he obtains the loan of a horse, or the hire of a car with the intention of returning it at the end of the period of loan or hire—or even at the end of some later period—and this even though he never intends to pay the rent agreed. The same is true where D obtains ownership which he intends to restore.

[248] The constituents of "intent permanently to deprive" have been sufficiently examined in connection with theft.[12] The elaboration by s. 6 of the

---

3 *Williams* (1836), 7 C. & P. 354.
4 *Hamilton* (1845), 1 Cox C.C. 244.
5 *Carpenter* (1911), 22 Cox C.C. 618; *Welham* v. *D.P.P.*, [1961] A.C. 103; [1960] 1 All E.R. 805.
6 *McCall*, [1971] Crim. L.R. 237 following *Carpenter* (footnote 5, above.).
7 *Hamilton* (footnote 4, above).
8 *Naylor* (1865), L.R. 1 C.C.R. 4. *Cf.* the discussion of *Williams* (1953) (above, para. [121] *et seq.*).
9 *Carpenter* (footnote 5, above).
10 *Potger* (1971), 55 Cr. App. Rep. 42 at 44. In *Waterfall* (below para. [265]) it was assumed that D was not dishonest if he believed that he would be able to get the money to pay for the taxi-ride. This seems to be inconsistent with the cases cited above.
11 *Kilham* (1870), L.R. 1 C.C.R. 261.
12 Above, para. [130].

meaning of the term applies for the purposes of s. 15 with the necessary adaptation of the reference to appropriation.[13] Reference may, therefore, be made to the discussion above.[14]

(d) With or without a view to gain

[249] There is no provision corresponding to that for theft that "it is immaterial whether the appropriation is made with a view to gain . . .".[15] It can hardly be doubted, however, that no further element of this nature is required in addition to the elements of *mens rea* described above. The draftsman perhaps took the view that the intention to obtain property, which is implicit in the subsection, in itself constituted a view to gain so[16] that any further express requirement would be superfluous. The terms of the Act make it clear that if D appropriates P's diamond and throws it into a deep pond, intending to deprive both P and himself permanently of it, he is guilty of theft. It does not, in express terms, say that D is guilty of deception if he obtains the ownership in or possession of P's diamond by deception with the intention of throwing the diamond into the pond and depriving P and himself permanently of it. It is submitted, however, that the obtainer of the diamond would be guilty of obtaining by deception. It is desirable that the same principles should govern s. 15 as s. 1. If the property in the diamond did not pass, D might be charged under either section. It has been suggested above[17] that it will save a great deal of difficulty if, in such cases, the charge is always brought under s. 15. This advice would be vitiated if s. 15 were construed to require a view to gain.

(e) Intention to obtain property

[250] It is submitted that an intention to obtain property for oneself or another is a constituent of the *mens rea*. The *actus reus* of the offence is not committed where D, dishonestly and by deception, causes P to be deprived of his property but neither D nor anyone else obtains it. An intention to deprive another of property is therefore not a sufficient *mens rea* for the offence.

[251] If D dishonestly tells P that a work of art owned by P is obscene, that it is being looked for by the police and that the best thing he can do is to burn it, D is not guilty of an offence under the section if P complies. Suppose then, that D's object is to cause loss to one person, but that this will, incidentally, bring profit to another. For example, D induces P to exclude E from his will by telling P false stories of E's misconduct. D does not know or care who will profit as a result of E's exclusion from the will. Someone almost certainly will. Suppose that P, having substituted S's name for E's, dies and the executors pay the legacy to S. There is no doubt that D has dishonestly obtained property by deception for S. The *actus reus* is complete. Is it a defence for D to say that he did not *intend* to obtain property for anyone, that his only intention was to ensure that E did *not* benefit and that he would have been perfectly content with the outcome if P had decided to spend all his money in his lifetime?

---

[13] Section 15 (3).
[14] See paras. [130]–[148].
[15] Section 1 (2), above, para. [117].
[16] See below, para. [250].
[17] See para. [30].

It is submitted that the essence of the offence is the obtaining of property; that, in this example, the obtaining of the advantage is merely incidental to the fulfilment of D's plan and that, accordingly, D should not be guilty. If he were to be convicted, the iniquity of his conduct (when he came to be sentenced) would be found to lie in his malicious deprivation of E; but that is not an offence. This is to say, in effect, that a direct and not merely an oblique intention[18] to obtain property for oneself or another, should be regarded as a constituent of the offence.

2 OBTAINING A PECUNIARY ADVANTAGE BY DECEPTION

[252] The draft bill proposed by the Criminal Law Revision Committee would have created two offences of (i) obtaining credit by deception and (ii) inducing an act by deception with a view to gain. The former offence was designed to replace the offence of obtaining credit by fraud contrary to the Debtors' Act 1869 and to extend its scope; the latter was to provide for relatively minor cases which did not amount to the obtaining either of property or credit by deception, but which, it was felt, should be punishable.[19] Instead of providing for each of the relatively minor cases by a detailed provision, the Committee proposed a definition in broad, general terms. This attracted a great deal of criticism and, in consequence, a new provision was introduced to create the offence of obtaining a pecuniary advantage by deception. This was intended to, and appears to succeed in, encompassing cases of obtaining credit by deception and the minor cases which the Committee sought to cover. Section 16 provides:

"(1) A person who by any deception dishonestly obtains for himself or another any pecuniary advantage shall on conviction on indictment be liable to imprisonment for a term not exceeding five years.

(2) The cases in which a pecuniary advantage within the meaning of this section is to be regarded as obtained for a person are cases where—

(a) any debt or charge for which he makes himself liable or is or may become liable (including one not legally enforceable) is reduced or in whole or in part evaded or deferred; or

(b) he is allowed to borrow by way of overdraft, or to take out any policy of insurance or annuity contract, or obtains an improvement of the terms on which he is allowed to do so; or

(c) he is given the opportunity to earn remuneration or greater remuneration in an office or employment, or to win money by betting.

(3) For purposes of this section 'deception' has the same meaning as in section 15 of this Act".

[253] It is submitted that s. 16 creates only one offence. Subsection (2) merely describes the various types of pecuniary advantage the obtaining of which will amount to an offence, just as s. 4 describes the property which may

---

18 Smith and Hogan, 37–39.
19 The *Report*, Cmnd. 2977, at p. 45.

be stolen under s. 1. It is however important that the particulars of the offence should specify precisely what is the pecuniary advantage which the accused is alleged to have obtained. "If you indict a man for stealing your watch, you cannot convict him of attempting to steal your umbrella;"[20] and, equally a man who is charged with obtaining a pecuniary advantage of one sort should not be convicted of obtaining a pecuniary advantage of a completely different sort. So a conviction was quashed where D was charged with obtaining a pecuniary advantage within the meaning of s. 16 (2) (*a*) and the court held that he had obtained a pecuniary advantage, not within that provision, but within s. 16 (2) (*c*)[1]. A case which seems to go to extreme lengths is *Hickmott* v. *Curd*[2] where the particulars alleged a pecuniary advantage within s. 16 (*a*) and the evidence established a pecuniary advantage within that provision; but the offence proved was committed at a different point in time (though on the same occasion) from that alleged; the deception was a different deception and the advantage obtained was a different advantage; yet the conviction was upheld.

A. THE DECEPTION

[254] Since "deception" has the same meaning as in s. 15, reference should be made to the discussion of the word in connection with that section.[3] Exactly the same considerations seem to be applicable as in obtaining property by deception.

B. PECUNIARY ADVANTAGE

[255] The meaning of this term is limited to the cases set out in the three paragraphs of s. 16 (2).

(*a*) *Section* 16 (2) (*a*)

[256] (i) *Liability for a debt or charge.*—It must be proved that there is a "debt or charge for which [D] makes himself liable or is or may become liable." It seems that the offence may be committed in the three following ways:

(*i*) A debt for which D *makes himself* liable is reduced, evaded or deferred;

(*ii*) A debt for which D *is* liable is reduced, evaded or deferred;

(*iii*) A debt for which D *may become* liable is reduced, evaded or deferred.

It is convenient to look first at case (*ii*). This contemplates an existing debt owed by D to P. D deceives P with the result that P agrees to accept a less sum in full satisfaction (reduction) or to forgive the debt altogether (evasion), or to accept payment of the whole sum at a date later than it is due (deferment). D, a tenant, owing his landlord, P, £10 of back rent, tells P a false hard luck story with the object and effect of causing P to agree that he need pay only £5 (reduction); or that he need pay nothing (evasion); or that he may have a month to pay (deferment). D's agreement may not be binding on him, not only because it has *ex hypothesi* been obtained by fraud and is therefore voidable, but also because there is no consideration for it; but that is immaterial.

---

[20] *McPherson* (1857), Dears. & B. 197 at 200, *per* Cockburn, C.J.
[1] *Aston and Hadley*, [1970] 3 All E.R. 1045; below, para. **[263]**.
[2] [1971] 2 All E.R. 1399; below para. **[267]**. *Cf.* commentary at [1971] Crim. L.R. 485.
[3] Above, paras. **[200]**-**[238]**.

Just as in theft it is enough that D assumes the rights of an owner though he does not obtain those rights in law, so here it is enough that he induces P to treat him as a debtor with a reduced or deferred obligation or as completely forgiven, even though the debt remains unaltered in law. It is sufficient if *either*

(a) the *payment* of the debt is reduced, evaded or deferred;[4] or

(b) the *debt itself* is reduced in amount or the *obligation* to pay it is evaded or deferred by an agreement effective (though voidable) in law.

[**257**] Case (*i*) presents greater difficulties. It appears to contemplate a situation in which fraud is practised before any debt has come into existence. It will be noted that the present tense governs both the incurring of the liability to pay the debt and the reduction of the debt. The debt is incurred and its amount reduced, etc. at the same time. It has been argued by Professor Elliott[5] that:

> "The statute could have made it a pecuniary advantage to get a reduced debt, but it does not; it makes it a pecuniary advantage to get a debt reduced, i.e. the full unreduced debt is the one for which [D] must make himself liable or is or may become liable."

It is submitted, however, that while the paragraph may be unhappily expressed, its meaning is plain. The debt for which D makes himself liable is a smaller debt than P would have agreed to had the deception not been practised; or it is payable at a later date than P would have agreed to had the deception not been practised. (Consideration of evasion is postponed for the moment.) How else can one both incur a debt and get it reduced or deferred by deception *at the same time*? In other words, the section, perhaps clumsily, *does* make it an offence to get a reduced debt or a deferred debt.

For example, P, a hairdresser, advertises that he charges lower rates for old age pensioners. On entering P's shop, D falsely states that he is a pensioner, whereupon P quotes the lower rate, cuts D's hair and charges him accordingly. Or a club, which allows credit to its permanent members, has a rule requiring temporary members to pay cash. D, who is a temporary member, falsely states that he is a permanent member and so induces the club to supply him with goods or services on credit.

[**258**] Elliott argues that cases like these are not within the section, on the ground that the debt which D gets reduced or deferred is not one for which he makes himself liable: the debt which is reduced is the hairdresser's full charge, for which D never makes himself liable; the debt which the club defers is that which would arise on a cash sale and D never makes himself liable for that, since the only contract of sale he makes is a credit sale.

The difficulty with this interpretation is that it confines the operation of the section to case (*ii*), that is, where there is an existing debt. It gives no meaning to the words "makes himself liable" or "may become liable." It is submitted

---

[4] *Locker*, [1971] 2 All E.R. 875 (C.A.).
[5] "Obtaining Credit by Fraud", [1969] Crim. L.R. 339 at 342. See the author's reply, [1971] Crim. L.R. 448.

that these words must be taken to add something; and that the only reasonable construction is that stated above.

[**259**] The most difficult situation is that of *evasion* under case (*ii*). If D, by deception, induces P to render for nothing some service for which P would normally charge him, it is argued by Elliott[6] that there is no "debt . . . for which D makes himself liable or is or may become liable . . ." If this is correct, it does indeed seem to follow that there is no offence. It is submitted, however that it is not correct. P, has been induced by deception to render to D some service for which D knows he would normally be charged. If, on discovering the truth, P were to sue for the value of the service rendered, it is submitted that he would recover. His cause of action would be in quasi-contract and the money would be recovered as a debt due from D to P from the moment that the service was rendered.[7] If this is correct—and it is, of course, a question of civil law—D has by deception, evaded a debt for which he makes himself liable by requesting and enjoying the service rendered by P. When P has rendered the service, he believes he has no right to recover any debt from D; but, in truth, he has such a right. This, it is submitted, is the evasion of a debt by deception. It may be noted that, if this argument is correct, it provides an alternative explanation for the situation under case (*i*) where the debt is reduced. D may be made liable in quasi-contract for the unreduced sum and so is paying less than he is obliged to pay.

[**260**] Case (*iii*) appears to contemplate a possible future debt. This would seem to cover the case of conditional liability. D is to become liable to pay money to P, if a certain event occurs. It would seem immaterial whether this potential liability arises under an existing contract or is in the course of negotiation. D, by deception, persuades P that the amount due should be less than an existing agreement provides, or than P would agree to in a contract being negotiated; or that there should be no liability; or that the liability shall arise later than an existing agreement provides or than P would agree to in a contract being negotiated, as the case may be. For example, D has entered into a contract to pay certain sums of money to P in the event of P incurring certain disabilities. D, by deception, induces P to agree that sums be reduced; or not payable at all; or payable a month later than the time specified in the contract. Similarly if D and P are negotiating such a contract and D by deception secures similar improvements in the terms.

Case (*iii*) would also cover the situation where D makes a false statement in his income tax return whereby his assessment to tax is reduced. Case (*i*) does not apply because D does not *make himself* liable; liability is imposed by law. Case (*ii*) does not apply because D *is* not liable—yet. But it is a debt for which he *may become* liable. This is a new weapon which the Inland Revenue does not appear to have wielded yet.

[**261**] (ii) *The effect of the deception.*—The essence of the offence is that the deception operates on P's mind and causes him to confer the pecuniary advan-

---

[6] *Ibid.*
[7] This argument is more fully developed in [1971] Crim. L.R. 448 at 453 *et seq.* Note that the provision would also be satisfied in the case where D induces P to look for payment for the service to be rendered to D, not to D but to E. *Cf. Royle,* [1971] 3 All E.R. 1359, discussed in [1972] Crim. L.R. 4.

tage. Since the advantage must be obtained by deception, it must be P who reduces, forgives or defers the debt.

> "... to be relevant, the deception, for the purposes of s. 16 (2) (*a*), must at least normally be a deception which operates on the mind of the person deceived so as to influence him to do or to refrain from doing something whereby the debt is evaded or deferred.[8]"

Thus no offence was committed in the leading case of *Locker*,[9] where D owed two months rent to his landlord, P, and gave P a cheque for the amount due, drawn on a bank at which D had no account. The argument that D had caused the payment of the debt to be deferred by deception was rejected by a Full Court of the Court of Appeal:

> "When the cheque was received by [P] he thought the debt was being paid; he thought that this was the quickest and obvious way in which his obligation was going to be satisfied. It never, on the evidence, crossed his mind that he was being invited to wait for his money, or that in any sense the actions of the appellant were intended to induce him to wait."[10]

Where a creditor takes a cheque in payment of an existing debt there is an inevitable time-lag between the receipt of the cheque and its being credited to the creditor's account or cashed. It was held that inducing a creditor to accept payment by cheque does not amount to deferring the debt. Receipt of a cheque is regarded as a present, though conditional payment. It would be otherwise, of course, if D induced P to accept a post-dated cheque, for example by representing falsely that a large cheque would be paid into his account in a week's time.

[262] (iii) *Obtaining credit.*—If the deception causes P to enter into a contract under which he gives credit to D, it is submitted that D has obtained the deferment of a debt by deception. Since the whole contract is procured by the deception, so is the term under which payment is deferred. It was held under the old law that one who obtained a meal in a restaurant by fraud had obtained "credit" by fraud.[11] "Credit" was simply the postponement of the obligation to pay for the meal until after the meal had been supplied and eaten. If the postponement of the obligation was obtained by the deception, it follows that the deferment of the debt was likewise obtained: it is the same thing; obtaining credit *is* deferring a debt.

[263] It is otherwise where the debt is payable immediately, and no credit is given. P may have been induced by deception to allow D to incur the debt, but that is not an offence. In *Aston and Hadley*,[12] D1 and D2 went to a betting-shop and made out a betting-slip for a bet of £70 on a dog. The bet was accepted by the manager and the slip was given to the cashier to ring up the bet on her till. It was well understood that the bet was payable immediately in cash. As the manager tendered the receipt and demanded the money, D1 counted out the notes extremely slowly. The progress of the race could be heard on a

---

[8] *Aston and Hadley*, [1970] 3 All E.R. 1045 at 1048 (C.A.).
[9] [1971] 2 All E.R. 875. See comment at [1971] Crim. L.R. 423.
[10] [1971] 2 All E.R. 875 at 880.
[11] *Jones*, [1898] 1 Q.B. 119.
[12] [1970] 3 All E.R. 1045.

broadcast relay in the shop and, when it became obvious that the dog in question was not going to win, the accused gathered the money and left in haste. It was alleged that they had evaded a debt for which D1 had made himself liable, by the false representation that D1 intended to pay immediately the sum of £70. The prosecution argued that the slow counting of the money was the deception. The convictions were quashed on the ground that the slow counting did not constitute such a representation and did not operate on P's mind in such a way as to bring about the evasion of the debt. The court thought, however, that there was evidence of a misrepresentation of an intention to pay as soon as the bet was accepted which influenced P to allow the bet to be placed—i.e., to *create* the debt. The court thought that this constituted an offence under s. 16 (2) (*c*). It seems implicit that the court did not think it an offence under s. 16 (2) (*a*) and it is submitted that it was not; though the debt was induced by deception, it was not evaded or deferred by deception.

[264] (iv) *Deferment and evasion achieved otherwise than by deception.*—It is not an offence under the section to defer or evade payment otherwise than by deception. If D, having consumed a meal in a restaurant, were to decide to leave without paying, he might evade payment of the debt but he clearly would not do so by deception. It would make no difference if he were to practise a deception in order to make good his escape. Suppose he points through the window, shouts "The town hall is on fire" and departs while the attention of the waiters is distracted, he does not offend against the section since no one has been deceived into agreeing that payment or the obligation to pay be deferred or avoided. If D, seeing P, the rent-collector, at the door, sends his son to say, "Sorry, Daddy's out," with the result that P goes on his way, D has evaded payment of the debt and he has also practised a deception, but he has not persuaded the rent-collector to defer or forgive the debt any more than if he had hidden under the bed or run away.[13] Payment is probably not evaded or deferred by deception while the creditor continues to press for payment.

[265] The principle laid down in *Locker*[14] must apply equally on a charge of evasion as it does on a charge of deferment; it must be proved that P *agreed* that the obligation to pay the debt be avoided or be not enforced; and it is not enough that D in fact evades payment. Prosecutors and courts seem to have been slow to recognise this. Thus, in *Waterfall*,[15] where D induced P, a taxi-driver, to drive him from Southampton to London by falsely stating that he had the money to pay, the Court of Appeal thought it was quite clear that he had obtained a pecuniary advantage in that he had made himself liable to a debt which he had evaded. This is very difficult to follow. It is true that in fact D never paid the debt so he evaded it in that sense; but P was never induced by any deception to agree that D be released from his obligation to pay or that the obligation to pay be not enforced. P was deceived into giving D a ride and into allowing him credit; and, if the indictment had alleged that he obtained not the evasion but the deferment of the debt, then it is submitted that it would have been correct.

---

[13] The author has changed his view about this difficult example since the first edition; see para. [329] of that edition.
[14] Above, para. [261].
[15] [1970] 1 Q.B. 148; [1969] 3 All E.R. 1048. Criticised by Griew, (1970), 33 M.L.R. 217.

[**266**] In the unsatisfactory case of *Page*,[16] D obtained the hire of a car by drawing a cheque on his account, knowing that it was overdrawn and that he had no authority to overdraw. It was held that he had evaded the debt by deception. In *Locker*,[17] the Full Court held that *Page* was right in that it held that evading payment was evading the debt: "In so far, therefore, as there might be any question of the correctness of the decision in *Page* on that point, we would confirm it."[18] The words, "on that point," appear to be significant, for it is difficult to see that *Page* can stand with the decision in *Locker*. The cases are indistinguishable on the facts: in both P took the cheque as present payment of the debt. It is true of course that a person who receives a "dud" cheque and supposes he is paid, is deceived and induced into refraining from pressing for payment. If this constitutes evasion by deception, then there was an evasion in *Locker* as well as in *Page*. In that event, it is very surprising that the court did not say so, even if it did not uphold the conviction. The result would be that all payments of debts by cheques known to be invalid would be offences under s. 16. Some may think this a very desirable result; but it is very doubtful if the section is intended to go so far and *Locker* seems to decide it does not. It is thought that *Page* was wrongly decided.

[**267**] A similar criticism must be made of *Hickmott* v. *Curd*.[19] D was charged with obtaining a pecuniary advantage by evading a debt by deception by representing that he had no money with which to pay for three double brandies. It was found that no one believed his statement that he had no money so that the particulars as set out were not satisfied. He had, however, before obtaining the drink, represented that he intended to pay for it, not merely by ordering it (which would have been enough) but by displaying his money. The court held that these facts disclosed an offence contrary to s. 16 and it was immaterial that the particulars were inaccurate. ". . . the appellant . . . knew perfectly well what he was there to meet, i.e. dishonestly and by deception obtaining these three brandies . . ." Obtaining the *brandies* was of course an offence against s. 15, not s. 16; and while, no doubt, the obtaining of credit did amount to an offence under s. 16, it did not consist in the *evasion* but the *deferment* of the debt.

Would there have been an evasion if D's story that he had no money (his money was hidden in his boot) had been believed? It is thought not. The debt would not have been forgiven. There would have been at most a deferment. If a creditor believes that his debtor has no money and consequently says that he may have a month to pay, there has certainly been a deferment; but is this so if the creditor simply ceases to press for payment because he believes it is useless to do so? If his demand for present payment is continuing, it is difficult to see that he has been deceived into deferring the debt or the payment of it.

[**268**] (v) *Reduction, evasion or deferment of a charge.*—Where D enters into a contract to do something other than pay money he may, by deception, obtain a "pecuniary advantage" in the literal sense of that term. If he is a seller,

---

[16] [1971] 2 All E.R. 870.
[17] Above, para. [**261**].
[18] [1971] 2 All E.R. at 880.
[19] [1971] 2 All E.R. 1399.

his dishonesty may enable him to get a higher price; and, as the price will usually be property, he will be guilty of an offence under s. 15. In that case there is no need to consider his liability under s. 16. There are cases of dishonesty where no property is obtained and no debt is reduced, evaded or deferred, but the justification for criminal sanctions is no less than in those cases. Whether these cases are offences depends on the meaning of the word "charge" in s. 16 (2) (*a*). This is obscure. One very tenable view is that " 'charge for which [one] is . . . liable' means simply what one is bound to pay as a charge for something—as when one speaks of being charged a price or charged for a service or privilege."[20]

If this is correct, the word is of no significance because it adds nothing to "debt." At the other extreme, "charge" might be given a very wide meaning: "a charge in its general sense is an obligation or liability."[1] If this be the proper meaning of the word, then it adds a great deal. But the use of the word in this very broad sense is rather unusual. More commonly, it is used in an intermediate sense to signify an encumbrance on property, such as a "land charge", a mortgage or a lien.

[**269**] It is impossible to predict with confidence what interpretation will be adopted. Everything depends on the choice of principles of statutory construction which commend themselves to the court to which the task falls. Only Lord Wilberforce's "fair, large and liberal" construction[2] could result in the broad meaning being preferred. The principle of strict construction of penal statutes would point to the narrow meaning.[3] Perhaps some *via media* is the most likely route.

The kind of case where the problem arises is that where the parties agree to an exchange of services, the performance of one service to be postponed to the other. For example:

D promises P that, if P will dig D's garden, D will give him a night's lodging. P digs the garden and D, as he intended all along, refuses to give him the lodging. D has obtained no property, so it is not an offence under s. 15; and he has not incurred a debt, so it is not an offence under s. 16, unless "charge" can be given the broad meaning. If it can be given that meaning, then there is an offence of obtaining the deferment of the charge by deception—just as the debt is deferred in the case where credit is obtained by deception in a restaurant.[4] There seems to be no reason why the criminal law should not cover this situation, as it would have done if D had offered £1 instead of lodging.

Even if the broad meaning be not adopted, the provision might be held to cover the reduction, evasion or deferment of an encumbrance on property. For example, the following type of fraud was common at one time.

"A reluctant vendor [of land] may make the title appear ineligible or defective, merely to induce a purchaser to forego the specific performance of a beneficial contract."[5]

---

[20] Griew, 6-34.
[1] Jowitt, *The Dictionary of English Law*, I, 350. [2] Above, para. [8].
[3] The narrow view is supported by *Fisher* v. *Raven*, [1964] A.C. 210, in which the House of Lords held, in effect, that "debt or liability" in the Debtors Act 1869 meant "debt" even though liability was defined to mean liability to pay money or moneys' worth.
[4] Above, para. [**262**].
[5] *Abstracts of Title* by Richard Preston, (1818) I, 35. Preston thought "a person playing this game, merits severe animadversion, and even punishment."

The purchaser's rights against the land may well be described as a charge; and, if so, the charge has been evaded by deception.

[270] (vi) *Unenforceable debts or charges.*—The rule under the Debtors Act 1869 was that the debt or liability had to be legally enforceable in order to constitute credit. So it was held that no offence was committed where credit was obtained under a wagering contract which was void in law[6] or under a contract which was illegal as contravening a statutory regulation relating to hire purchase.[7] The same would no doubt have been true of the case where P, a prostitute, allowed D to have intercourse with her on a promise of payment which D never intended to fulfil.[8]

Section 16 (2) (*a*) specifically covers debts or charges which are "not legally enforceable". It is arguable that, under the Theft Act, there must still be a debt or charge recognised as such by the law, whether enforceable or not. The law does recognise such a thing as an "unenforceable obligation"—for example, an otherwise valid contract which is not supported by a memorandum in writing under the Statute of Frauds, the Law of Property Act 1925 or the Hire-Purchase Act 1938.[9] It is clear that a debt due under such a contract is one which is "not legally enforceable" under s. 16 (2) (*a*). On the other hand it might be argued with some force that the so-called "debt" due to the bookmaker under a wagering contract is a complete nullity in law[10] and thus not a "debt" within the meaning of the subsection at all. The mischief rule of interpretation, however, suggests that "not legally enforceable" should apply to this case. There was no case before the Act where a charge of obtaining credit by fraud failed merely because the debt was unenforceable under the Statute of Frauds or any similar act. It is at cases like *Garlick*[11] that these words are aimed; and in *Aston and Hadley*,[12] the court had no doubt that a wagering debt was within the section.

[271] The wager is void by statute, but not illegal. The "debt" due to the prostitute, on the other hand, is the fruit of a contract which is illegal at common law; that due under the hire-purchase agreement which contravenes the statutory regulation is the fruit of a contract which is illegal by statute. Should this distinction between voidness and illegality make a difference? It might be argued that, while the court can go to the lengths of affording the protection of the criminal law to the holder of a merely void "debt", it should not do so where the "debt" is tainted with illegality. This may be answered, however, by observing that the criminal law will protect even the thief in the possession of his stolen property against those who would dispossess him without right or claim of right. If D dishonestly takes from a robber, P, the proceeds of the robbery, D is guilty of theft. If D obtains the proceeds of the robbery by

---

[6] *Leon*, [1945] K.B. 136.
[7] *Garlick* (1958), 42 Cr. App. Rep. 141.
[8] *Cf. Caslin*, [1961] 1 All E.R. 246.
[9] Cheshire and Fifoot, *Law of Contract* (7th ed.), 166-189.
[10] All contracts or agreements, whether by parole or in writing, by way of gaming or wagering, shall be null and void . . . : Gaming Act 1845, s. 18.
[11] Above, footnote 7.
[12] [1970] 3 All E.R. 1045 at 1047; above, para. **[263]**.

deception from P, he will be guilty of an offence under s. 15 of the Act.   Why, if P is protected in the possession of the illegally obtained money, should he not equally be protected in respect of the illegal debt?   A possible answer is that the money undeniably exists and P's possession of it is recognised by the law; but that the debt does not exist, for the law refuses to recognise it.

[272] It is submitted, however, that these theoretical difficulties should not stand in the way of an interpretation of the Act which will remedy the mischief at which it is aimed, and which is not confined to the case of merely void obligations.   P should not be deprived of the protection of the criminal law because, when he was defrauded, he was committing some other offence against a statutory regulation or was engaging in immoral conduct upon which the law frowns.   Bookmakers and prostitutes, though their activities are looked upon with varying degrees of disfavour by the law, are entitled to be protected against fraud.

(b) Section 16 (2) (b)

[273] It is curious that the draftsman thought it necessary to make a special reference to borrowing by way of overdraft.   When D overdraws on his account, he does not become presently liable to repay the debt which he owes to the bank.   Why not?   Only because the bank has been deceived into deferring liability.   He thus makes himself liable for a debt which is deferred and therefore is expressly covered by s. 16 (2) (a) as well as (b).[13]

It may be that insurance and annuity contracts were singled out because they are cases where the insurer is peculiarly dependent on the assured's good faith, since the special facts which affect the risk lie peculiarly within the latter's knowledge.   It may, therefore, have been thought that the insurer needs special protection against the assured's fraud.

These cases are not within s. 16 (2) (a) since the situation is one in which the liability or potential liability of a debtor is increased.   If the increased sum were actually paid, the payment would probably be too remote[14] from the deception to constitute an offence under s. 15.

[274] Contracts of insurance are contracts *uberrimae fidei*, so that, under the civil law, there is an obligation to make disclosure of any material circumstance.[15] Failure to do so renders the contract voidable.   No action will lie for damages, however—i.e., the non-disclosure is not "deceit"—and it is submitted that a mere non-disclosure will not amount to a deception ("by words or conduct") for the purposes of s. 16, unless the non-disclosure makes, and is known by the accused to make, the words or conduct which have been used positively misleading.[16]

---

[13] Griew, 6-38, takes a different view.
[14] See above, paras. **[187]**-**[188]**.
[15] Chitty, *Contracts*, I, 159-160.
[16] *Kylsant*, [1932] 1 K.B. 442; [1931] All E.R. Rep. 179.   A case where ". . . a document has been put forward . . . in such a form that though it stated every fact correctly, fact by fact, and everything was correctly stated by the card, yet the true effect of what was said was completely false and completely misleading."

(c) Section 16 (2) *(c)*

[275] Obtaining an office or employment by false pretences did not amount to an offence under the Larceny Act 1916, and will probably not be an offence under s. 15 of the Theft Act since the obtaining of the salary or wages is too remote from the false pretence or deception.[17] This case is now specifically dealt with. D commits an offence if he obtains an appointment by stating that he has a qualification which he does not possess; or if he obtains the appointment at a higher salary by stating that he has that qualification. The offence is also committed by one who obtains an appointment, or an appointment on better terms, for another in a similar way.

[276] It is not an offence under the section to obtain the opportunity to earn remuneration otherwise than in an office or in employment. The exact scope of the provision is doubtful. It has been argued[18] that a freelance author does not earn money *"in* employment" by his publishers, nor a solicitor *"in* employment" by his client; that " 'employment' seems to be confined to a fairly narrow range of relationships and may in fact be limited to the relationship of master and servant." If this is so, it is unfortunate; but it may be that the provision is not so severely limited. The following cases which have actually occurred (without giving rise to any authoritative decision) might reasonably be regarded as instances of earning "in employment":

D calls at P's house and says, falsely, that the Forestry Commission has said that a tree in P's garden should be cut down and that he will do the job for £8. P employs him to cut down the tree.

D offers to clean P's windows. P says E is his regular window cleaner. D says, falsely, that E has retired. P employs D to clean the windows.

These are instances of the "employment" of independent contractors. Even the solicitor and the author may be said to be employed—in the "simple language . . . used and understood by ordinary literate men and women"—[19] and, if they are employed, their remuneration is surely earned "in employment."

[277] Before the Act, it was no offence where D induced P to take bets on credit by false pretences. If the horse backed by D happened to win, the money, it was held, was paid out because D had backed a winning horse, not because he had made a false pretence.[20] That case is also specifically dealt with; and D would apparently now be guilty whether he was allowed to bet on cash or credit terms.

C. THE MENS REA

(a) Deliberate or reckless

[278] The deception must be deliberate or reckless, as in the case of obtaining property by deception and precisely the same considerations apply as in the case of s. 15.[1]

---

[17] *Lewis* (1922), Russell, 1186.
[18] Griew, 6-40.
[19] *Treacy* v. *D.P.P.*, [1971] A.C. 537 at 565; [1971] 1 All E.R. 110 at 124, *per* Lord Diplock.
[20] *Clucas*, [1949] 2 K.B. 226.
[1] Above, para. [200].

(b) Dishonesty

[**279**] The two questions which arise here are (i) whether D is dishonest if he intends to give full value in money or money's worth for any pecuniary advantage he obtains; and (ii) whether a claim of right to the advantage is a defence.

[**280**] (i) *Intention to give full value not a defence.*—It seems from the examples given in s. 16 (2) that an intention to give full value in return for the pecuniary advantage which has been obtained by deception is unlikely to afford a defence. Suppose that D, by making false statements as to his assets, persuades his bank manager to allow him to borrow by way of overdraft. Section 16 (2) (*b*) says that he is to be regarded as having obtained a pecuniary advantage. It seems that it will be no answer to the charge for D to say that he intended (and was able) to repay the loan with interest in the agreed time. In a sense he has not obtained a "pecuniary advantage" at all, since he is going to give a full economic return for what he gets;[2] but he is guilty. Similarly, it would seem, if D, aged 48, applies for an appointment for which the maximum age is 45, stating that he is 44. He is guilty of the offence if he is appointed (and of an attempt if he is not) and it is no answer for him to say, truthfully, "I was the best qualified candidate and would have earned every penny of my salary if appointed". It is true that s. 16 (2) (*c*) defines only "pecuniary advantage" and the advantage must be obtained "dishonestly"; but it is thought that it would defeat the intention behind s. 16 (2) if the meaning given to "dishonestly" excluded these cases.

An intention to give full value was never a defence to a charge of obtaining by false pretences[3] and would still not be a defence under the law of obtaining by deception;[4] so it is, perhaps, consistent that it should not be a defence here either.

[**281**] (ii) *A claim of right to the advantage.*—It has been submitted above that a claim of right to the property obtained should be a defence to a charge of obtaining by deception, contrary to s. 15. If this is correct, it is submitted that it must follow that such a claim is also a defence to a charge under s. 16. This, of course, is quite different from the situation considered in the previous paragraph. An intention to give full value is not a defence; but a belief that one has already given full value and is entitled to the pecuniary advantage may be a defence. Suppose that D enters into a contract with P that P shall do certain work for £50. P does the work and asks for payment. D is firmly convinced that he paid £50 in cash at the time the contract was made. P, also in good faith, denies this and threatens to sue. D offers to give P a pencil which he says is of 15 carat gold if P will (i) accept £20 in satisfaction; or (ii) forgive the debt altogether; or (iii) wait a month for payment. D knows that the pencil is not made of gold. The debt has been reduced, or evaded, or deferred, by deception. If P honestly (though wrongly) believes that there is no debt, he does not believe he is obtaining anything to which he is not entitled. By analogy to obtaining property, it would seem that this cannot be an offence.

---

[2] *Cf.* the similar problem which arises in connection with the meaning of "a view to gain", below, para. [**353**].

[3] *Hamilton*, (1845) 1 Cox C.C. 244; *Berg v. Sadler and Moore*, [1937] 2 K.B. 158; [1937] 1 All E.R. 637.

[4] Above, para. [**249**].

E

(c) *Intention to obtain a pecuniary advantage*

[282] Causing a pecuniary disadvantage to another is not necessarily the same thing as obtaining a pecuniary advantage for oneself or another. An exactly similar argument to that employed in relation to obtaining property by deception[5] may be relied on here. Suppose that D's object is to cause loss to one person, but that this will, incidentally, bring a pecuniary advantage to another. For example, E is a candidate for an appointment with P. D sends to P a reference containing false statements, so as to ensure that E will not be appointed. D does not know who the other candidates are, but, if his deception is the reason why E is not appointed, one of them will obtain a pecuniary advantage as the direct result of D's deception. Suppose that the deception is successful and, consequently, S is appointed and E is not. There is no doubt that D has dishonestly obtained a pecuniary advantage by deception for S. The *actus reus* is complete. Is it a defence for D to say that he did not *intend* to obtain a pecuniary advantage for anyone, that his only intention was to ensure that E did *not* obtain a pecuniary advantage and that he would have been perfectly content with the outcome if P had decided not to make an appointment at all?

It is submitted that the essence of the offence is the obtaining of the advantage; that, in this example, the obtaining of the advantage is merely incidental to the fulfilment of D's plan and that, accordingly, D should not be guilty.

In the recent case of *Royle*[6], Edmund Davies, L.J., said that s. 16 has created a "judicial nightmare" and expressed the hope of the Court of Appeal that it would soon be replaced by a simpler provision. That hope is echoed here.

---

[5] Above, para. [250].
[6] [1971] 3 All E.R. 1359.   See the author's attempt to restate the effect of s. 16 as interpreted by the courts in [1972] Crim. L.R. 4.

CHAPTER V

OTHER OFFENCES INVOLVING FRAUD

1 FALSE ACCOUNTING

[**283**] Section 17 of the Theft Act replaces ss. 82 and 83 of the Larceny Act 1861 and the Falsification of Accounts Act 1875. It provides:

"(1) Where a person dishonestly, with a view to gain for himself or another or with intent to cause loss to another,—

(a) destroys, defaces, conceals or falsifies any account or any record or document made or required for any accounting purpose; or

(b) in furnishing information for any purpose produces or makes use of any account, or any such record or document as aforesaid, which to his knowledge is or may be misleading, false or deceptive in a material particular;

he shall, on conviction on indictment, be liable to imprisonment for a term not exceeding seven years.

(2) For purposes of this section a person who makes or concurs in making in an account or other document an entry which is or may be misleading, false or deceptive in a material particular, or who omits or concurs in omitting a material particular from an account or other document, is to be treated as falsifying the account or document".

A. THE ACTUS REUS

[**284**] The two new offences created by this section may be committed by anyone whereas the 1861 offences applied only to officers of companies and the 1875 Act was confined to "any clerk, officer or servant". The new provisions, unlike the old, would apply, for example, to the honorary treasurer of a members' club who is not a servant.

[**285**] The section is confined to records or documents "for any accounting purpose". In the context, this plainly means accounting in the financial sense. The wording is clearly wide enough to cover an account produced by mechanical means, as in the case of a taxi-meter.[1] Falsifying the gas-meter or electricity-meter would seem to be an offence within the section, although previously it was an offence punishable only summarily with a £5 fine.[2] On the other hand, dishonestly to falsify the mileometer of a car with a view to gain would not normally be an offence under this section since the mileometer of a car is not usually a record made or required for any accounting purpose. It would be otherwise, however, if the mileometer reading were used to calculate a mileage allowance due to the driver. It would then be indistinguishable from the taximeter case.

---

[1] *Cf. Solomons,* [1909] 2 K.B. 980.
[2] Gas Act 1948, s. 29; Electric Lighting Act 1882, s. 12, incorporating s. 38 of the Gasworks Clauses Act 1871.

B. THE MENS REA

[286] The act must be done:

(i) dishonestly,

(ii) with a view to gain for himself or another or with intent to cause loss to another and, in the case of s. 17 (1) (b),

(iii) with knowledge that the document is or *may be* misleading, false or deceptive in a material particular. Recklessness is sufficient.

[287] As to dishonesty, reference may be made to the discussion of this element in other crimes.[3] Similar problems arise here. For example, the bookmaker's clerk may "borrow" his employer's money to place bets (with a view to gain) and falsify the accounts, to cover up his action but with every intention and expectation of replacing the money before it is missed. Is he dishonest?

[288] As to the view to gain or intent to cause loss, see the discussion of these elements in connection with other crimes.[4] Suppose D falsifies the accounts so as to deceive his employer into thinking that D's department is more profitable than it really is, in order to ensure that D's employment will not be terminated.[5] It may be argued that D has no view to gain in such a case, since he intends to give full economic value for the wages he receives;[6] but, whether or not this is a sound argument (and it is probably not) he perhaps has an intent to cause loss in that he knows that the effect of his deception will be that his employer will keep open an uneconomic department. This, however, is only an "oblique" intention[7] and it is arguable that a direct intention must be proved.

[289] Has D a view to gain or an intent to cause loss where he falsifies an account in order to conceal losses or defalcations which have already occurred? Since, by s. 34 (2) (a)[8]:

"(i) 'gain' includes a gain by keeping what one has, as well as a gain by getting what one has not; and

(ii) 'loss' includes a loss by not getting what one might get, as well as a loss by parting with what one has;"

the answer will be generally in the affirmative. At least one of the objects which D will have in view will be that of avoiding or postponing making restitution—"keeping what one has" and preventing P from getting what he might. The Court of Appeal has said[9] that putting off the evil day of having to pay, is a sufficient gain. If D's *sole* object is to avoid prosecution, he will not be guilty of the offence. This result has been criticised[10] but it is perhaps not unreasonable. Telling lies to avoid prosecution, whether in an account or elsewhere, if it is to be an offence, would more naturally find a place in the offence of

---

[3] Above, paras. [118]–[129] and [240]–[246].
[4] Below, paras. [347]–[353].
[5] *Cf. Wines*, [1953] 2 All E.R. 1497.
[6] See below, paras. [351]–[352].
[7] Smith and Hogan, 37-39.
[8] Below, para. [347].
[9] *Eden* (1971), 55 Cr. App. Rep. 193 at 197.
[10] Griew, 6-49.

perverting the course of justice[11] than in the Theft Act. If D is penniless, there may be a difficulty in proving that he intended to do more than avoid prosecution; but, if he is employed, he may find it difficult credibly to deny that one of his objects was the continuance of his wages; and, as has been seen, this is almost certainly enough. Gain need not be D's sole object.

2 LIABILITY OF COMPANY OFFICERS FOR OFFENCES UNDER SECTIONS 18 AND 19

[**290**] Section 18 of the Act provides:

"(1) Where an offence committed by a body corporate under section 15, 16 or 17 of this Act is proved to have been committed with the consent or connivance of any director, manager, secretary or other similar officer of the body corporate, or any person who was purporting to act in any such capacity, he as well as the body corporate shall be guilty of that offence, and shall be liable to be proceeded against and punished accordingly.

(2) Where the affairs of a body corporate are managed by its members, this section shall apply in relation to the acts and defaults of a member in connection with his functions of management as if he were a director of the body corporate."

An offence can be committed by a body corporate only through one of its responsible officers.[12] In every case where a corporation is guilty of an offence, then, there must be at least one of the officers referred to in the section who consented or connived. If he is unidentifiable, then only the corporation may be convicted; if he can be identified, he will, in the great majority of cases be guilty of an offence under ss. 15, 16 and 17 independently of s. 18, either as a principal offender or as a secondary party. Connivance or an express consent to an offence would seem sufficient to found liability under the general law,[13] apart from s. 18. The section is intended to go farther than this:

"The clause follows a form of provision commonly included in statutes where an offence is of a kind to be committed by bodies corporate and where it is desired to put the management under a positive obligation to prevent irregularities, if aware of them. Passive acquiescence does not, under the general law, make a person liable as a party to the offence, but there are clearly cases (of which we think this is one) where the director's responsibilities for his company require him to intervene to prevent fraud and where consent or connivance amounts to guilt."[14]

[**291**] The "positive obligation" clearly does not go so far as to impose liability for negligence;[15] you cannot consent to that of which you are unaware,[16]

---

[11] Smith and Hogan, 512-514.
[12] Smith and Hogan, 105–109; Tesco Supermarkets v. Nattrass, [1971] 2 All E.R. 127.
[13] *Ibid.*, 65–75.
[14] The *Report*, Cmnd. 2977, para. 104. See, for examples of similar provisions, Building Control Act 1966, s. 9 (5); Prices and Incomes Act 1966, s. 22; Industrial Development Act 1966, s. 10; Veterinary Surgeons Act 1966, s. 20 (5); and Sea Fisheries Regulation Act 1966, s. 11 (6).
[15] Compare the provisions in the statutes referred to in footnote 14, above, all of which include the phrase, "or to be attributable to any neglect on the part of . . .".
[16] *Re Caughey, Ex parte Ford* (1876), 1 Ch. D. 521 at 528 (C.A.), *per* Jessel, M.R. and *Lamb* v. *Wright & Co.*, [1924] 1 K.B. 857 at 864.

and "connivance" involves turning a blind eye, which has always been regarded as equivalent to knowledge.[17] Even "passive acquiescence" has sometimes been held sufficient to found liability as a secondary party, under the general law, but probably only on the ground that inactivity was a positive encouragement to others to commit the unlawful act in question.[18] Section 14 may go a little beyond this, though that is not entirely clear and the provision does not seem yet to have been interpreted by the courts.[19] At least it eases the Crown's task to the extent that they have proved their case if they prove consent and they do not have to go on to establish that the consent amounted to an aiding and abetting, etc.

3 FALSE STATEMENTS BY COMPANY DIRECTORS, ETC.

[**292**] Section 19 (see page 204, below) replaces s. 84 of the Larceny Act 1861. It is wider than the earlier provision in that it applies to officers of unincorporated as well as incorporated bodies—for example, the chairman of a club. It is narrower in that:

(i) there must be an intent to deceive *members or creditors*, whereas the earlier provision extended to an intent to induce *any person* to become a shareholder or partner, or to advance money, etc.;

(ii) the written statement or account must be about the body's affairs.

[**293**] Examples of the kind of case to which the section is intended to apply are:

"A prospectus might include a false statement, made in order to inspire confidence, that some well-known person had agreed to become a director. It might also include a false statement, made in order to appeal to persons interested in a particular area, that a company had arranged to build a factory in that area."[20]

[**294**] The *mens rea* consists in:

(i) an intent to deceive;

(ii) knowledge that the statement is or may be misleading, false or deceptive in a material particular.

Though no intent to *defraud* is required, the effect seems to be much the same, since the statement must be false in a *material* particular. A particular is hardly likely to be held to be material unless the person to whom it is addressed is likely to take action of some kind on it and, thus, almost invariably, to be defrauded in the wide meaning now given to "fraud"[1].

---

[17] Edwards, *Mens Rea in Statutory Offences*, 202–205; *Williams*, C.L.G.P. 159; Smith and Hogan, 73.

[18] Smith and Hogan, 83–84.

[19] *Cf.* the draconian provision in the Borrowing (Control and Guarantees) Act 1946, s. 4 (2), criticised by Upjohn, J. in *London and County Commercial Property Investments, Ltd.* v. *A.-G.* [1953] 1 All E.R. 436 at 441.

[20] The *Report*, Cmnd. 2977, para. 105. False statements in prospectuses are also punishable by two years' imprisonment under the Companies Act 1948, s. 44. Offences under that section may, however, be committed negligently and the onus of disproving negligence is on the accused; whereas under s. 19 of the Theft Act the Crown must prove at least recklessness.

[1] *Welham* v. *D.P.P.*, [1961] A.C. 103; [1960] 1 All E.R. 805.

As the Criminal Law Revision Committee thought, statements made recklessly will be within the section.[2]   It is enough that D knows that the statement is or *may be* false, etc.

4 SUPPRESSION, ETC., OF DOCUMENTS

[295] Section 20 (1) replaces an elaborate group of offences in ss. 27–30 of the Larceny Act 1861. These offences have been little used in recent times and the Criminal Law Revision Committee had doubts as to whether any part of them should be retained, but s. 20 (1) was included because:

> "It seemed to us that it might provide the only way of dealing with a person who, for example, suppressed a public document as a first step towards committing a fraud but did not get so far as attempting to commit the fraud."[3]

It should be noted that the subsection does not apply to local government documents, the Committee being of the opinion that these were adequately protected by existing statutory provisions.

The main constituents of the offence are considered in connection with other offences.[4]

Section 20 (2) reproduces the substance of the offence under the Larceny Act 1916, s. 32 (2), modified so as to conform to the scheme of the Theft Act.[5]

---

[2] The *Report*, Cmnd. 2977, para. 104.
[3] The *Report*, Cmnd. 2977, para. 106.
[4] As to "dishonestly", see above, paras. **[118]**–**[129]** and **[240]**–**[246]**; "with a view to gain" and "with intent to cause loss", see below, paras. **[347]**–**[353]**.
[5] As to "deception" see above, paras. **[201]**–**[238]**; and as to the other constituents of the offence see footnote 4, above.

CHAPTER VI

REMOVAL OF ARTICLES FROM PLACES OPEN TO THE PUBLIC

[**296**] By s. 11 of the Theft Act:

"(1) Subject to subsections (2) and (3) below, where the public have access to a building in order to view the building or part of it, or a collection or part of a collection housed in it, any person who without lawful authority removes from the building or its grounds the whole or part of any article displayed or kept for display to the public in the building or that part of it or in its grounds shall be guilty of an offence.

For this purpose 'collection' includes a collection got together for a temporary purpose, but references in this section to a collection do not apply to a collection made or exhibited for the purpose of effecting sales or other commercial dealings.

(2) It is immaterial for purposes of subsection (1) above, that the public's access to a building is limited to a particular period or particular occasion; but where anything removed from a building or its grounds is there otherwise than as forming part of, or being on loan for exhibition with, a collection intended for permanent exhibition to the public, the person removing it does not thereby commit an offence under this section unless he removes it on a day when the public have access to the building as mentioned in subsection (1) above.

(3) A person does not commit an offence under this section if he believes that he has lawful authority for the removal of the thing in question or that he would have it if the person entitled to give it knew of the removal and the circumstances of it.

(4) A person guilty of an offence under this section shall, on conviction on indictment, be liable to imprisonment for a term not exceeding five years."

[**297**] It has been seen that an intention permanently to deprive is an essential constituent of theft, as it was of larceny. The Criminal Law Revision Committee considered the matter and came down against either (i) extending theft to include temporary deprivation, or (ii) creating a general offence of temporary deprivation of property.

"The former course seems to the Committee wrong because in their view an intention to return the property, even after a long time, makes the conduct essentially different from stealing. Apart from this either course would be a considerable extension of the criminal law, which does not seem to be called for by an existing serious evil. It might moreover have undesirable social consequences. Quarrelling neighbours and families would be able to threaten one another with prosecution. Students and young people sharing accommodation who might be tempted to borrow one another's property in disregard of a prohibition by the owner would be in danger of acquiring a criminal record. Further, it would be difficult for the police to avoid being involved in wasteful and undesirable investigations into alleged offences which had no social importance."[1]

[**298**] The question whether temporary deprivation should be criminal attracted more attention than any other issue, both in and out of Parliament, during the passage of the Theft Bill;[2] but the government stuck firmly to the view expressed by the Committee. In two instances, the Committee found that there was a case for making temporary deprivation an offence, though not theft. These two cases are the subjects of this and the following chapter.

[**299**] Section 11 undoubtedly owes its existence to one particular and very unusual case—the removal from the National Gallery of Goya's portrait of the Duke of Wellington. The portrait was returned after a period of four years. There was evidence that the taker tried to make it a condition of his returning it that a large sum should be paid to charity. It has been argued above[3] that this should constitute a sufficient intent to deprive, but the accused was acquitted of larceny of the portrait, though convicted of larceny of the frame which was never recovered. The Criminal Law Revision Committee referred to two other cases, both of a very unusual nature.

". . . an art student took a statuette by Rodin from an exhibition, intending, as he said, to live with it for a while, and returned it over four months later. (Meanwhile the exhibitors, who had insured the statuette, had paid the insurance money to the owners, with result that the statuette, when returned, became the property of the exhibitors.[4]) Yet another case was the removal of the coronation stone from Westminster Abbey."

It may well be doubted whether these instances amounted to a case for the creation of a special offence but the government acted on the Committee's suggestion and produced a clause which, after much debate and amendment, became s. 11. The object of the section is to protect things which are put at hazard by being displayed to the public. Where, however, the purpose of the display is "effecting sales or other commercial dealings", it was thought reasonable to expect the person mounting the exhibition to bear the resulting hazards and to take adequate precautions against them.

A. THE ACTUS REUS

[**300**] The ingredients of the offence are as follows:
(i) The *public* must have access. So the contents of a building will not be protected where only a particular small class of persons is permitted to have access; as where the owner opens the building to the members of a club, school or similar body.

---

1 The *Report*, Cmnd. 2977, para. 56.
2 See Samuels, 118 N.L. J. 281; Hadden, 118 N.L.J. 305; Smith, 118 N.L.J. 401. Parl. Debates, Official Report (H.L.), Vol. 289, cols. 1305–1325, 1480–1485, Vol. 290, cols. 51–71, 1390–1421, Vol. 291, cols. 59–71; (H.C.) Standing Committee H, cols. 3–18.
3 See para. [**138**].
4 If this had been foreseen by the taker then he might have been held to have an intention permanently to deprive; but this kind of foresight could probably only be attributed to a lawyer!

[301] (ii) The public must have access *to a building in order to view*. If the public have access to the building for this purpose, then articles in the grounds are protected. If the public do not have access to the building or have access only for some purpose other than viewing, articles in the grounds to which they do have access in order to view are not protected. If an exhibition of sculpture is put on in the grounds of a house, it will not be an offence to "borrow" an item unless the public are also invited into the house for the purpose of viewing. If one piece of sculpture is displayed in the hall, then the fifty pieces in the grounds will also be protected. If, however, the public are invited into the house for some purpose other than viewing—for example, to have tea—none of the articles will be protected. It follows, of course, that exhibitions in streets and squares are not protected.

[302] (iii) The article must be *displayed or kept for display*. If D, while touring the art gallery, removes the fire extinguisher, he commits no offence against this section. If the article is in a store, it may be "kept for display" though not presently displayed.

[303] (iv) If the article is displayed in a building, it must be removed *from the building*. If it is displayed in the grounds of the building, it must be removed *from the grounds*. Presumably it would be enough to take the article from the grounds into the building. If D is apprehended in the course of removing the article either from the grounds or the building then, no doubt he is guilty of an attempt.

[304] (v) The thing taken must be an *article*. The meaning of the word depends on its context. The expression, "any article whatsoever," in the Public Health Act 1936 was held not to include a goldfish, the court evidently taking the view that the word did not cover animate things.[5] On the other hand, a horse has been held to be an article for the purposes of a local Act dealing with exposure for sale at a market.[6] Bearing in mind the mischief at which the section is aimed, it is submitted that, if the other conditions are satisfied, any thing is protected, from an elephant in the London Zoo to a flower growing in the grounds of the stately home to which the public have access.

[305] (vi) Where the article is in the building or its grounds as forming part of or being on loan for exhibition with, a collection intended for permanent exhibition to the public, the offence may be committed at any time.[7] So it may be committed during the night when the building is closed, or on Sunday, even though the public are not admitted on Sunday, or in the middle of a month when the building is closed for renovation. Where this condition is not satisfied, then the article is protected only on a day when the public have access to the building. If P opens his stately home to the public on Easter Monday, then for the duration of that day only, articles displayed to the public in the building or its grounds are protected by the section. If D hides in the building until after midnight and removes an article on Tuesday he commits no offence under this section.

[306] (vii) If the public are admitted to view *the building* or part of it, then anything displayed is protected. If they are not admitted to view the building

---

[5] *Daly v. Cannon*, [1954] 1 All E.R. 315.
[6] *Llandaff and Canton District Market Co. v. Lyndon* (1860), 8 C.B.N.S. 515.
[7] Section 11 (2).

or part of it, then articles are protected only if a collection or part of a collection is displayed. Where a cathedral is open to the public to view and D removes an article which is displayed there, it is immaterial whether a collection is displayed or not. The term "collection" was used because it helps to indicate the intended purpose of the section—to protect articles assembled as objects of artistic or other merit or of public interest. It seems clear that it is not necessary that the contents should have been brought together for the purposes of exhibition in order to amount to a collection. If that were so, the contents of the stately home might be excluded from protection, for they were brought together for the edification of the collector, not for exhibition. It is no doubt sufficient that articles are preserved together. A single article could hardly constitute "a collection"; but, if it were on loan from a collection, might it not be "part of" a collection? A single article, not forming part of a collection, which was displayed to the public, would not be protected unless the public were admitted to view the building in which it was housed, as well as the article. Thus, if it were exhibited in a Nissen hut, it would not be protected, but it might be otherwise if the surroundings were more elegant.

[**307**] (viii) If the public are admitted to view a collection made or exhibited for the purpose of effecting sales or other commercial dealings, the articles will not be protected.[8] If the public are admitted to view the *building*, it would seem that articles will be protected even though they do form part of an exhibition for the purpose of effecting sales or commercial dealings. This will be so even where the public are admitted for the dual purpose of viewing the building and the collection; when the public are admitted to view a building, any article which is displayed is protected.

[**308**] The definition of "collection" excludes not only commercial art galleries but also shops, salerooms and exhibitions for advertising purposes. Had it not been for this limitation, it is obvious that the scope of the section would have been immensely wider than is necessary to deal with the narrow class of cases at which the provision is aimed. Of course, a particular collection may be protected if the conditions of the section are satisfied, even though it is housed in a sale room, as where Christie's gave an exhibition in their sale room of articles which had been purchased from them and were lent by public galleries all over the world.

[**309**] (ix) It should be emphasised that the protection of the section is not lost because the articles displayed are for sale. It is a question of the purpose of the exhibitor in inviting the public to attend. Thus, it is clear that the pictures displayed at the Royal Academy exhibitions are protected, even though they are for sale. Neither sale, nor any other commercial dealing is the purpose of the Royal Academy in mounting the exhibition—though it may be the purpose of individual artists. There may be a difficult question where the exhibition has a dual purpose. Perhaps this is a case where it would be proper to have regard to the dominant purpose.

It is also clear that articles do not lose the protection of the section because a charge is made for admission with the object of making money in excess of the cost of upkeep. The sale or commercial dealing which is contemplated is one which is consequent upon the viewing of the exhibition.

---

[8] Section 11 (1).

B. THE MENS REA

[**310**] The *mens rea* of the offence is an intention to remove the article, knowing that there is no lawful authority for doing so and that the owner would not have authorised removal had he known of the circumstances. This closely follows the *mens rea* required for taking conveyances under s. 12. If the building were on fire and D removed a picture from it, he might well suppose that P would have authorised him to remove the picture had he known of the circumstances. The onus is, of course, on the Crown, once D has laid a foundation for such a defence, to prove beyond reasonable doubt that D did not so believe.

[**311**] As with s. 12, "dishonesty" is not a constituent of the offence. Where students borrow some article for the purpose of a "rag", it might be debatable whether they are dishonest or not; but the question need not be considered on a charge under s. 11; it is enough that they know that the removal is not and would not have been authorised by the owner had he known of it.

CHAPTER VII

TAKING A MOTOR VEHICLE OR OTHER CONVEYANCE WITHOUT AUTHORITY

[**312**] Section 12 of the Act replaces the offence under s. 217 of the Road Traffic Act 1960. Some important modifications in the nature of the offence are made and these are considered below. Section 12 (1) provides:

"Subject to subsections (5) and (6) below, a person shall be guilty of an offence if, without having the consent of the owner or other lawful authority, he takes any conveyance for his own or another's use or, knowing that any conveyance has been taken without such authority, drives it or allows himself to be carried in or on it."

There seem to be two offences here and it is convenient to treat them separately.

1 TAKING A CONVEYANCE

A. TAKES

[**313**] The concept of "taking" which has been eliminated from stealing still survives here, but, fortunately, it seems to have given little trouble in connection with this offence. "Taking" suggests the acquisition of possession. It was held in *Mowe* v. *Perraton*[1] that a van driver who, at the end of his day's work and before returning the van to his employer's garage, drove the van on an unauthorised private errand, was not guilty because "he had taken and driven the motor vehicle as part of his work". That case was distinguished in *Wibberley*[2] on the ground that D, in the earlier case, had not finished his day's work (because this included returning the van to the garage) when he drove the van for his own purposes; it was merely a case of deviation from an authorised route during working hours. In *Wibberley* the day's work was done and, though D could lawfully have left the vehicle outside his house, his use of it for a purpose of his own was a taking within the meaning of the Act.

[**314**] It is clear that in both cases, D had custody of the vehicle, possession remaining in the employer. It is submitted that the distinction is that in *Wibberley* D "took" because he had altered the character of his control over the vehicle, so that he no longer held as servant but assumed possession of it in the legal sense; whereas in *Mowe* v. *Perraton*, D continued to hold as servant, as would a lorry driver who deviated from his authorised route to visit a favourite café[3]. The fact that the day's work is unfinished can hardly be conclusive evidence against a taking. If, in the middle of the day, D were to decide to

---

[1] [1952] 1 All E.R. 423.
[2] [1965] 3 All E.R. 718.
[3] *Quaere* whether such a conclusion could properly be drawn from the facts in *Mowe* v. *Perraton* and whether the case can really stand with *Wibberley*.

take his employer's van away for a fortnight's holiday, it is submitted that he would clearly "take" it. As soon as he departed from his authorised route with that intent, he would control the vehicle for his own purposes and not those of his employer.

[315] It is clear that a hirer under a hire-purchase agreement cannot commit the offence because he is the "owner" for this purpose.[4] Other bailees, however, may commit the offence. A bailee, unlike a servant, has possession of the thing entrusted to him; yet if he operates the conveyance after the purpose of the bailment has been fulfilled, that subsequent use may be held to amount to a taking, though he has never given up possession. In *McGill*,[5] D borrowed a car to take his wife to the station on the express condition that he brought it straight back. He did not return it that day, and the following day drove it to Hastings. It was held that his use of the car after the purpose of the borrowing was fulfilled constituted a taking. Once the conveyance has been *taken* by D, however, subsequent movement of it does not constitute a fresh taking,[6] unless he has abandoned and then resumed possession; though it may be an offence under the second limb of the section.[7]

[316] Under the Road Traffic Acts, the offence was not committed unless the vehicle was "driven away" as well as taken. This requirement led to some very subtle distinctions. It was held that, for example, a vehicle was not being driven where D released the handbrake so that it ran down a hill or where it was being towed or pushed by another vehicle. It would seem that there is a taking in each of these cases and convictions would now be possible, if the other constituents of the offence were present[8].

[317] This seems to be a very desirable change in the law. It was never clear what part *driving* played in the mischief of the offence. The offence appears to be designed to protect the owner of a conveyance from temporary deprivation of it. Yet, under the old law, the offence would clearly not have been committed by loading a vehicle on to a transporter by crane and taking it away for a month—otherwise, presumably, if it had been driven on to the transporter.[9] It is not clear why the former case should not equally be an offence, and there is no doubt that it may be under the Theft Act. One of the constituents of the offence, however, is that the conveyance must be taken for "his own or another's use"—a new requirement, not found in the Road Traffic Acts. This would seem to exclude allowing the conveyance to run (or float) away out of malice. Probably driving, whatever the motive, would be held to be "use" as would, for example, the display of the vehicle in an exhibition of veteran cars.

---

[4] Section 12 (7) (*b*), below, page 201.
[5] [1970] R.T.R. 209 (C.A.). See commentaries at [1970] Crim. L.R. 291 and 480.
[6] *Pearce*, [1961] Crim. L.R. 122.
[7] Below, para. [324].
[8] In *Roberts*, [1964] 2 All E.R. 541, the court thought it "possible" that D's releasing the handbrake and allowing the vehicle to run down the hill amounted to a taking. It would clearly be a sufficient taking for the purposes of larceny—suppose D had had an intent permanently to deprive, as by allowing the vehicle to run over a cliff into the sea; and it is thought that the requirements of this section should not be more stringent.
[9] According to the Criminal Law Revision Committee, under the old law, ". . . the essence of the offence is stealing a ride" (the *Report*, Cmnd. 2977, at para. 84); but there was more to it than that, as appears if the offence is compared with that of unlawful riding on public transport, where the authority is not deprived of the vehicle.

[**318**] The elimination of the requirement of "driving" may bring within the section (or, at least, the first part of it) certain conveyances which otherwise would be outside it—that is any conveyance with accommodation for a passenger or passengers which has no means of self-propulsion and so cannot be driven but must be towed.

B. A CONVEYANCE

[**319**] By s. 12 (7) (*a*) of the Act:
" 'conveyance' means any conveyance constructed or adapted for the carriage of a person or persons whether by land, water or air, except that it does not include a conveyance constructed or adapted for use only under the control of a person not carried in or on it, and 'drive' shall b' construed accordingly."

Thus conveyances for the carriage of goods are excluded, but only where the conveyance has no place for a driver. A lorry is clearly within the protection of the Act, since it is constructed for the carriage of at least one person. A goods trailer, however, would not be so protected, nor a barge with no provision for a passenger. A vehicle, such as some milk floats, which is operated by a man walking beside it, is expressly excluded.

[**320**] Bicycles are also expressly excluded by s. 12 (5):
"Subsection (1) above[10] shall not apply in relation to pedal cycles; but subject to subsection (6) below,[11] a person who, without having the consent of the owner or other lawful authority,[12] takes a pedal cycle for his own or another's use, or rides a pedal cycle knowing it to have been taken without such authority, shall on summary conviction be liable to a fine not exceeding fifty pounds."

C. "WITHOUT HAVING THE CONSENT OF THE OWNER OR OTHER LAWFUL AUTHORITY"

[**321**] These words again import into the offence a concept which was very troublesome in the law of larceny and is now happily disposed of. It would seem clear that, as in larceny, a consent extracted by intimidation would not amount to a defence.[13] In principle, a consent induced by fraud would be no consent if the mistake induced in the owner was as to the identity of the taker or the nature of the transaction. Fraud going to less fundamental matters would not be sufficient. Thus if, for example, D borrowed P's car on a pretence that he wished to drive to Derby to visit his sick grandmother, when really he wanted to go there to see his girl-friend, he would not commit the offence; but it is thought that he would do so if his real intention was not to go to Derby at all, but to drive the car on the Monte Carlo rally. Against this view is the decision in *Peart*.[14] D induced P to lend his van, for a payment of £2, by representing that he wanted to drive to Alnwick and would return the van by 7.30 p.m. Instead, as presumably he intended all along, he drove to Burnley

---

[10] Above, para. [**312**].
[11] Above, para. [**323**].
[12] Above, para. [**321**].
[13] *Hogdon*, [1962] Crim. L.R. 563.
[14] [1970] 2 Q.B. 672; [1970] 2 All E.R. 823.

where he was found at 9 p.m. It was held that there was no taking; the mis-representation did not vitiate P's consent. The court reserved the question whether a misrepresentation can ever be so fundamental as to vitiate consent for the purposes of this crime. The case is difficult to reconcile with the earlier case of *McGill*.[15] If, when a conveyance has been borrowed for a particular purpose, it is "taking" to use it for a quite different purpose *after* the declared purpose has been fulfilled, it is difficult to see why it is not "taking" to use it *immediately* for a purpose quite different from that declared. It is submitted that *McGill* is to be preferred to *Peart*. Similar principles should apply to a consent obtained without fraud, but under a mistake by P known to D.

[**322**] "Other lawful authority" would apply to the removal of a vehicle, in accordance with a statutory power such as the regulations made under s. 43 of the Road Traffic Act 1960, where the vehicle had been parked in contra-vention of a statutory prohibition, or in a dangerous situation, or in such circumstances as to appear to have been abandoned.

It would also cover any removal of a vehicle in pursuance of a common law right such as that of abating a nuisance,[16] or of a contractual right such as that of a letter under a hire-purchase agreement to resume possession in certain circumstances.

D. THE MENS REA

[**323**] Section 12 (6) provides:

> "A person does not commit an offence under this section by anything done in the belief that he has lawful authority to do it or that he would have the owner's consent if the owner knew of his doing it and the circum-stances of it."

It is clear then that the prosecution must prove that D knew that he was taking the vehicle without the owner's consent and did not believe that the owner would have consented if asked. This is an important change in the law for, under s. 217 of the Road Traffic Act 1960, the onus was on D to satisfy the court, on a balance of probabilities, that he acted in the *reasonable* belief that he had lawful authority, etc. This was a highly unsatisfactory situation. Suppose D had been charged with (i) taking and driving away and (ii) stealing petrol, both charges arising out of his taking P's car, and had raised the defence in both cases that he believed he had P's authority to drive the vehicle. It would have been necessary to direct as to (i), that the onus was on D to prove his belief on a balance of probabilities and that the defence was made out if only the belief was reasonable; and as to (ii) that the onus was on the Crown to disprove his belief beyond reasonable doubt and that if they failed to do this, he was entitled to be acquitted even if his belief was an unreasonable one. This was preposterous. The Act brings the law of taking and driving away into line with that of stealing.[17] On the facts envisaged, the direction in relation to both charges would now be the same.

---

[15] Above, para. [**315**].
[16] *Cf. Webb* v. *Stansfield*, [1966] Crim. L.R. 449.
[17] *Cf.* the discussion of s. 2 (1) (*a*), above, para. [**119**].

2 DRIVING OR ALLOWING ONESELF TO BE CARRIED BY A "TAKEN" CONVEYANCE

A. THE ACTUS REUS

[**324**] D was not (and is not) guilty of taking a conveyance by driving or allowing himself to be carried in or on a conveyance which had been so taken, provided that he was not a party to the taking.[18] Special provision was made to meet this case in the Road Traffic Act 1962, s. 44 and that provision is reproduced in s. 12 of the Theft Act. It seems clear that at least one offence, separate and distinct, from taking a conveyance is created; and there are two such offences if *driving*[19] and *allowing oneself to be carried* cannot be regarded as alternative modes of commission of a single offence. It does not seem to matter greatly whether the provision is construed as creating two offences or one. It is true that if the courts should adopt the latter construction it would dispense with the necessity for proving which of several accused was driving a taken vehicle—a matter which might sometimes be difficult—since all would be principal offenders in the same offence. Even if "driving" is a separate offence, so long as it is clear that one of several passengers was driving, all may be convicted of driving, provided the necessary knowledge can be proved, although the actual driver cannot be identified, since each of them, if he was not the principal, was an aider and abettor.[20] One case in which it would matter would be where there was no evidence of *mens rea* against one of two or more possible drivers of the vehicle. If that person were the driver, there was no principal offender and there are difficulties about convicting of aiding and abetting where there is no principal offender.[1] The chance that he was the driver might thus create a reasonable doubt whether any of the parties was guilty of driving, even though there was conclusive evidence of *mens rea* against some of them.

[**325**] The vehicle must actually have been taken; one cannot know a thing to be so, unless it is so.[2]

The provision is intended to deal with persons other than the original taker, but it is not limited to such persons. The taker would appear to commit another offence on each subsequent occasion when he drives the vehicle or allows himself to be carried in or on it. Where the original taking is not an offence because of lack of *mens rea*, a subsequent driving of it may make the taker liable. For example, D takes P's car, wrongly supposing that P consents to his doing so. The car has been taken without P's consent but no offence has been committed. Having learned that P does not consent to his having the

---

[18] *Stally*, [1959] 3 All E.R. 814; *D. (Infant) v. Parsons*, [1960] 2 All E.R. 493.

[19] "Driving" now includes the activity of a person who sets in motion and controls an aircraft, hovercraft, boat or any other conveyance: s. 12 (7) (*a*). It is conceivable that the old technicalities of what is "driving" might arise again here. It is submitted that D is driving when he is in or on the vehicle and is in control of its forward or backward motion. *Cf. Wallace v. Major*, [1946] K.B. 473; *Saycell v. Bool*, [1948] 2 All E.R. 83; *Shimmel v. Fisher*, [1951] 2 All E.R. 672; *Spindley*, [1961] Crim. L.R. 486; *Roberts*, [1964] 2 All E.R. 541; *Arnold*, [1964] Crim. L.R. 664.

[20] *Du Cros v. Lambourne*, [1907] 1 K.B. 40; *Swindall and Osborne* (1846), 2 Car. & Kir. 230.

[1] Smith and Hogan, 91–94.

[2] D might possibly be guilty of an attempt where he wrongly thought he knew that the vehicle had been taken. *Cf.* above, para. [**51**].

car, D continues to drive it. He appears to commit the offence though it is arguable that a "taken" conveyance is one taken with *mens rea*.

B. THE MENS REA

[326] It must be proved that D knew that the conveyance had been taken without authority when he drove it or allowed himself to be carried in or on it as the case may be. Probably "wilful blindness" would be enough as in the case of other statutes.[3] Such a state of mind is, however, barely distinguishable from that of *belief* that the conveyance had been so taken. The Criminal Law Revision Committee thought that belief was not knowledge for the purposes of the old law of receiving[4] and made special provision for that state of mind in the new offence of handling.[5] It is inevitable that comparison will be made between s. 12 (1) and s. 21 (1), with the implication that belief will not do in the case of s. 12; but it is submitted that such an argument should not be accepted.[6]

3 SENTENCE

[327] The maximum punishment for the offences is raised from one to three years' imprisonment. In this case, the increase *does* represent an invitation to the court to impose stiffer penalties: the Criminal Law Revision Committee thought that the penalties under the old law were

". . . far too low having regard to the prevalence of the offence, to the danger, loss and inconvenience which often result from it and to the fact that courts are commonly called on to deal with offenders who have committed the offence many times."[7]

---

[3] Smith and Hogan, 73; Edwards, *Mens Rea in Statutory Offences*, 202-205; Williams, *C.L.G.P.* 159.
[4] The *Report*, Cmnd. 2977, para. 134; below, para. [488].
[5] See s. 22 (1), para. [430].
[6] Below, para. [488].
[7] The *Report*, Cmnd. 2977, para. 82.

CHAPTER VIII

ABSTRACTING OF ELECTRICITY

[**328**] The Larceny Act of 1916 made special provision for the stealing of electricity because, no doubt, it was not capable of being taken and carried away. The notion of appropriation in the Theft Act might perhaps have been applied without incongruity to the abstraction of electricity but the unique nature of this kind of property was thought to call for a special provision. Section 13 of the Act provides:

"A person who dishonestly uses without due authority, or dishonestly causes to be wasted or diverted, any electricity shall on conviction on indictment be liable to imprisonment for a term not exceeding five years."

Thus the offence would be committed by an employee who dishonestly used his employer's electrically-operated machinery without authority; by a householder who, having had his electricity supply cut off, reconnected it or who by-passed the meter; and by a tramp who, having trespassed into a house to obtain a night's shelter, turned on the electric fire to keep himself warm.

[**329**] The tramp would not be guilty of burglary, since abstracting electricity is not one of the ulterior offences specified in s. 9 (1) (b);[1] unless the court should think that abstracting electricity *is* theft, after all—a conclusion difficult to sustain, perhaps, in view of the specific provision in s. 12. Yet, oddly, it would seem that the person who did the acts described in the previous paragraph would be guilty of theft if it were gas he consumed, instead of electricity; so the tramp would be a burglar, if it were a gas fire. Not a very happy result.

[**330**] There is nothing in the section to suggest that the electricity must come from the mains. Therefore it is probable that D commits the offence if he borrows my flashlight or portable radio and uses the dry battery.[2] Is the offence committed then by the dishonest "borrower" of a conveyance, such as a motor car, which consumes electricity from the battery when it is operated? If so, we have the incongruous result that the—merely incidental—use of the electricity is a more serious offence than the use of the vehicle as a whole.[3] It might be argued that if, as will usually be the case, the battery is charging properly, there will be as much electricity stored in it at the end of the journey as the beginning; and that, therefore, the use is not dishonest. An analogy might be drawn with the case where D takes P's coins, intending permanently to deprive him of them but to replace an equivalent sum from D's own money, not causing any injury to P.[4] It is not a fair analogy, however. In the case of

---

[1] Below, para. [**404**].
[2] Or if he operates an electrically-powered milk-float or similar vehicle. Taking such a vehicle is not an offence under s. 11 if the operator is not carried in or on it.
[3] This incongruity has always been present with regard to the petrol which is consumed.
[4] Above, para. [**121**].

the coins, the replacements are D's property; in the case of the electricity, the replacement is generated by the use of P's petrol and P's machinery and belongs to P as much as the electricity consumed. It seems likely, therefore, that the dishonest borrower of a motor vehicle (or motor boat, aircraft, etc.) does commit an offence against s. 13.[5]

[**331**] What if D obtains the benefit of the use of the electricity by fraud? Lord Airedale put the case[6] of a woodworking company allowing sea scouts to use their electrically-operated machinery and D's obtaining the use of the machinery by falsely stating that he is a sea scout. Lord Airedale thought D might escape because he had obtained authority, albeit by false pretences, and was therefore not acting "without due authority". One answer to this might be that some meaning should be given to the word "due"; and that, while D was acting with actual authority, he was not acting with "due" authority, since the authority was voidable on the ground of fraud. But the best answer probably is that D should be charged under s. 16. He has, by deception, obtained for himself a pecuniary advantage within s. 16 (2) (*a*).

[**332**] The corresponding provision in the Larceny Act was sometimes used to deal with persons who dishonestly used a telephone and this would seem to be perfectly possible under the Theft Act. For example, the employee who dishonestly uses his employer's telephone for his own private purposes would seem to be in no different situation from the employee who uses any other electrically operated machine. Specific provision for the dishonest use of a *public* telephone or telex is now made by the insertion of a new section, s. 65A, in the Post Office Act 1953.[7] This creates a merely summary offence. It is submitted that such cases should now be prosecuted as summary offences and not under s. 13; but where the telephone is a private one, there is no reason why s. 13 should not be invoked.

---

[5] This incongruity would not have arisen under the draft bill proposed by the Criminal Law Revision Committee, since the draft clause contained the words, "with intent to cause loss to another". These words were cut out by the House of Lords.

[6] Parl. Debates (H. of L.), Vol. 190, col. 154.

[7] See Schedule 2, para. 8, below.

CHAPTER IX

BLACKMAIL[1]

[**333**] "Blackmail" is the name which was commonly given to the group of offences contained in ss. 29–31 of the Larceny Act 1916. That term is officially adopted for the first time as the name of the offence which replaces the sections of the Larceny Act. Section 21 (1) of the Theft Act provides:

"A person is guilty of blackmail if, with a view to gain for himself or another or with intent to cause loss to another, he makes any unwarranted demand with menaces; and for this purpose a demand with menaces is unwarranted unless the person making it does so in the belief—

(a) that he has reasonable grounds for making the demand; and

(b) that the use of the menaces is a proper means of reinforcing the demand."

I THE ACTUS REUS

[**334**] The *actus reus* consists in a demand with menaces; and the two problems here are to determine the meaning of the expressions, "demand" and "menaces".

A. DEMAND

[**335**] Under the Larceny Act, the demand had to be for "any property or valuable thing"[2] or something capable of being stolen[3] or for an appointment or office of profit or trust.[4] The Theft Act is not so limited. Section 21 (2) provides:

"The nature of the act or omission demanded is immaterial, and it is also immaterial whether the menaces relate to action to be taken by the person making the demand."

[**336**] In effect, this is limited by the requirement that the demand be made with a view to gain or intent to cause loss[5] so that the change in the law is probably slight. In the vast majority of cases, the blackmailer will be demanding money or other property, intending both a gain to himself and a loss to another. It is clearly intended that the demand for a remunerated appointment or office[6] be covered, though whether such a case satisfies the requirement of "view to gain or loss" requires further consideration.[7] It would seem, however, that a demand for an unremunerated office, which would formerly have been an offence, would now, *prima facie*, not be. To threaten one believed to have influence in these matters, if he did not procure D's appointment as a justice of the peace, or Lord Lieutenant of the County, or Chairman of the

---

1 The *Report*, Cmnd. 2977, paras. 108–125.
2 Sections 29 and 31 (a).
3 Section 30.
4 Section 31 (b).
5 See below, para. [**347**].
6 The *Report*, Cmnd. 2977, para. 117.
7 Below, para. [**353**].

Trustees of the British Museum would appear no longer to be an offence of blackmail. The limitation would seem to be in pursuance of a general policy of limiting the provisions of the Act to the protection of economic interests. Had there been no such limitation, the section would have extended to such cases as that where D demands with menaces that P shall have sexual intercourse with him—a case which is obviously outside the scope of an enactment dealing with "theft and similar or associated offences" and which is provided for by other legislation.[8]

[**337**] In other respects, the Act extends the scope of the law. To demand with menaces that a person abandon a claim to property or release D from some legal liability of an economic nature may now be an offence. To demand with menaces that P discontinue divorce proceedings would not, however, be within the section.

[**338**] Whereas under s. 29 of the Larceny Act the demand had to be in writing, it is quite immaterial whether the demand under the Theft Act be oral or written.

[**339**] Whether an utterance amounts to a "demand" seems to depend on whether an ordinary literate person would so describe it.[9] A demand is made when and where a letter containing it is posted; and it probably continues to be made until it arrives and is read by the recipient.[10] To post such a letter in England addressed to P in Germany amounts to an offence in England. To post the letter in Germany addressed to P in England would be an offence here, at least if it arrived within the jurisdiction and, according to Lord Diplock,[11] even if it did not.

An oral demand would appear to be made when uttered, though unheard by the person addressed. If an emissary, other than the Post Office, be despatched bearing a demand, whether written or oral, it would seem that it could scarcely be held to be "made" until delivered.[12] The test would seem to be whether D has done, personally or through an agent, the final act necessary in the normal course to result in a communication. The Post Office, though sometimes treated as such, is not an agent in any real sense. The posted letter is as irrevocable as the bullet expelled from a gun. Any emissary other than the Post Office, whether he carries a demand or a loaded gun, may be recalled; so the principal of the one has, as yet, no more demanded than the principal of the other has shot. As was the case under the old law, it is likely that there may be a demand although it is not expressed in words, "a demand may be implicit or explicit".[13] It is probably enough that "the demeanour of the accused and the circumstances of the case were such that an ordinary reasonable man would understand that a demand . . .was being made upon him . . .".[14] There may also be a demand although it is couched in terms of request and

---

[8] Sexual Offences Act 1956, s. 2.
[9] *Treacy* v. *D.P.P.*, [1971] A.C. 537 at 565; [1971] 1 All E.R. 110 at 124, *per* Lord Diplock.
[10] *Ibid.*
[11] *Ibid.*
[12] See Griew, 7–12, and the discussion by Lord Reid (dissenting) in *Treacy* : [1971] A.C. at 550, and [1971] 1 All E.R. at 111.
[13] *Clear*, [1968] 1 All E.R. 74 at 77.
[14] *Collister and Warhurst* (1955), 39 Cr. App. Rep. 100 at 102.

obsequious in tone;[15] the addition of the menace is sufficient to show that it is truly a demand that is made.

B. MENACES

[**340**] The Criminal Law Revision Committee stated:[16]

"We have chosen the word 'menaces' instead of 'threats' because, notwithstanding the wide meaning given to 'menaces' in *Thorne's* case . . . we regard that word as stronger than 'threats', and the consequent slight restriction of the scope of the offence seems to us right."

It is reasonably clear then, that it was the intention that the old law should be preserved here. In the case referred to, *Thorne* v. *Motor Trade Association*,[17] Lord Wright said:

"I think the word 'menace' is to be liberally construed and not as limited to threats of violence but as including threats of any action detrimental to or unpleasant to the person addressed. It may also include a warning that in certain events such action is intended."

[**341**] In view of the breadth of this definition, it is apparent that any restriction imposed by the use of the word "menaces" rather than "threats" must be slight. In most cases, there is no need to spell out the meaning of the word to a jury, since it is "an ordinary English word which a jury could be expected to understand."[18]

The one limitation is that the threat does not amount to a menace unless "it is of such a nature and extent that the mind of an ordinary person of normal stability and courage might be influenced or made apprehensive so as to accede unwillingly to the demand".[19] If the threat is "of such a character that it is not calculated to deprive any person of reasonably sound and ordinarily firm mind of the free and voluntary action of his mind",[20] then it does not amount to a menace; but it has been said this doctrine should receive "a liberal construction in practice"[1]—that is, the court should be slow to hold that the threat would not influence an ordinary man.

[**342**] If the threat is one of so trivial a nature that it would not influence anybody[2] to respond to the demand, it is certainly reasonable to say that it is not a menace. The doctrine is satisfactory enough, then, where the person to whom the demand is addressed is a person of normal stability and courage, but it has been said that "persons who are thus practised upon are not as a rule of average firmness".[3] Suppose that P is a weak-minded person, likely to be swayed by a fanciful or trivial threat which an ordinary person would ignore; and that this is known to the threatener. It is submitted that the threat should be regarded as a menace; and that to hold the contrary would be hardly more

---

[15] *Robinson* (1796), 2 East P.C. 1110; *Studer* (1915), 11 Cr. App. Rep. 307.
[16] The *Report*, Cmnd. 2977, para. 123.
[17] [1937] A.C. 797 at 817 (H.L.).
[18] *Lawrence*, [1971] Crim. L.R. 645.
[19] *Clear*, [1968] 1 All E.R. 74 (C.A.).
[20] *Boyle and Merchant*, [1914] 3 K.B. 339 at 345 (C.C.A.).
[1] *Tomlinson*, [1895] 1 Q.B. 706 at 710, *per* Wills, J.; *Clear* (*supra*) at 80.
[2] *Cf. Tomlinson* (*supra*), *per* Wills, J.; *Boyle and Merchant*, [1914] 3 K.B. at 344.
[3] *Tomlinson*, [1895] 1 Q.B. at 710, *per* Wills, J.

reasonable than to say that robbery was not committed because the victim allowed himself to be overcome by a degree of force which a courageous man would have successfully resisted; or that there was no obtaining by deception because the victim was excessively gullible and was taken in by a pretence which anyone with his wits about him would have seen through.

[**343**] Whether a threat amounts to a menace within this principle appears, at first sight, to be an objective question to be answered by looking at the actual facts of the case. It appears from the recent case of *Clear*,[4] however, that the question is to be answered by reference to the facts known to the accused, if these are different from the actual facts—that, in effect, the question is one of intention. In that case, D had received a sub-poena to appear as a witness in an action in which P was the defendant. D demanded money from P with a threat that, if the money were not paid, he would alter the statement he had made to the police and so cause P to lose the action. P was quite unmoved by this threat since the action was being defended by his insurers and, if the action succeeded, it was they and not he who would pay. D's conviction was upheld. It might be said that, in the actual circumstances of the case, the words used could not influence a person of normal stability and courage; but the court appears to have held that regard must be had, not to the actual circumstances, but to the circumstances as they appeared to the person making the demand:

"There may be special circumstances unknown to an accused which would make the threats innocuous and unavailing for the accused's demand, but such circumstances would have no bearing on the accused's state of mind and of his intention. If an accused knew that what he threatened would have no effect on the victim it might be different."[5]

[**344**] It is submitted, therefore, that there is a sufficient menace if, in the circumstances known to the accused, the threat might:

(i) influence the mind of an ordinary person of normal stability and courage, whether or not it in fact influences the person addressed; or
(ii) influence the mind of the person addressed, though it would not influence an ordinary person.

It is assumed, of course, that in both cases there is an intention to influence the person addressed to accede to the demand by means of the threat.

2 THE MENS REA

[**345**] The *mens rea* of blackmail comprises a number of elements:

(1) An intent to make a demand with menaces.[6]
(2) A view to gain for himself or another, *or* intent to cause loss to another.
(3) Either
(a) no belief that he has reasonable grounds for making the demand, *or*
(b) no belief that the use of the menaces is a proper means of reinforcing the demand.

---

4 *Supra*, [1968] 1 All E.R. at 80.
5 *Ibid.*
6 Above, paras. [**334**]–[**344**].

[**346**] It is clear that the onus of proof of each of these elements is on the Crown; but it is enough to establish (1) and (2) and *either* (3) (*a*) or (3) (*b*). It may well be that, once the Crown has introduced evidence of elements (1) and (2), an evidential burden is put upon the accused as regards (3); that is he must introduce some evidence of his belief of *both* (*a*) and (*b*), whereupon it will be for the Crown to prove that he did not believe one, or the other, or both. Where, on the face of it, the means used to reinforce the demand are improper, and D does not set up the case that he believed in its propriety, the jury need not be directed on the point.[7] It will be noted that whether or not a demand is "unwarranted" is exclusively a question of the accused's belief, as to which no one is better informed than he; and the phraseology of the section—"a demand with menaces is unwarranted unless . . ."—suggests that it is for the accused to assert that his demand was warranted.

Where, however, D does not set up such a defence, but the evidence is such that a jury might reasonably think he had the beliefs in question, it is the duty of the judge to direct the jury not to convict unless satisfied that he did not have the beliefs or one of them.[8] The first element requires no further consideration.

A. A VIEW TO GAIN OR INTENT TO CAUSE LOSS

[**347**] "Gain" and "loss" are defined by s. 34 (2) (*a*) of the Theft Act:

" 'gain' and 'loss' are to be construed as extending only to gain or loss in money or other property, but as extending to any such gain or loss whether temporary or permanent; and

(i) 'gain' includes a gain by keeping what one has, as well as a gain by getting what one has not; and

(ii) 'loss' includes a loss by not getting what one might get, as well as a loss by parting with what one has."

[**348**] As has already been noted,[9] this definition limits the offence to the protection of economic interests. Without it, the scope of s. 21—demanding with menaces the performance of *any act or omission*—would have been very wide indeed and would certainly have extended far beyond "theft and similar or associated offences" which it is the object of the Theft Act to revise. In most cases, the blackmailer is trying to obtain money to which he knows he has no right and there will be no doubt about his view to gain. It is clearly not necessary, however, that there should be evidence of a direct demand for money or other property. It is enough that D's purpose in demanding the act or omission, whatever it may be, is gain or loss in terms of money or other property. Suppose that D demands with menaces that P should marry him. If P is an heiress and D's object is to enrich himself, he is guilty of blackmail. But if D's object is the satisfaction of his carnal desires, or the social advancement which the marriage will bring, then he is not guilty. No doubt it is

---

[7] *Lawrence*, [1971] Crim. L.R. 645.

[8] "It is always the duty of the judge to leave to the jury any issue (whether raised by the defence or not) which, on the evidence in the case, is an issue fit to be left to them": *Palmer* v. *R.*, [1971] 1 All E.R. 1077 at 1080 (P.C.), *per* Lord Morris.

[9] Above, para. [**336**].

enough that the acquisition of money or other property is one of several objects
which D has in mind in making the demand.

[**349**] Is it enough that D foresees that the fulfilment of his demand will
result in a gain to him, even though gain is not one of the objects of the demand?
D is so consumed with desire for the heiress that he would have made exactly
the same demand with menaces even if she had been a pauper: but he knows
that the marriage will be profitable. It is thought that this will probably not
be enough. Where it is a case of causing loss rather than making a gain, "intent"
is specifically required and this is likely to be construed to require a desire that
loss should ensue. D demands with menaces that P should jump into a muddy
pool. D's object is that P, who has offended him, should suffer discomfort and
humiliation. As D foresaw, P's clothes are ruined by immersion in the pool
and so he suffers a loss. It is probable that D is not guilty. If that be correct
with regard to "intent to cause loss", it would seem appropriate that a similar
principle should govern "view to gain".

(a) Belief in a right to the gain

[**350**] It is not necessarily a good defence that D believes he has a right to
the gain. If he has such a belief, then he certainly believes that he has reasonable grounds for making the demand, but it will be recalled that this does
not cause the demand to be warranted unless it is coupled with a belief that
the use of the menaces is a proper means of reinforcing the demand. Section 21
does not use the word "dishonestly" which, in ss. 1, 15, 16, 17 and 20, ensures
that a claim of right to the property is a defence. It is clear that the Criminal
Law Revision Committee intended that the offence might be committed where
D had both a claim of right and an actual right to the property which he intended to acquire.[10]

> "A may be owed £100 by B and be unable to get payment. Perhaps A
> needs the money badly and B is in a position to pay; or perhaps A can
> easily afford to wait and B is in difficulty. Should it be blackmail for
> A to threaten B that, if he does not pay, A will assault him—or slash the
> tyres of his car—or tell people that B is a homosexual, which he is (or
> which he is not)—or tell people about the debt and anything discreditable
> about the way in which it was incurred? On one view none of these threats
> should be enough to make the demand amount to blackmail. For it is no
> offence merely to utter the threats without making the demand (unless
> for some particular reason such as breach of the peace or defamation);
> nor would the threat become criminal merely because it was uttered to
> reinforce a demand of a kind quite different from those associated with
> blackmail. Why then should it be blackmail merely because it is uttered
> to reinforce a demand for money which is owed? On this view no demand
> with menaces would amount to blackmail, however harsh the action
> threatened, unless there was dishonesty. This is a tenable view, though an
> extreme one. In our opinion it goes too far and there are some threats
> which should make the demand amount to blackmail even if there is a
> valid claim to the thing demanded. For example, we believe that most

---

[10] The *Report*, Cmnd. 2977, para. 119.

people would say that it should be blackmail to threaten to denounce a person, however truly, as a homosexual unless he paid a debt. It does not seem to follow from the existence of a debt that the creditor should be entitled to resort to any method, otherwise non-criminal, to obtain payment. There are limits to the methods permissible for the purpose of enforcing payment of a debt without recourse to the courts. For example, a creditor cannot seize the debtor's goods; and in *Parker*[11] it was held (as mentioned in paragraph 92) that a creditor who forged a letter from the Admiralty to a sailor warning him to pay a debt was guilty of forgery notwithstanding the existence of the debt."

[**351**] Acts of Parliament, however, do not always carry out the intention of those who frame them, and it has been argued that the use of the words "with a view to gain" will defeat the object of the Committee in this case:[12] "There is surely no gain or loss where a person merely secures the payment of that which he is owed."

The argument might be elaborated as follows:

". . . If I liquidate a just debt, I suffer no economic loss. In my personal balance sheet, the amount of cash in hand on the credit side is reduced, but this is offset by a corresponding reduction on the debit side in the item 'sundry creditors'."[13]

If the debtor has suffered no economic loss it follows that the creditor has acquired no economic gain for, while his cash in hand will increase, his credit balance under "sundry debtors" will diminish. If "gain in money or other property" means economic enrichment, then, it is arguable that D has no view to gain when he demands that to which he is entitled.

[**352**] The answer turns on the meaning of the word "gain". That word has frequently been the subject of interpretation in other statutes.[14] The meaning given to a word in one statute is by no means conclusive as to that which it should bear in another; but it may give some guidance. "Gain" certainly might mean "profit"[15] and if that is its meaning in the Theft Act, then the argument in the preceding paragraph seems a sound one. On the other hand, Jessel, M.R. has said " 'Gain' means exactly acquisition . . . Gain is something obtained or acquired."[16] Though he found that there was a profit, and therefore a gain, in that case, it would seem that he did not think that gain was necessarily to be equated with profit. If then, "gain" includes acquisition, whether at a profit or not, the difficulty disappears. A man may properly be said to have *acquired* that which he is entitled to have, if he secures ownership or possession of it. Apart from the intentions of the Committee which have been

---

[11] (1910), 74 J.P. 208.

[12] Hogan, [1966] Crim. L.R. at 476.

[13] R. N. Gooderson, [1960] C.L.J. 199 at 205, discussing the meaning of "fraud" in relation to *Welham* v. *D.P.P.*, [1961] A.C. 103.

[14] Particularly the Companies Acts and Factories Acts. See Companies Act 1948, s. 434 (1) and Factories Act 1961, s. 175 (1). See also Obscene Publications Act 1964, and *Chief Constable of Blackpool* v. *Woodhall*, [1965] Crim. L.R. 660.

[15] "Any gain consequent on death" in the New Zealand Law Reform Act 1939, means "any increase in financial resources", *per* Ostler, J. in *Alley* v. *Alfred Bucklands & Sons, Ltd.*, [1941] N.Z.L.R. 575.

[16] *Re Arthur Average Association* (1875), 10 Ch. App. 542 at 546.

quoted above, the Act itself suggests that this is the right view, (a) through the omission of the word "dishonestly", which would have imported a defence of claim of right, (b) because s. 21 requires not merely a belief that D is entitled to the thing demanded but also a belief that the use of the menaces is proper, and (c) because "gain" is defined to include "getting what one has not." It is submitted therefore that "gain" includes the acquisition of money or other property whether it is due in law or not.[17]

(b) *Intention to return an economic equivalent*

[353] If the view expressed in the preceding paragraph is wrong, similar problems arise where D intends to restore to P an economic equivalent of the alleged gain which he has in mind. As a starting point, suppose that D wishes to acquire a particular florin belonging to P which has a sentimental value for both P and D. D demands of P with menaces that he exchange the desired florin for another. Obviously D intends to acquire the florin but he does not intend to make any profit in terms of money.[18] If there were no view to gain in this situation, many cases would be excluded from the section which it is reasonably clear that it is intended to cover. If D demands with menaces that he be given an appointment, he may have every intention of doing a good day's work and earning his wages.[19] The runner who, by menaces, gains admission to a race may have every intention of supplying a first-class performance which will be worth as much or more in terms of money to the organisers of the meeting as any prize he may win. The gambler who, by menaces, causes the bookmaker's clerk to let him bet on credit may have every intention of paying up if the horse backed loses—he is prepared to pay the full economic value of the chance he has bought. In each of these examples, D has a view to the acquisition of money or other property—his wages, the prize, the winnings—and in each case it is submitted that he is guilty of blackmail.

If this be correct, the same principle must govern "loss". D intends P to suffer a loss if he intends him to be deprived of particular money or property, though he may also intend that P be fully compensated in economic terms.

(c) *Temporary gain and loss*

[354] The intent permanently to deprive which is an essential ingredient of theft, robbery and obtaining property by deception is not a requisite of blackmail. Suppose that D, by menaces, causes P to let him have a car on hire for a week. If D intends to return the car at the end of the week, he cannot be guilty of theft or of robbery.[20] He has, however, a view to a temporary gain which is sufficient under s. 21 and he is guilty of blackmail.

This may seem strange, but it is consistent with the theory that it is the method of obtaining the property—the demand with menaces—which is the gist of the offence and not the unlawful profit made or contemplated by D or the

---

[17] *Cf. Lawrence*, [1971] Crim. L.R. 645, where it appears that D believed the debt to be due.

[18] Of course, the problem under consideration would not arise if the coin had a higher market value than its nominal value. *Cf. Moss* v. *Hancock*, [1899] 2 Q.B. 110.

[19] Lord Denning has expressed the view that, in such a case, there is no intention to cause economic loss to the employer: *Welham* v. *D.P.P.*, [1961] A.C. at 131. It follows that the employee has no intention to make an economic gain.

[20] Above, para. **[130]**.

corresponding loss to P. As we have seen D may be demanding property which he is entitled to have.

(d) *Intent to cause loss*

[355] In most cases "a view to gain" and an "intent to cause loss" will go hand in hand; P's loss will be D's gain. The phrase, "intent to cause loss" is not, however, superfluous. There may be circumstances in which D intends to cause a loss to P without any corresponding gain to D. If P has written his memoirs and D demands with menaces that P destroy them, D has an intent to cause loss but no view to gain.

Another instance would be the case where D demands with menaces that P dismiss Q from a remunerated office or employment or that P should not promote Q. D intends to cause Q a loss (by not getting what he might get[1]) and it is immaterial whether D has in view any gain to himself or another. Likewise where D demands with menaces that P resign his own appointment, or not apply for, or refuse promotion.

(e) *Gain by keeping and loss by not getting*

[356] A view to gain includes an intent to keep what one has; and intent to cause a loss includes causing another not to get what he might get.[2] Thus if D owes P £10 and, by menaces, he induces him to accept £5 in full satisfaction he has caused a gain and a loss within the meaning of s. 21.

[357] If D, knowing that P is in financial difficulties and in urgent need of money, takes advantage of this situation in order to induce P to accept a less sum in satisfaction, he may be in danger of conviction of blackmail. D can hardly say, to any effect, that he had reasonable grounds for making the demand if he knew the larger sum was due; and in that case it is immaterial whether the use of the menaces is a proper means of reinforcing the demand. The Court of Appeal has taken the view that it is "intimidation" and holding a creditor "to ransom" to say "We cannot pay you the £480. But we will pay you £300 if you will accept it in settlement. If you do not accept it on those terms you will get nothing. £300 is better than nothing".[3] This suggests that that court, at least, would regard such pressure on a creditor as a "menace".

(f) *Remoteness*

[358] Where a number of intermediate steps are required between the act caused by D's menace and the acquisition by him of any gain, problems of remoteness may arise.

If D gains admission to an Inn of Court by menacing the Under-Treasurer,[4] is he guilty of an offence under the section? If he intends ultimately to practise and thereby to earn fees it would seem that his action is taken with a view to gain—though this is rather far to seek. But if he has no intention to practise and merely wants the prestige of the barrister's qualification, it is difficult to see that he can have committed the offence. It must appear that D at least con-

---

[1] Below, para. [357].
[2] Section 34 (2) (i) and (ii), above, para. [347].
[3] *D. & C. Builders* v. *Rees*, [1966] 2 Q.B. 617 at 625, *per* Lord Denning, M.R.
[4] *Cf. Bassey* (1931), 22 Cr. App. Rep. 160.

templated the *possibility* of using his qualification to earn money, probably that this was his actual intention.

What, then, if D menaces the headmaster of the public school with a view to gaining admission for his newly-born son? If D believes that the only advantage of education at that school is that it will produce a more cultured person with a greater capacity for the enjoyment of life than education in a state school, he has no view to gain. If, however, he believes and is motivated by his belief that his son will (in about twenty years' time) have a greater earning power, is it to be said that he has a view to gain? Literally he does. Yet the gain is so distant in time and subject to so many contingencies that its connection with the demand with menaces may be thought too remote. A stronger case is that of a candidate for a university examination who menaces the examiner with a view to passing or getting a better class degree than he would otherwise obtain. Most candidates have an eye on their earning capacity and this might be *prima facie* evidence of a view to gain.

B. UNWARRANTED DEMANDS

[**359**] Whether a demand is "warranted" or not appears to be exclusively a question of the accused's belief. Theoretically a demand with menaces may be unwarranted although D is entitled to recover the property demanded and the menace is a perfectly proper means of enforcing the demand. Suppose P has stolen and disposed of D's picture. D threatens to report him to the police unless he pays D £1,000. D believes the picture is only worth £100; so he does not believe that he has reasonable grounds for making the demand. The picture is in fact worth £1,000, so he does actually have reasonable grounds. D who has looked up an out-of-date law book believes that it is the offence of compounding a felony to accept any consideration for not disclosing a theft; so he does not believe that the use of the menace is a proper means of enforcing the demand. But by the Criminal Law Act 1967, s. 5 (1) it is lawful to accept reasonable compensation for making good the injury or loss caused by an arrestable offence, in consideration for not disclosing it. The use of the menaces then—or so it seems—is a proper means of reinforcing the demand. Looking at the facts objectively, D has done nothing wrong; but he is guilty of blackmail: "It is all in the mind!" This is something of a new departure in English law.

[**360**] It does not seem likely that this will be a serious issue in practice. Where D's conduct is objectively innocent, it is unlikely that a prosecution will ever be instituted. If it is, the onus of proof on the Crown will be very difficult to satisfy. The usual way of satisfying the jury that D did not have the beliefs referred to in s. 21 (1) (*a*) and (*b*) will be by showing that no reasonable person could have held such a belief. For example, if D says that he believed that he had reasonable grounds for demanding £1,000 from his neighbour in return for not disclosing to the neighbour's wife that her husband had committed adultery, it is safe to assume, in the absence of some extraordinary circumstances, that the jury will disbelieve him and be satisfied beyond reasonable doubt of his guilt. They will be so satisfied because they will feel that no

man in his right mind could entertain such a belief for a moment.[5]   If then, D's beliefs are entirely reasonable, the normal mode of proof fails; and, in the absence of some confession by D as to his belief in the unreasonableness of his demand, or the impropriety of his threat, conviction will be impossible.

[**361**] The problem that is likely to arise is the converse. That is, the grounds for making the demand were not reasonable but D asserts that he believed they were; the use of the menaces is not a proper means of reinforcing the demand but D asserts that he believed it was. The question for the jury then is simply whether D is speaking the truth. Juries have to determine this question often enough; but the difference about this case is that it is not a question of the accused's belief in *fact*, but the accused's belief in *standards*.

[**362**] This provision of the Act has been criticised by a judicial writer:[6]
   "If a defendant has acted disgracefully by making a certain demand reinforced by threats of a particular kind, I see no injustice in holding him responsible in a criminal court, even though he may have acted according to his own standard in these matters. On the other hand I see some danger to our general standards of right and wrong, if each man can claim to act according to his own, however, low that standard may be. That is one objection. Another is the difficulty of the jury's ascertaining the defendant's standard, so that it may be decided whether in the case before them he acted in accordance with it. A man whose standard is below the general may fail in a particular case to observe even his own standard in which event he would, I suppose, be punishable under clause 17 [now section 21]. But are questions of this kind triable?"

[**363**] In reply to this it has been argued[7] that what the section does is to make a moral, as well as a legal claim of right a defence to a charge of blackmail and that this is proper.   Miss Bernhard was acquitted of blackmail contrary to s. 30 of the Larceny Act 1916 because she believed, on the advice of a Hungarian lawyer, that she had a legal right to the money demanded.[8]
   "Oddly enough—at least it has always seemed odd to me—she would have been convicted of blackmail had she known the law but felt with the deepest sincerity that she was morally entitled to something".[9]

[**364**] If Robin Hood, having demanded "Your money or your life!" is charged with robbery, it will not avail him in the slightest to say, however sincerely and convincingly, that, according to his moral code, robbing the rich to pay the poor is the most laudable of social activities; but suppose he has been charged instead with blackmail, contrary to s. 21? It is impossible to suppose that he can be acquitted. He has, after all, to believe he has *reasonable* grounds. The answer, it is suggested, is not simply a question of the accused's own moral code. The question "when does a man believe he has reasonable grounds for

---

   [5] The ultimate question is as to the state of mind of the accused person and this should always be stressed to a jury. References to the reasonable or ordinary man in a direction to a jury are dangerous: *Cf.* Criminal Justice Act 1967, s. 8; *Wallett*, [1968] 2 Q.B. 367; [1968] 2 All E.R. 296.
   [6] Sir Bernard MacKenna, "Blackmail: A Criticism", [1966] Crim. L.R. 467 at 472.
   [7] By Brian Hogan, [1966] Crim. L.R. 474.
   [8] [1938] 2 K.B. 264.
   [9] Hogan, above, footnote 7, at 478.

making a demand?" should perhaps be answered "When he believes that reasonable men generally would regard the grounds as reasonable."[10] Modern Robin Hoods know very well that reasonable men generally do not regard it as reasonable to rob the rich, even to reward the poor.

[**365**] It is not difficult, however, to envisage situations in which, though D has no claim of legal right, he may suppose that reasonable men generally would regard his demand as justified. For example, D demands payment of money won on a wager with P, though he knows that wagers are unenforceable in law; D demands money promised to her by P in return for immoral services rendered to P: D demands payment of a statute-barred debt, being aware of the statute of limitations. A jury might very well say, in these circumstances, that they believed D, when he said that he believed that his act would not be condemned as wrongful by ordinary men.

[**366**] The same approach may be made to the second limb of "warranted". D, believing his wages to be due and being unable to get payment, demands them at the point of a dagger. The question is, it is submitted, "Did D believe that people generally would regard this as a proper means of enforcing the demand?" The answer is very likely to be in the negative, with the result that D, though not guilty of robbery or attempted robbery,[11] would be guilty of blackmail.

[**367**] On the other hand D's plea might very well be accepted in the following cases. D, a bookmaker, being unable to obtain payment of a wagering debt due from P, another bookmaker, threatens to report P to Tattersalls if he does not pay up. D threatens P that she will tell P's wife of their immoral relationship if P does not pay her the money he promised her. D threatens that he will warn his friends against doing business with P if P does not pay up the statute-barred debt.

[**368**] If this view is accepted, the law is certainly lacking in precision; but this is a branch of the law in which precision is not easily obtainable. From the point of view of justice, however, the law seems unexceptionable. The defendant is not to be held liable unless it is proved that he knew he was doing something which he ought not to do, in the broad sense described, *either* in making the demand, *or* in making the threat. D, believing that she has been indecently assaulted by P, tells him that she will "summons" him if he does not compensate her.[12] No doubt the size of the demand in such a case will influence the jury in deciding whether they believe P's assertion that she thought both the demand and the menaces to be reasonable.

---

[10] *Cf.* the test proposed under the M'Naghten Rules in *Codere* (1916), 12 Cr. App. Rep. 21 at 27: ". . . whether according to the ordinary standard adopted by reasonable men the act was right or wrong." As it was put by the appellant's counsel (at 25) ". . . it would probably be sufficient to render him punishable, if he knew—that is understood and appreciated—that the act would be condemned and regarded as wrong by his fellow-creatures."

[11] *Skivington*, [1968] 1 Q.B. 166; above, para. [**153**].

[12] *Cf. Dymond*, [1920] 2 K.B. 260.

CHAPTER X

BURGLARY AND AGGRAVATED BURGLARY

1 BURGLARY

[**369**] The law relating to burglary and other breaking offences contained in the Larceny Act 1916, ss. 24–27, was very complicated.[1] The Theft Act effects a considerable simplification of the law. The Act eliminates entirely the concept of "breaking" which was a requisite of burglary and most forms of house-breaking under the Larceny Act. "Breaking" was a highly technical term on which there was a great deal of case law and it no longer served a useful purpose in the definition of the offences. The Act also gets rid of the distinction between breaking "in the night" and breaking "in the day" which was the most conspicuous difference between the old offences of burglary and housebreaking. So far as the definition of the new offence is concerned, the concept of "dwelling house" is also eliminated; but, unfortunately, it will still be necessary to distinguish between "dwellings" and other buildings for the purposes of ascertaining the jurisdiction of magistrates' courts.[2] The new offences of burglary will comprehend all[3] that was formerly burglary and house-breaking—and a good deal more besides.

[**370**] Section 9 of the Act provides:

"(1) A person is guilty of burglary if—

(*a*) he enters any building or part of a building as a trespasser and with intent to commit any such offence as is mentioned in subsection (2) below; or

(*b*) having entered any building or part of a building as a trespasser he steals or attempts to steal anything in the building or that part of it or inflicts or attempts to inflict on any person therein any grievous bodily harm.

(2) The offences referred to in subsection (1) (*a*) above are offences of stealing anything in the building or part of a building in question, of inflicting on any person therein any grievous bodily harm or raping any woman therein, and of doing unlawful damage to the building or anything therein.

(3) References in subsections (1) and (2) above to a building shall apply also to an inhabited vehicle or vessel, and shall apply to any such

---

[1] Smith and Hogan (1st ed.), 397–401.
[2] Section 29 (2), below, para. [**499**].
[3] With some unimportant exceptions.

vehicle or vessel at times when the person having a habitation in it is not there as well as at times when he is.

(4) A person guilty of burglary shall on conviction on indictment be liable to imprisonment for a term not exceeding fourteen years."

Paragraphs (a) and (b) of s. 9 (1) create separate offences. A person indicted under one paragraph, may not be convicted of an offence under the other.[4] When there is a doubt as to which offence was committed, it is desirable to have two counts.

A. THE ACTUS REUS

(a) Enters

[371] In the vast majority of cases the proof of an entry will present no problems; but there are bound to be borderline cases where difficulties arise. Suppose that D climbs up a drainpipe and puts his arm through a window in order to pull himself inside. Has he entered? If not, is it necessary that his entire body should be within the building? The man with his arm through the window was not "in" a building for the purposes of "being found" there, under s. 28 of the Larceny Act 1916;[5] but he had made a sufficient entry for the purposes of burglary at common law and under the Larceny Act 1916, to which the common law principles applied. As the Theft Act gives no express answer to these problems, it is at least possible that the courts will resort to the common law cases in the interpretation of "enters"; and, indeed, it seems to have been assumed in Parliament[6] that the common law rules would apply.

[372] The common law rule is that the insertion of any part of the body, however small, is a sufficient entry. So where D pushed in a window pane and the forepart of his finger was observed to be inside the building, that was enough.[7] But the common law goes farther than that. If an instrument is inserted into the building for the purpose of committing the ulterior offence, there is an entry even though no part of the body is introduced into the building. So it is enough that hooks are inserted into the premises to drag out the carpets[8] or that the muzzle of a gun is introduced with a view to shooting someone inside.[9] It would amount to an entry if holes were bored in the side of a granary so that wheat would run out and be stolen by D,[10] provided that the boring implement emerged on the inside. On the other hand, the insertion of an instrument for the purpose of gaining entry and not for the purpose of committing the ulterior offence, is not an entry if no part of the body enters.[11] If D bores a hole in a door with a centre bit for the purpose of gaining entry, the emergence of the point of the bit on the inside of the door is not an entry.

---

[4] Hollis, [1971] Crim. L.R. 525.
[5] Parkin, [1950] 1 K.B. 155.
[6] Parl. Debates, Official Report (H.L.), Vol. 290, cols. 85–86.
[7] Davis (1823), R. & R. 499.
[8] (1583), 1 Anderson 114.
[9] 2 East P.C. 49.
[10] State v. Crawford (1899), 46 L.R.A. 312 (Alabama).
[11] Hughes (1785), 1 Leach 406; but cf. Tucker (1844), 1 Cox C.C. 73.

[373] Even if the courts are willing to follow the common law in holding that the intrusion of any part of the body is an entry, they may be reluctant to preserve these technical rules regarding instruments, for they seem to lead to outlandish results. Thus it seems to follow from the common law rules that there may be an entry if a stick of dynamite is thrown into the building or if a bullet is fired from outside the building into it.[12] What then if a time bomb is sent by parcel post? Has D "entered", even though he is not on the scene at all?—perhaps even abroad and outside the jurisdiction? Whether D enters or not can hardly depend on how far away he is and the case seems indistinguishable from the others put. Yet this is hardly an "entry" in the "simple language as used and understood by ordinary literate men and women" in which the Act is said to be written.[13]

[374] There is, however, a cogent argument in favour of the common law rules which may be put as follows. If D sends a child, under the age of ten, into the building to steal, this is obviously an entry by D,[14] through an "innocent agent", under ordinary principles. Suppose that, instead of a child, D sends in a monkey. It is hard to see that this should not equally be an entry by D. But if that point be conceded, it is admitted that the insertion of an *animate* instrument is an entry; and are we to distinguish between animate and inanimate instruments? Unless we are, the insertion of the hooks, etc., must also be an entry.

If D puts a child under ten through the window, so that child may open a door and admit D who will himself steal, it is by no means so clear that the innocent agency argument is open; and the common law rule regarding instruments would suggest it is not an entry; since the child is being used to gain entry and not to commit the ulterior offence.

(b) As a trespasser

[375] Trespass is a legal concept and we must resort to the law of tort in order to ascertain its meaning.[15] It would appear that any intentional, reckless or negligent entry into a building is a trespass if the building is in fact in the possession of another who does not consent to the entry. Mistake is no defence to an action in tort; so that, if D on a very dark night were to enter the house next door in mistake for his own, this would be regarded as an intentional entry and a trespass. This would apparently be so even if D's mistake was a reasonable one, *a fortiori* if it were negligent as, for example, if he made the mistake because he was befuddled with drink. It is submitted, however, that it is not sufficient (though it is necessary) that D is a trespasser in the civil law. In the criminal law he must be shown to have *mens rea*. If he is charged under s. 9 (1) (a), it must appear that, when he entered, he knew the facts which caused him to be a trespasser or at least that he was reckless whether those facts existed.[16] A merely negligent entry, as where D enters another's house,

---

[12] 1 Hawk. P.C., c. 17, s. 11; 2 East P.C. 490; *contra*, Hale, 1 P.C. 554.
[13] Above, para. [8], footnote 8, and see Griew, 4–06.
[14] Hale, 1 P.C. 555; Smith and Hogan, 81.
[15] Salmond on *Torts* (15th ed.), 48; Winfield on *Tort* (8th ed.), 323; Street, *Law of Torts* (4th ed.), 13, 63.
[16] The absence of the word "knowingly" should not deter the court from importing a requirement of *mens rea*: Roper v. *Taylor's Central Garage (Exeter), Ltd.*, [1951] 2 T.L.R. 284 at 288, *per* Devlin, J.

honestly but unreasonably believing it to be his own, should not be enough. So too a belief in a *right* to enter the house of another should be a defence, for then there is no intention to enter *as a trespasser*. Suppose that D, being separated from his wife, wrongly supposes that he has a right to enter the matrimonial home of which she is the owner-occupier and does enter with intent to inflict grievous bodily harm upon her. Even if he is in law a trespasser, it is submitted that he is not a burglar.

[376] If D's entry is involuntary, he is not a trespasser and cannot be guilty of burglary. So if he is dragged against his will into P's house and left there by his drunken companions and he steals P's vase and leaves, this is not burglary. If, however, D had intentionally entered the building, believing it to be his own house and committed theft on discovering the truth, it appears from the previous paragraph that he would have committed theft after entering as a trespasser and thus committed the *actus reus* of burglary. In this case it seems that D has *mens rea* as well, for burglary under s. 9 (1) (*b*) is committed, not at the time of entry, but when the ulterior crime is committed; and at that time, he knows that he has entered as a trespasser.

[377] (i) *Trespass ab initio.*—Under a doctrine of the common law, which is now of doubtful validity,[17] where D's entry into a building is lawful because of the authority of the law, as distinct from the consent of the owner, and he commits a trespass to the building, the original entry may, retrospectively, become a trespass for the purposes of the law of tort. So if a constable were to enter a house to search for stolen goods under the authority of s. 26 of the Theft Act[18] and to attempt to steal a plaque fixed to the wall of the house, he would become a trespasser *ab initio*. By a legal fiction he has now entered as a trespasser and he has actually attempted to commit theft. Is he then to be guilty of burglary? It is submitted that he is not. The Act uses the words "enters . . . as a trespasser" and it is submitted that this means that the accused must actually be a trespasser at the time of entry. Moreover, if the submission in the previous paragraph is correct, the constable cannot be convicted because he did not *intend* to enter as a trespasser, nor was he reckless.

[378] Trespass *ab initio* has no application in the situation where D has entered with the permission of the occupier and subsequently committed theft. It would be very strange if liability to conviction of burglary should depend on whether a lawful entry was by authority of law or by consent of the owner. Particularly in view of the doubtful status of the doctrine in the civil law, it is submitted with some confidence that it has no relevance to the new offence of burglary.

[379] (ii) *Entry under false pretences.*—Since trespass is an entry without consent, difficulties may arise where consent is obtained by fraud. If the fraud is such as to render the transaction void, then it is safe to say that any apparent consent is not real consent and a trespass will be committed.

For example (to borrow the characters from a well-known civil case), if Blenkarn by pretending to be the well-known firm of picture cleaners, Blenkiron

---

[17] See *Chic Fashions (West Wales), Ltd.* v. *Jones,* [1968] 2 Q.B. 299 at 313 and 317; [1968] 1 All E.R. 229 (C.A.) at 236 and 239.
[18] Below, para. [494].

& Co.,[19] causes P to enter into "a contract" with him for the cleaning of P's pictures and thereby gains admission to P's premises, he does so as a trespasser and will be guilty of burglary if he steals while on the premises.

Similarly if D, by impersonating X who has a reader's ticket, gains admission to the P University library with intent to steal the books.

[**380**] Mistake as to identity in these examples rendered the contract, in the first case, and licence, in the second case, void. The problem is more difficult where the fraud is such as to render the transaction not void but merely voidable.

For example, D, by producing forged references, causes P to enter into a contract with him, D, for the cleaning of P's pictures. D obtains a reader's ticket to the P University library by falsely pretending that he, D, is reading for a degree at another university. In these situations, the contract and the licence are not void but voidable. It may therefore be argued that since D enters the premises under an existing contract or licence, he does not do so as a trespasser. P may rescind the transaction but, until he does so, it is a perfectly good contract or licence. If this argument is sound, the consequences could be serious, for some acts which were (and rightly) burglary or housebreaking under the old law would be outside the terms of s. 9. For example, D gains admission to P's house by falsely pretending that he has been sent by the B.B.C. to examine the radio set in order to trace disturbances in transmission. It was held,[20] under the old law, that there was a constructive breaking since the householder had been deceived by a trick and he would not have admitted the man had he known the true facts. "Breaking" is no longer an issue and the sole question is whether there was a trespassory entry.

[**381**] There are English and Commonwealth authorities which suggest that there is a trespass in all the examples considered in paragraph [**380**]. In *Taylor* v. *Jackson*[1] D had permission to go on P's land and hunt for rabbits. He went there to hunt for hares and the divisional court held that this was evidence of trespass in pursuit of game, contrary to the Game Act 1831, s. 30. In *Hillen and Pettigrew* v. *I.C.I. (Alkali), Ltd.*[2] members of a stevedore's gang employed to unload a barge were held to be trespassers when they placed kegs on the hatch covers, knowing that this was a wrong and dangerous thing to do. They were, therefore, not entitled to damages when the hatch covers collapsed and they were injured. Lord Atkin said:

"As Scrutton, L.J. has pointedly said: 'When you invite a person into your house to use the staircase you do not invite him to slide down the bannisters.'[3] So far as he sets foot on so much of the premises as lie outside the invitation or *uses them for purposes which are alien to the invitation* he is not an invitee but a trespasser, and his rights must be determined accordingly. In the present case the stevedores knew that they ought not to use the covered hatch in order to load cargo from it; for them *for such a purpose it was out of bounds*: they were trespassers."

---

[19] *Cf. Cundy* v. *Lindsay* (1878), 3 App. Cas. 459.
[20] *Boyle*, [1954] 1 Q.B. 292.
[1] (1898), 78 L.T. 555.
[2] [1936] A.C. 65.
[3] *The Carlgarth*, [1927] P. 93 at 110.

[382] In *Gross* v. *Wright*[4] the defendant agreed with the plaintiff to build a party wall, twenty-four inches thick and half on the land of each of them. In breach of the agreement, he narrowed the wall on each succeeding storey above the first, keeping the wall perpendicular on the plaintiff's side, but setting it back on his own side. It was held by the Supreme Court of Canada that the defendant had entered upon the plaintiff's land as a trespasser. Anglin, J. said:

> "The determination to build the wall otherwise than as agreed upon having been arrived at before the work was begun the original entry itself was not authorised by the licence given by the agreement."[5]

[383] In *Farrington* v. *Thomson and Bridgland*[6] one of the defendant police officers entered the plaintiff's hotel and ordered him to close it on the ground that he had committed "a third offence" against the Victorian Licensing Act and *ipso facto* forfeited his licence. The defendants knew they had no power to close the hotel and, in purporting to exercise a power which they knew they did not possess, they were guilty of the tort of misfeasance in a public office. Because the officer had entered for the purpose of committing a tort, the defendants were held by Smith, J. to be guilty of trespass.

The learned judge said:[7]

> "The evidence indicates, I think, that the part of the hotel entered and traversed by Bridgland was at the material time open to the public. The plaintiff's situation in relation to this part of his hotel would seem to have been comparable with that of a shopkeeper in relation to that part of his shop which is open to the public. Such a person is, in general, regarded as extending a tacit invitation to the public to enter that part of the premises for the purpose of discussing or transacting any business which concerns him: compare *Indermaur* v. *Dames*;[8] *Mackay* v. *Abrahams*;[9] *Davis* v. *Lisle*.[10] But this general principle appears to me to require some qualification. The tacit invitation cannot, I think, be taken to extend to persons entering for the purpose of committing a criminal offence, or a tort against the occupier, merely because the intended wrongful act relates to the occupier's business."

Later in his judgment, he said:[11]

> ". . . Bridgland's entry on the premises for the purpose of committing that tort was not within the scope of any tacit invitation or licence that he may have had from the plaintiff, and that therefore his entry onto the premises, . . . was a trespass: Compare Smith's *Leading Cases* (13th ed.), at p. 139; Salmond on *Torts* (12th ed.), at pp. 158-9; *Taylor* v. *Jackson*;[12] *Hillen* v. *I.C.I.* (*Alkali*), *Ltd.*"[13]

---

[4] [1923] 2 D.L.R. 171.
[5] *Ibid.*, at 185. See also Brodeur, J. at 188. Duff, J. did not insist, as Anglin, J. did, that the original entry should be a trespass; "The moment he began to reduce the thickness of the wall on his own side while maintaining unreduced its thickness on the other side, he became a trespasser."
[6] [1959] V.R. 286.
[7] *Ibid.*, at 292.
[8] (1866), L.R. 1 C.P. 274.
[9] [1916] V.L.R. 681.
[10] [1936] 2 K.B. 434.
[11] [1959] V.L.R. at 297.
[12] (1898), 78 L.T. 555.
[13] [1936] A.C. 65.

[384] (iii) *Entry for a purpose alien to a licence to enter.*—Such cases are not only authority for saying that all the hypothetical examples considered above are cases of trespass and therefore of burglary, but they go much further. In the examples, a false pretence is made with a view to gaining entry. These authorities suggest that it is enough to negative a licence to enter, that entry is made with a secret unlawful intent, even though no false pretence is made. If this is right, D, who enters a shop for the purpose of shoplifting, is a burglar. This is perhaps fair enough. Few would object to the conviction of burglary of intending bank robbers who enter the bank flourishing pistols; yet banks are no more and no less open to the public than shops—that is, an invitation is extended by both to those members of the public who wish to enter for the transaction of the business for which the premises exist—the sale of goods, the cashing of cheques, the opening of an account and so on. One decision goes against this view. In *Bryne* v. *Kinematograph Renters Society, Ltd.*[14] Harman, J. held that it was not trespass to gain entry to a cinema by buying tickets with the purpose, not of seeing the film, but of counting the patrons. It is submitted that this decision is against the weight of authority and should not be followed.

[385] This is not to say that all shoplifters will now become burglars. In order to convict of burglary, it will be necessary to prove that D entered with intent to steal and this will often be difficult or impossible. If D entered the shop in order to make a purchase or to look at the stock in order to decide whether to make a purchase, he is not a trespasser. If he then yields to temptation and steals, he probably becomes a trespasser but it remains a fact that he did not *enter* as a trespasser. Where there is evidence that the shoplifting was pre-meditated, as a previous conspiracy, or system, or preparatory acts, as the wearing of a jacket with special pockets, then a conviction for burglary may be possible.

[386] (iv) *Who is the victim of the burglary?*—Trespass is an interference with possession. Burglary is therefore committed against the person in possession of the building entered. Where the premises are let, the burglary is committed against the tenant and not against the landlord. Even if the tenant is only a tenant at will, he may maintain trespass. So may a deserted wife, though she has no proprietary interest in the matrimonial home.[15] On the other hand, "The guest at a hotel will not ordinarily have sufficient possession of his room to enable him to sue in trespass."[16] As under the old law, the indictment should allege that the burglary was committed in the building of the hotelier,[17] —if it is thought necessary to lay the property in anyone.[18] It has been held that, where a servant occupies premises belonging to his master for the more convenient performance of his duties as servant, he cannot maintain an action for trespass against the master.[19] In such a case it is, of course, necessary to

---

[14] [1958] 2 All E.R. 579 at 593.
[15] *National Provincial Bank, Ltd.* v. *Ainsworth,* [1965] A.C. 1175.
[16] Street, *Torts* (3rd ed.), 67.
[17] Hale, 1 P.C. 557; *Prosser* (1768), 2 East P.C. 502.
[18] Below, para. [388].
[19] *Mayhew* v. *Suttle* (1854), 4 E. & B. 347; *White* v. *Bayley* (1861), 10 C.B.N.S. 227.

look at the precise terms of the arrangement between the parties; if the servant has been given exclusive possession, he and not the master is the victim of a trespass. And it does not necessarily follow that, because the servant in a particular case may not maintain trespass against the master, he cannot do so against third parties.[20]

[**387**] The position of a lodger depends on the precise terms of his contract. If he has exclusive possession so that he can refuse entry to the landlord then, no doubt, he may maintain trespass. Many lodgers, however, do not have such possession and in such cases an unauthorised entry by a third party is a trespass against the landlord.

It seems to follow that burglary is not committed where an innkeeper enters the room of a guest, even though the entry is without the guest's consent and with intent to steal; and that, depending on the terms of the contract, the same may be true in the case of a master entering premises occupied by his servant for the purposes of his employment and a landlord entering the rooms of his lodger.

[**388**] It may be that an indictment will lie although it does not allege that the building was the property of anyone. Whereas the Larceny Act 1916 required that the breaking and entering be of the dwelling house *of another*, there is no such expression in the Theft Act. The requirement of trespass means that evidence must be offered that someone other than the accused was in possession. If that is all that is necessary, evidence that A or B was in possession should suffice—it is equally a trespass in either event. But if a statement of ownership is required in the indictment, "A or B" will hardly do. It is submitted, therefore, that it should be sufficient that indictment alleges that D trespassed in a building without alleging who is the owner of the building.

(c) Any building or part of a building

[**389**] The meaning of "building" in various statutes has frequently been considered by the courts. Clearly the meaning of the term varies according to the context and many things which have been held to be buildings for other purposes will not be buildings for the purpose of the Theft Act—for example, a garden wall, a railway embankment or a tunnel under the road. According to Lord Esher, M.R., its "ordinary and usual meaning is, a block of brick or stone work, covered in by a roof."[1] It seems clear, however, that it is not necessary that the structure be of brick or stone to be a building within this Act. Clearly all dwelling houses are intended to be protected and these may be built of wood; while "the inhabited vehicle or vessel" which is expressly included is likely to be built of steel or of wood. More helpful is the view of Byles, J., that a building in its ordinary sense is "a structure of considerable size and intended to be permanent or at least to endure for a considerable time."[2]

---

[20] Though in *White* v. *Bayley* (above, footnote 19) Byles, J. thought, *obiter*, that an action could not have been maintained by the servant against a stranger (10 C.B.N.S. at 235).

[1] *Moir* v. *Williams*, [1892] 1 Q.B. 264.

[2] *Stevens* v. *Gourley* (1859), 7 C.B.N.S. 99 at 112. For other descriptions, see *Stroud's Judicial Dictionary* (4th ed.), 1, 334.

[390] To be a building, the structure must have some degree of permanence and it seems clear that it would not include a tent even though the tent was someone's home. It is again a question of the meaning of the word in the language of ordinary literate men; and this perhaps suggests that a telephone kiosk is not a building. If it is, the wreckers of these places are probably burglars.

[391] The outbuildings of a house seem to be buildings for the purposes of the Act so that burglary may now be committed in a detached garage, a wooden toolshed or a greenhouse. Similarly, farm buildings such as a stable, cow-byre, pig-stye, barn or silo and industrial buildings such as factories, warehouses and stores. Other cases are more difficult. It is not uncommon for trespassers to enter unfinished buildings and do damage. If they enter with intent to cause damage by fire or explosion are they now guilty of burglary? An unfinished building was a building within s. 6 of the Malicious Damage Act 1861.[3] Why not for the purposes of burglary? Clearly there is a difficult question as to the point in its erection at which a structure becomes a building. In *Manning*,[4] Lush, J. said:

". . . it is sufficient that it should be a connected and entire structure. I do not think four walls erected a foot high would be a building."

In that case all the walls were built and finished and the roof was on. It may be that a roof will be thought necessary for a structure to be a building under the present Act, for it clearly is not intended to extend to a walled garden, yard or paddock. What if there is a roof but no walls, as in the case of a bandstand?[5] There is no obvious answer to borderline cases such as this but they are likely to be rare.

[392] (i) *Part of a building.*—It is sufficient if the trespass takes place in part of a building so that one lodger may commit burglary by entering the room of another lodger within the same house, or by entering the part of the house occupied by the landlord. A guest in a hotel may commit burglary by entering the room of another guest. A customer in a shop who goes behind the counter and takes money from the till during a short absence of the shopkeeper would be guilty of burglary even though he entered the shop with the shopkeeper's permission. The permission did not extend to his going behind the counter. Suppose P takes D, a tramp, home for a meal. While they are sitting in the drawing room D becomes unpleasant and P tells him to go. If D walks straight out, helping himself to some money he sees on the hall-table as he does so, he is not guilty of burglary; he cannot be trespassing by going where P tells him to go. But if he remains, against P's will, for another hour he is a trespasser. Clearly he is not committing burglary by remaining ensconced in P's armchair, drinking P's whisky (though this is theft). What if he now walks out and takes the money as before? He was a trespasser and he has entered a part of the house (the hall) and stolen therein. But since P wanted him to go that way, it is difficult to see that he entered that part of the house "as a

---

[3] *Manning* (1871), L.R. 1 C.C.R. 338.
[4] *Ibid.*, at 341.
[5] Held to be a building for the purposes of a private act regulating the provision of public entertainments in buildings: *A.G.* v. *Eastbourne Corporation* (1934), 78 Sol. Jo. 633.

trespasser". Probably he ceased to be a trespasser when he began to leave, belatedly, but in accordance with P's continuing wish.

[**393**] What is "a part" of the building may be a difficult and important question. Take a case put by the Criminal Law Revision Committee.[6] D enters a shop lawfully[7] but conceals himself on the premises until closing time and then emerges with intent to steal. When concealing himself he may or may not have entered a part of the building to which customers are not permitted to go; but even if he did commit a trespass at this stage, he may not have done so with intent to commit an offence in that part of the building into which he has trespassed. For example, he hides in the broom cupboard of a super-market, intending to emerge and steal tins of food. Entering the broom cup-board, though a trespass committed with intent to steal, is not burglary, for he has no intent to steal in the part of the building which he has entered as a trespasser. When he emerges from the broom cupboard after the shop has closed, he is a trespasser and it is submitted that he has entered a part of the building with intent to steal. He is just as much a trespasser as if he had been told in express terms to go, for he knows perfectly well that his licence to remain on the premises terminated when the shop closed.[8] Suppose, however, having entered lawfully, he merely remained concealed behind a pile of tins of soup in the main hall of the supermarket. This was not a trespass because he had a right to be there. When he emerged and proceeded to steal, still in the main hall of the supermarket, was he entering another part of the building? It is submitted that every step he took was "as a trespasser", but it is difficult to see that he entered any part of the building as a trespasser; the whole trans-action took place in a single part of the building which he had entered lawfully.

[**394**] It would seem that the whole reason for the words "or part of a building," is that D may enter or be in part of a building without trespass and it is desirable that he should be liable as a burglar if he trespasses in the remainder of the building with the necessary intent. It is submitted that the building need not be physically divided into "parts". It ought to be sufficient if a notice in the middle of a hall stated, "No customers beyond this point". These considerations suggest that, for present purposes, a building falls into two parts only: first, that part in which D was lawfully present and, second, the remainder of the building. This interpretation avoids anomalies which arise if physical divisions within a building are held to create "parts".[9]

[**395**] (ii) *The extent of a "building" and its "parts".*—Under the old law, the entry had to be into a particular dwelling house, office, shop, garage, etc. A single structure might contain many dwelling houses—for example a block of flats—many offices, shops or garages. If D broke into Flat 1 with intent to pass through it, go upstairs and steal in Flat 45, the breaking and entering of Flat 1 was neither burglary nor housebreaking for D did not intend to to commit a felony

---

[6] The *Report*, Cmnd. 2977, para. 75.

[7] *I.e.*, without intent to steal; above, para. [**385**].

[8] The Criminal Law Revision Committee thought "The case is not important, because the offender is likely to go into a part of the building where he has no right to be, and this will be a trespassory entry into that part". But he has no right to be in any part of the building after closing time and the only question, it is submitted, is whether he went into *another* part.

[9] See para. [**397**]; Griew, 4–09, n. 17, finds this interpretation "desirable but strained" and rejects it.

therein.[10] It was probably not even an attempt, not being sufficiently proximate to the intended crime. If D broke into a flat above a jeweller's shop with intent to break through the ceiling and steal in the shop, he could be convicted of burglary in the flat only if it could be said that he broke and entered the flat with intent to commit a felony therein, namely to break and enter the shop.[11] The difficulty about this argument is that while the breaking may reasonably be said to have occurred in the flat, the entering, strictly speaking, took place in the shop. On that view, there was no intent to commit a felony in the flat and it was not, therefore, burglary or housebreaking to break and enter it.

[396] The effect on this situation of the Theft Act depends on what is the extent of a "building". In its ordinary natural meaning, this term could certainly include a block of flats. If that meaning be adopted, D's entering Flat 1 as a trespasser with intent to pass through it, go upstairs and steal in Flat 45 is an entry of a building as a trespasser with intent to steal therein—that is, it is burglary. Similarly the intending jewel thief would be guilty of burglary when he entered the flat above the jeweller's shop as a trespasser. The effect would be to make the full offence of what was previously, at the most, an attempt, and probably was only an act of preparation. There seems no good reason, however, why the law should not be extended in this way. On the contrary, there is everything to be said for enabling the police to intervene at the earliest possible moment to prevent such offences; and for forestalling defences such as "I had no intention to steal in the flat—I was only using it as a passage to another flat which I never reached". It is submitted therefore that the word "building" should be given its natural meaning.

[397] Suppose, however, that D is lawfully in Flat 1, and that he can get to Flat 45 where he intends to steal only by trespassing into Flat 2. Suppose he is apprehended in Flat 2. He is guilty of burglary only if he can be shown to have intended to steal in "the part of the building in question". If Flat 2 is a separate part, he had no such intention and his act is probably too remote to constitute an attempt to enter Flat 45. But it is very odd that entering Flat 1 (from outside where D lawfully was) as a trespasser with intent to steal in Flat 45 should be burglary, and entering Flat 2 as a trespasser (from Flat 1 where D lawfully was) with intent to steal in Flat 45 should be nothing. It is therefore submitted that, as physical divisions are *unnecessary* to create "parts", so the existence of such divisions is insufficient to create them. If the building is divided into the part into which D may lawfully go and the part into which he may not, then Flats 2 and 45 are in the same "part" of the building and D is guilty of burglary as soon as he enters Flat 2.

[398] Is a row of terrace houses a single building?[12] Suppose D breaks into no. 1,

---

10 *Cf. Wrigley*, [1957] Crim. L.R. 57.
11 *Cf.* comment on *Wrigley*, [1957] Crim. L.R. 58.
12 In *Hedley* v. *Webb*, [1901] 2 Ch. 126, Cozens-Hardy, J. held that two semi-detached houses were a single building for the purpose of determining whether there was a sewer within the meaning of the Public Health Act 1875, s. 4. In *Birch* v. *Wigan Corporation*, [1953] 1 Q.B. 136, the Court of Appeal (Denning, L. J. dissenting) held that one house in a terrace of six was a "house" within the meaning of s. 11 (1) and (4) of the Housing Act 1936 and not "part of a building" within s. 12 of that Act. But, since the sections were mutually exclusive, the house could not be both a "house" and "part of a building" for the purpose of the Act. Otherwise, Denning, L. J. would have been disposed to say that the house was both and Romer, L. J. also thought that "for some purposes and in other contexts two 'houses' may constitute one building."

climbs into the rafters and makes his way above no. 2, intending to continue to no. 36, descend into the house and steal therein. Has he already committed burglary? It is difficult to discern any satisfactory principle by which this case can be distinguished from those of the block of flats and the flat above the shop considered above. In both the block of flats and the terrace a series of dwelling houses are contained within a single structure and it cannot matter that the arrangement is horizontal rather than vertical. It is true that there is internal communication between the flats; but it can hardly be said that the block of flats would cease to be "a building" because access to them was confined to an external staircase. In policy and in principle there seems to be no reason why "building" should not include the whole terrace.

[**399**] (iii) *Inhabited vehicle or vessel.*—The obvious cases which are brought within the protection of burglary by this provision are a caravan or a houseboat which is someone's home. There seems to be no reason whatever why a home should lack the ordinary protection of the law because it is mobile and this extension is welcome. Its limits should be noted. "Inhabited" implies, not merely that there is someone inside the vehicle, but that someone is *living* there. My saloon car is not an inhabited vehicle because I happen to be sitting in it when D enters against my will. The caravan or houseboat which is a man's home is, however, expressly protected, whether or not he is there at the time of the burglary. He may, for example, be away on his holidays.

[**400**] The provision is not free from difficulty. Many people now own "dormobiles" or motorised caravans which they use for the ordinary purposes of a motor car during most of the year but on occasions they live in them, generally while on holiday. While the vehicle is being lived in, it is undoubtedly an inhabited vehicle. When it is being used for the ordinary purposes of a motor car, it is submitted that it is not an inhabited vehicle. The exact moment at which the dormobile becomes an inhabited vehicle may be difficult to ascertain. Is it when the family have loaded it with their belongings before departing on their holiday? When they take to the road on their journey to the sea-side? When they park the vehicle at the place where they intend to sleep? Or when they actually go to sleep in the vehicle? It can hardly be later than that. Since the vehicle is not really distinguishable from any other family car going on holiday until it reaches its destination, it probably becomes "inhabited" when it reaches the place at which it is to be used as a home. But does it then cease, for the time being, to be inhabited, if the family go for a spin in it next day? Is it burglary if a thief enters it in the car park of the swimming pool where they have gone for a swim? Similar problems arise when the holiday is concluding. If the answer tentatively suggested above regarding the beginning of the holiday is correct, then it ought to follow that when the vehicle embarks on its homeward journey, after the last night on which it is intended to sleep in it, it then ceases to be inhabited.

[**401**] Very similar problems will arise in connection with boats with living accommodation. Ships where the passengers or crew sleep aboard, are clearly covered. The person who trespasses into a passenger's cabin on the Queen Elizabeth in order to steal is clearly guilty of burglary.[13]

---

[13] Presumably, in such a case, the trespass is committed against the owners since, under modern conditions, they, and not the master, are in possession of the ship: *The Jupiter* (No. 3), [1927] P. 122 at 131; affirmed, [1927] P. 250. The passengers would seem to be in the same situation as the guests in a hotel. See above, para. [**387**].

[**402**] Difficult problems of *mens rea* may arise. According to ordinary principles, D should not be convicted unless he knew of the facts which make the thing entered "a building" in law. Suppose D enters a dormobile parked by the side of the road. If he knew that P was living in the vehicle, there is no problem. But what if he did not know? In principle it would seem that he ought to be acquitted of burglary, unless it can be shown that he was at least reckless whether anyone was living there or not; and this seems to involve showing that the possibility was present to his mind.

B. THE MENS REA

(a) Intention to enter as a trespasser; or knowledge of having trespassed

[**403**] As argued above,[14] it is submitted that it must be proved on a charge under s. 9 (1) (*a*) that D intended to enter, knowing of the facts which, in law, made his entry trespassory; or, at least, being reckless whether such facts existed; and, on a charge under s. 9 (1) (*b*), that, at the time of committing the ulterior offence, D knew of or was reckless as to the facts which had made his entry a trespass. If, in a case under either paragraph, D sets up an honest belief in a right to enter, it should be for the Crown to prove the belief was not held.

(b) The ulterior offence

[**404**] It must be proved that D, *either*—

  (i) entered with intent to commit one of the following offences:
    (*a*) stealing,
    (*b*) inflicting grievous bodily harm,
    (*c*) rape,
    (*d*) unlawful damage to the building or anything therein;
  or
  (ii) entered and committed or attempted to commit one of the following offences:
    (*a*) stealing,
    (*b*) inflicting grievous bodily harm.

[**405**] Under the draft bill proposed by the Criminal Law Revision Committee, the ulterior offences were the same whether the case was one of entering with intent under s. 9 (1) (*a*) or entering and committing under s. 9 (1) (*b*); that is, it would have been burglary to enter and commit rape or unlawful damage even though there were no such intent at the time of entry. Where there is evidence that a man has actually committed rape, it was thought by Parliament that there is no need for the burglary charge because rape, being punishable with life imprisonment, is the more serious offence. Stealing and grievous bodily harm, on the other hand, are less heavily punishable than burglary. If, however, it should emerge at the trial that D was guilty only of an *attempt* to rape, he will be liable only to seven years' imprisonment instead of the fourteen years to which he would have been liable, had this been retained as an offence of burglary. The logic of the argument which led to the exclusion of rape from s. 9 (1) (*b*) should have required the inclusion of unlawful damage,

---

[14] See para. [**376**].

for that is usually a less serious offence than burglary. As it is, the modification made by Parliament means that D is not guilty of burglary if he enters in order to have a sleep and wrecks the place before he leaves, whereas he is guilty of burglary if he steals anything.

It is unfortunate that the simpler proposal of the Committee has not been retained. It is a curious logic which says that a trespasser should not be a burglar because the offence he has committed in the building is so serious as to carry a sentence of more than fourteen years, whereas if it had been less serious and less severely punishable, burglary would have been an appropriate charge.

[**406**] (i) *Stealing.*—This clearly means theft, contrary to s. 1.[15] So it is not enough to prove that D has entered with intent to commit an offence contrary to s. 15 or s. 16 of the Act. If the *Lawrence* (C.A.) principle[16] is valid, virtually all s. 15 offences are theft, contrary to s. 1; but, if it is not, the old distinction between larceny by a trick and obtaining by false pretences becomes important here. Thus D gains admission to P's house or place of business by pretending to be the agent of E, a person well-known to P. This is an entry as a trespasser.[17] D then induces P to sell goods to E, and departs, taking the goods and leaving a forged cheque. There is, of course, no contract with E, the ownership in the goods remains in P, and D has dishonestly appropriated property belonging to another with the intention of permanently depriving the other of it. He is guilty of theft (as well, of course, as obtaining by deception) and, therefore, he is guilty of burglary. But the position is different where D gains admission to P's building by pretending that her (D's) husband is ill and then, by the same pretence, induces P to lend her £20 intending to deprive P permanently of it. Here too D enters as a trespasser but (subject to the *Lawrence* (C.A.) principle) the offence committed inside is only obtaining by deception and not theft (because the ownership in the money passes to D) and therefore burglary is not committed. The difference lies in whether the property passes or not. If D goes into P's shop and induces P to let him have a television set on credit by giving a false address and false references, the nature of D's crime depends on the nature of the transaction in the civil law. If it is hire or hire-purchase, the ownership does not pass and D is guilty of theft as well as obtaining by deception; if it is a credit sale, the ownership passes and D is guilty only of obtaining by deception. Thus, it is burglary in the former case[18] but not in the latter.

[**407**] (ii) *Grievous bodily harm.*—The infliction of grievous bodily harm must be an "offence". There are three offences under the Offences against the Person Act 1861 in which the infliction of grievous bodily harm may be a constituent. They are causing grievous bodily harm with intent (s. 18) [19], unlawfully and maliciously inflicting grievous bodily harm (s. 20)[17] and unlawfully and maliciously administering poison so as to inflict grievous bodily harm (s. 23)[20].

---

[15] See s. 1 (1.) [16] Above, para. [**33**]. [17] Above, para. [**379**].
[18] Assuming that entry with intent to commit a fraud of this nature is a trespass: see above, para. [**384**].
[19] Smith and Hogan, 264. "Cause" is wider than "inflict." An intention to cause grievous bodily harm otherwise than by poison or assault seems to be insufficient *mens rea* for burglary.
[20] Smith and Hogan, 269.

[408] Where the charge is one of entering with intent under s. 9 (i) (*a*) it would seem that the evidence must establish an intent to commit the former and more serious of these two offences.[1] To satisfy the terms of s. 9 (1) (*a*), an actual intention to inflict grievous bodily harm must be proved. Under s. 9 (1) (*b*), however, the position seems to be different. Here it is only necessary to prove that D entered and committed an offence of inflicting grievous bodily harm. Suppose D enters P's house as a trespasser[2] and throws a stone intending to smash a vase, knowing that there is a risk that by so doing he might cause serious bodily harm and either not caring whether he does or not, or hoping that he does not not. He is not, so far, guilty of burglary. But, if he throws the stone and actually causes grievous bodily harm to P he is guilty of an offence under s. 20 of the Offences against the Person Act and therefore of burglary. If no more can be established than that the grievous bodily harm was caused negligently, then the offence of burglary is not made out.

What if D enters with intent to murder? It would be very strange if an entry with intent to inflict grievous bodily harm amounted to burglary, and an entry with intent to murder did not. It is submitted that the greater includes the less and that an intention to kill, whether by inflicting physical injuries or by poisoning is enough.

[409] (iii) *Rape*.—Rape is a common law offence consisting in having sexual intercourse with a woman without her consent. The punishment of life imprisonment is prescribed by s. 37 and Schedule 2 of the Sexual Offences Act 1956.[3] Few problems seem to arise in connection with this form of ulterior intent. One general problem which might be discussed in this context, however, is whether a conditional intent will suffice. D enters a dwelling-house as a trespasser intending to have sexual intercourse with P. He hopes she will consent but he intends to have intercourse anyway. Is he guilty of burglary as soon as he enters? There are obvious difficulties about proving such a state of mind, but, if it can be proved, it is submitted that it is a sufficient intent to rape.

[410] Is it necessary that the object of the ulterior crime be in the building before the trespassory entry? In other words, is it burglary if D drags P into a barn with intent to rob, or inflict grievous bodily harm on, or rape her? The words of the section do not supply a clear answer, but the purpose of the offence—the protection of persons and things in a building—suggests that the crime does not extend to these cases.

[411] (iv) *Unlawful damage to the building or anything therein*.—The damage intended must be such that to cause it would amount to an offence. It is an offence under s. 1 of the Criminal Damage Act 1971, intentionally or recklessly to destroy or damage any property belonging to another.

---

[1] The principal difference between the two offences is that in the former an actual intention must be proved, whereas in the latter it is enough that the accused was reckless whether or not he caused grievous bodily harm.
[2] But without intent to commit any of the offences referred to in s. 9 (1) (*a*).
[3] Smith and Hogan, 288.

2 AGGRAVATED BURGLARY

[**412**] By s. 10 of the Theft Act:

"(1) A person is guilty of aggravated burglary if he commits any burglary and at the time has with him any firearm or imitation firearm, any weapon of offence, or any explosive; and for this purpose—

(a) 'firearm' includes an airgun or air pistol and 'imitation firearm' means anything which has the appearance of being a firearm, whether capable of being discharged or not; and

(b) 'weapon of offence' means any article made or adapted for use for causing injury to or incapacitating a person, or intended by the person having it with him for such use; and

(c) 'explosive' means any article manufactured for the purpose of producing a practical effect by explosion, or intended by the person having it with him for that purpose.

(2) A person guilty of aggravated burglary shall on conviction on indictment be liable to imprisonment for life."

[**413**] The reason given by the Criminal Law Revision Committee for the creation of this offence is that "burglary when in possession of the articles mentioned . . . is so serious that it should in our opinion be punishable with imprisonment for life. The offence is comparable with robbery (which will be so punishable). It must be extremely frightening to those in the building, and it might well lead to loss of life."[4]

A. THE ARTICLES OF AGGRAVATION

[**414**] "Firearm" is not defined in the Act, except to the extent that it includes an airgun or air pistol. It would seem likely that the courts will seek guidance as to the meaning of this term from the definition in the Firearms Act 1968, s. 57 (1). The expression is given a wide meaning in that Act, however, and it does not necessarily follow that it should bear a similarly wide meaning in the Theft Act. Thus the definition includes any component part of a firearm, but the natural meaning of the term does not include parts. If I have the body locking pin of a Bren gun in my pocket, no one would say I was carrying a firearm. As the statutory definition has not been incorporated in the Theft Act, as could easily have been done, it is submitted that the word should not be given a meaning any wider than that which it naturally bears; and that, therefore, the term "imitation firearm" be similarly limited.

[**415**] The definition of "weapon of offence" is somewhat wider than that of "offensive weapon" in s. 1 (4) of the Prevention of Crime Act 1953. It would seem that (i) articles made for causing injury to a person, (ii) articles adapted for causing injury to a person, and (iii) articles which D has with him for that purpose are precisely the same as under the 1953 Act.[5] Thus, (i) would include a service rifle or bayonet, a revolver, a cosh, knuckleduster or dagger; (ii) would include razor blades inserted in a potato, a bottle broken for the purpose, a chair leg studded with nails; and (iii) would include anything that could cause

---

4 The *Report*, Cmnd. 2977, para. 80.
5 Smith and Hogan, 282.

injury to the person if so desired by the person using it—a sheath-knife, a razor, a shotgun, a sandbag, a pick-axe handle, a bicycle chain or a stone.[6] To these categories, however, s. 10 (1) (*b*) adds (iv) any article made for *incapacitating* a person, (v) any article adapted for *incapacitating* a person, and (vi) any article which D has with him for that purpose. Articles *made* for incapacitating a person might include a pair of handcuffs and a gag; articles *adapted* for incapacitating a person might include a pair of socks made into a gag, and articles *intended* for incapacitating a person might include sleeping pills to put in the night-watchman's tea, a rope to tie him up, a sack to put over his head, pepper to throw in his face, and so on.

In the cases of (i), (ii), (iv) and (v) the prosecution need prove no more than that the article was made or adapted for use for causing injury or incapacitating as the case may be. In the cases of (iii) and (vi) clearly they must go further and prove that D was carrying the thing with him with the intention of using it to injure or incapacitate, not necessarily in any event, but at least if the need arose.

[416] The definition of "explosive" closely follows that in s. 3 (1) of the Explosives Act 1875 which, after enumerating various explosives, adds:

"... and every other substance, whether similar to those above mentioned or not, used or manufactured with a view to produce a practical effect by explosion or by a pyrotechnic effect . . ."

[417] It will be observed that the definition in the Theft Act is narrower. The Explosive Substances Act, if read literally, is wide enough to include a box of matches—these produce a "pyrotechnic effect"; but it seems clear that a box of matches would not be an "explosive" under the Theft Act.

The main difficulty about the definition—and this is unlikely to be important in practice—lies in determining the meaning of "practical effect". Perhaps it serves to exclude fireworks which, so it has been said in connection with another Act, are "things that are made for amusement"[7]; but if the thing is *intended* to produce "a practical effect", it is immaterial that it was not manufactured for that purpose and that it is incapable of doing so.

B. "AT THE TIME" OF COMMISSION OF BURGLARY

[418] It must be proved that D had the article of aggravation with him *at the time* of committing the burglary. Where the charge is one of entry with intent this is clearly at the time of entry. Where the charge is one of committing a specified offence, having entered, it is at the time of commission of the specified offence.

C. "HAS WITH HIM"

[419] This again closely follows the wording of the Prevention of Crime Act 1953. It has been held that the words in that Act mean "*knowingly* has

---

[6] *Harrison* v. *Thornton*, [1966] Crim. L.R. 388.
[7] *Bliss* v. *Lilley* (1832), 32 L.J.M.C., *per* Cockburn, C. J. and Blackburn, J.; but Wightman, J. thought that a fog-signal was a "firework".

with him'', [8] in the sense that D must be proved to have known that he had the thing which is an offensive weapon. Whether it must also be proved that he knew that it possessed those characteristics which make it an offensive weapon within the meaning of the Act has not been decided. It does not follow that it will be so decided. It has been held under the law relating to possession of dangerous drugs, that a mental element must be proven to establish possession, but that element falls short of knowledge that the thing is a dangerous drug. [9] It would be enough that D knew that it was a drug; or that he had had a reasonable opportunity to ascertain its nature; or that he suspected that there was "anything wrong" with the thing and took or retained control regardless. Similarly, under the Firearms Act 1968 it is unnecessary to prove that D knew the thing he used was a firearm within the meaning of the Act [10]—though it is no doubt necessary to prove that he knew he had that thing.

It may be predicted with some confidence, therefore, that proof will be required that D knew that he had the article of aggravation with him at the appropriate time. It is submitted that, in principle, proof should also be necessary that he knew the thing had the characteristics of an article of aggravation.

[**420**] Suppose D enters P's house by using a jemmy, with intent to steal. While he is in the act of stealing he is interrupted by P and attacks him with the jemmy. If the more recent interpretation of the Prevention of Crime Act [11] is followed in construing the Theft Act, the jemmy will be held to be a weapon of offence on the ground that D had it with him for the purpose of causing injury, even though he had no thought of using it for causing injury until that moment. "If it is found that the accused did in fact make use of it for the purpose of causing injury, he had it with him for that purpose." [12] It is submitted that this is an unhappy construction of the provision and that an earlier ruling of the Court of Criminal Appeal [13] is preferable; but the fact must be faced that the later ruling is likely to be followed. If so, it follows that what is initially a simple burglary may develop into aggravated burglary. In such a case, however, it is submitted that aggravated burglary will lie only if D is charged with entering and committing and not if he is charged with entering with intent.

[**421**] In the case put, D was in the act of stealing and was therefore guilty of burglary under s. 9 (1) (*b*) because he had committed or was attempting to commit a specified offence. Suppose, however, that D had been interrupted after entry and before he had reached the stage of an attempt to steal. Even though the jemmy becomes a weapon of offence when it is used against P, D is not guilty of aggravated burglary (unless he inflicts or attempts to inflict *grievous* bodily harm) because he can now be charged only under s. 9 (1) (*a*) and the jemmy was not a weapon of offence at the time he committed that burglary. The courts may be tempted, however, to regard burglary as a con-

---

[8] *Cugullere*, [1961] 2 All E.R. 343 at 344.
[9] *Warner* v. *Metropolitan Police Commissioner*, [1969] 2 A.C. 256; [1968] 2 All E.R. 356.
[10] *Pierre*, [1963] Crim. L.R. 513; Smith and Hogan, 280–281.
[11] In *Woodward* v. *Koessler*, [1958] 3 All E.R. 557 (D.C.); *Powell*, [1963] Crim. L.R. 511 (C.C.A.); Smith and Hogan, 283-284.
[12] *Per* Donovan, J., [1958] 3 All E.R. at 558.
[13] *Jura*, [1954] 1 Q.B. 503. *Cf. Considine* v. *Kirkpatrick*, [1971] S.A.S.R. 73 at 81.

tinuing offence and to hold that it continues to be committed from the time D enters with intent until, he leaves the building. This would extend "aggravated burglary" to the case where D has entered and committed the specified offence, all without thought of using his jemmy as an offensive weapon, but is intercepted as he is about to leave and strikes a blow with it. It is impossible not to sympathise with a desire so to construe the statute so as to avoid the anomalies envisaged above. These anomalies, however, arise from an excessively wide construction of the term "offensive weapon" which, it is feared, will be followed in construing "weapon of offence". To redress the anomalies by adopting a wide interpretation of burglary would result in the statute being given an unduly extended meaning. It is submitted that a better course would be to reconsider the interpretation of "offensive weapon" adopted in *Woodward* v. *Koessler*[14] or not to follow it in construing "weapon of offence". It is submitted that aggravated burglary is really aimed at the criminal who sets out armed with a firearm, etc. It is not aimed at the burglar who sets out unarmed with any aggravating article but happens to make use of such an article in the course of the burglary.[15] If it were, the Act would have said "uses" rather than "has with him". The effect of the *Woodward* v. *Koessler* construction is that if D is interrupted in the course of stealing after a trespassory entry and he picks up an inkstand[16] (or any other object) and throws it with intent to cause injury, he becomes guilty of aggravated burglary. It is submitted that this goes beyond the purpose of this offence.

---

[14] Above, para. **[420]**.

[15] It is true, of course, that these arguments are equally applicable to the Prevention of Crime Act 1953, where they do not at present appear to be accepted.

[16] *Cf. Harrison* v. *Thornton*, [1966] Crim. L.R. 388.

CHAPTER XI

POSSESSION OF HOUSEBREAKING IMPLEMENTS, ETC.

[**422**] By s. 25 (1) and (2) of the Theft Act:

"(1) A person shall be guilty of an offence if, when not at his place of abode, he has with him any article for use in the course of or in connection with any burglary, theft or cheat.

(2) A person guilty of an offence under this section shall on conviction on indictment be liable to imprisonment for a term not exceeding three years."

This offence replaces the more complicated provisions contained in the Larceny Act 1916, s. 28. The 1916 Act was directed chiefly against[1], though it was not limited to, preparatory acts in contemplation of offences of breaking and entering. The new provision is expressed to be directed against acts preparatory to:

(i) burglary contrary to s. 9,
(ii) theft contrary to s. 1,
(iii) criminal deception contrary to s. 15[2],
(iv) taking and driving away a conveyance, contrary to s. 12.[3]

1 THE ACTUS REUS

A. ANY ARTICLE

[**423**] The *actus reus* consists in the accused's having with him any article. Clearly the article need not be made or adapted for use in committing one of the specified offences. It is sufficient that the *mens rea* is proved in respect of the article, that is, that the accused intended to use it in the course of, or in connection with, one of the specified offences. Thus, it might be a tin of treacle, intended for use in removing a pane of glass, a pair of gloves to be worn so as to avoid leaving fingerprints; a collecting box marked "Oxfam" when the possessor did not represent that organisation; and so on. There may occasionally be difficulty in deciding what is an "article". Does it include blacking on the face to prevent recognition, or "Bostik" on the fingers to prevent fingerprints? Having regard to the mischief at which the section is aimed, it is submitted that a substance so applied to the body, remains an "article".

[**424**] The offence is thus very wide in its scope. But there must be some limits. Thus D can hardly be committing an offence because he is wearing his

---

[1] The *Report*, Cmnd. 2977, p. 69.
[2] By s. 25 (5), "cheat" means an offence under s. 15.
[3] By s. 25 (5), "theft" in this section includes an offence of taking under s. 12 (1).

trousers when on his way to do a burglary. Yet he intends to wear them while he is committing the burglary and would not dream of undertaking such an enterprise without them. Similarly, he can hardly be committing an offence by wearing his shoes or any other item of everyday apparel. Yet it was suggested above that gloves for the avoidance of fingerprints would entail liability. This suggests that the article must be one which D would not be carrying with him but for the contemplated offence. If it is something which he would carry with him on a normal, innocent expedition, it should not fall within this section. So there might be a difference between a pair of rubber gloves and a pair of fur-lined gloves which D was wearing to keep his hands warm on a freezing night, even though he did intend to keep them on so as to avoid leaving fingerprints. The latter pair of gloves is hardly distinguishable, for this purpose, from D's overcoat which seems to fall into the same category as his trousers. If D is carrying a pair of plimsolls in his car to facilitate his cat-burgling, this seems a plain enough case; but what if he has simply selected his ordinary crepe-sole shoes for wear because they are less noisy than his hob-nails?

B. "HAS WITH HIM"

[**425**] The expression "has with him"[4] is the same as in s. 10 (1) of the Act. Questions as to D's knowledge of the nature of the thing can hardly arise here, since it must be proved that he intended to use it in the course of or in connection with a specified offence. No doubt D has an article with him if it is in his immediate possession or control; so that he will be guilty if the article is only a short distance away and he can take it up as he needs it; as where a ladder has been left in a garden by an accomplice and D enters the garden intending to use the ladder to make an entry. If the article is found in D's car some distance from the scene of the crime this will be evidence that D was in possession of the article when driving the car.

It is probable that again mere momentary possession will suffice,[5] as where D is apprehended on picking up a stone which he intends to use to break a window in order to commit burglary.

C. WHEN NOT AT HIS PLACE OF ABODE

[**426**] No offence is committed by being in possession of house-breaking implements in one's own home. There is no similar exemption for possession at one's place of work. The offence is committed as soon as D steps from his house into the street carrying the article with intent.

D. USE IN THE COURSE OF OR IN CONNECTION WITH

[**427**] It is not necessarily a defence that D did not intend to use the article while actually committing the contemplated crime. If, for example he intended to use it only in the course of making his escape after the commission of the offence, this would be enough, being use "in connection with" the offence. Similarly if he intended to use the article while doing preparatory acts. The

---

[4] See above, para. [**419**].
[5] Above, para. [**421**].

string used by D to tie himself up in *Robinson*[6] would seem to come within the provision, though it was to be used only in the course of a preparatory act and not in the course of the commission of the proposed criminal deception. Any insurance claim form he might have had, on the other hand, would have been for use in the course of commission of the offence.

2 THE MENS REA

[**428**] The *mens rea* for the offence would appear to consist in:

   (i) knowledge that one possesses the article; and
   (ii) an intention to use the article in the course of or in connection with any of the specified crimes.

[**429**] Section 25 (3) provides:

> "Where a person is charged with an offence under this section, proof that he had with him any article made or adapted for use in committing burglary, theft or cheat shall be evidence that he had it with him for such use."

This is probably no more than enactment of the general rules regarding proof of intent.[7] The jury may take this fact into account but it is entirely for them to say what weight, if any, is to be attached to it. If D offers no explanation then the jury may be told that there is evidence upon which they may find that he had the necessary intent; but it is submitted that they should be told so to find only if satisfied beyond reasonable doubt that he in fact had that intent.[8] If D does offer an explanation then the jury should be told to acquit if they think it may reasonably be true and to convict only if satisfied beyond reasonable doubt that the explanation is untrue.[9]

Where the article in question is not made or adapted for use in any specified offence[10], mere proof of possession without more will not amount to *prima facie* evidence—*i.e.*, the case will have to be withdrawn from the jury. But, in certain circumstances, possession of articles not made or adapted for committing offences may amount to very cogent evidence of intent.[11] It is a question of law for the judge, at what point proof of other incriminating circumstances amounts to a case fit for submission to the jury.

---

[6] (1915), 11 Cr. App. Rep. 124.
[7] *Cf.* Criminal Justice Act 1967, s. 8.
[8] *Cf.* the case where the alleged receiver is proved to have been in possession of recently stolen property and offers no explanation: *Abramovitch* (1914), 11 Cr. App. Rep. 45.
[9] The decision in *Patterson*, [1962] 2 Q.B. 429 that the onus of proof under Larceny Act 1916, s. 28 was on the accused, was based on the express wording of that section and is entirely inapplicable to the new provision.
[10] *Cf. Harrison*, [1970] Crim. L.R. 415.
[11] Griew, 4–27.

CHAPTER XII

HANDLING STOLEN GOODS

[**430**] The new offence created by s. 22 replaces both the indictable offences under the Larceny Act 1916, s. 33 and the summary offences under the Larceny Act 1861, s. 97. Section 22 provides:

"(1) A person handles stolen goods if (otherwise than in the course of the stealing) knowing or believing them to be stolen goods he dishonestly receives the goods, or dishonestly undertakes or assists in their retention, removal, disposal or realisation by or for the benefit of another person, or if he arranges to do so.

(2) A person guilty of handling stolen goods shall on conviction on indictment be liable to imprisonment for a term not exceeding fourteen years."

1 THE ACTUS REUS

A. STOLEN GOODS

[**431**] By s. 34 (2) (*b*):

" 'goods', except in so far as the context otherwise requires, includes money and every other description of property except land, and includes things severed from the land by stealing."

It will be noted that this definition differs from and is narrower than the definition of "property" for the purposes of theft in s. 4 (1).[1] Since, however, land generally is excluded from theft by s. 4 (2), the effect seems to be that, with small exceptions to be discussed below, the property which can be the subject of handling is co-extensive with that which can be the subject of theft.

(a) Things in action

[**432**] Things in action are expressly mentioned in s. 4 (1) and not in s. 34 (2) (*b*). They must however be included in the words "every other description of property except land". The remaining question is whether the context of s. 22 *requires* the exclusion of things in action. If s. 22 were confined, like the old law, to *receiving*, no doubt the context would so require. Receiving connoted taking possession or control of a physical thing and was wholly inapplicable to a thing in action. It may well be that this continues to be so under the Theft Act and that a charge of handling by receiving a thing in action, contrary to s. 22, would be bad. The new offence, however, is not confined to receiving but can be committed in a variety of ways.[2] "Removal"

---

[1] Above, para. [**83**].
[2] Below, para. [**469**].

may be thought appropriate only to a physical thing and possibly the same is true of "retention"; but "disposal" and "realisation" are both words which are perfectly apt to include dealings with a thing in action and therefore it would seem that the context does not require the exclusion of things in action from the definition of goods as the object of disposal or realisation. It is, of course, arguable that "goods" must mean the same for the whole of s. 22 and that its meaning should not vary according to the particular verb selected by the prosecution as appropriate to describe the accused's conduct. But, if it had been the intention to exclude things in action from handling, this would surely have been done expressly, as in the case of land. The definition of goods clearly leaves it open to the court to hold that it includes things in action where the context permits and, as handling is the only crime to which the definition is relevant, it seems to follow that provision is made for a variable meaning of "goods" within s. 22.

[**433**] Cases of handling a stolen thing in action are likely to be rare but they are certainly quite possible. E, an executor, dishonestly sells to F a copyright which belongs to a beneficiary under the will, P. Even if an indictment for receiving a thing in action will lie, this may not be handling by F, though he knows all the facts, because his participation may be "in the course of the stealing"—since the stealing consists in the sale.[3] The copyright is, however, stolen goods in F's hands. D then assists F to dispose of, or realise the copyright for F's benefit. D is guilty of handling and F is presumably guilty of aiding and abetting him in handling.

(b) Land

[**434**] "Land" which is stolen contrary to s. 4 (2) (*b*) can always be the subject of handling since the stealing necessarily involves severance of the thing in question. A fixture or structure which is stolen contrary to s. 4 (2) (*c*), on the other hand, may or may not be severed from the land. Only if it is severed can it be the subject of handling. If E, an outgoing tenant, dishonestly sells to D, the incoming tenant, a fixture belonging to P, D cannot be guilty of handling (whether or not his act is in the course of stealing) if the fixture is not severed; nor, of course, is F guilty of handling if he, knowing all the facts, takes over the premises, including the fixture, from D; yet he has knowingly taken possession of a stolen fixture.

Land which is stolen contrary to s. 4 (2) (*a*) will rarely be capable of being handled since the kind of conduct contemplated by 4 (2) (*a*) will not normally involve severance.

Land may be the subject of both obtaining by deception and blackmail. Again, severance may or may not take place and handling is possible only if it does so.

(c) Meaning of "stolen"

[**435**] By s. 24 (4):

"For purposes of the provisions of this Act relating to goods which have been stolen (including subsections (1) to (3) above) goods obtained in

---

[3] In that case F is, of course, guilty of aiding and abetting the theft.

England or Wales or elsewhere either by blackmail or in circumstances described in section 15 (1) of this Act shall be regarded as stolen; and 'steal', 'theft' and 'thief' shall be construed accordingly. "

By s. 24 (1):

"The provisions of this Act relating to goods which have been stolen shall apply whether the stealing occurred in England or Wales or elsewhere, and whether it occurred before or after the commencement of this Act, provided that the stealing (if not an offence under this Act) amounted to an offence where and at the time when the goods were stolen; and references to stolen goods shall be construed accordingly."

[**436**] Thus goods are "stolen" for the purposes of the Act if:

(i) they have been stolen contrary to s. 1;
(ii) they have been obtained by blackmail contrary to s. 21;
(iii) they have been obtained by deception contrary to s. 15 (1);
(iv) they have been the subject of an act done in a foreign country which was (a) a crime by the law of that country and which (b), had it been done in England, would have been theft, blackmail or obtaining by deception contrary to s. 1 or s. 21 or s. 15 (1) respectively.

These provisions narrow the previous law in two ways:

[**437**] (i) Section 33 (1) of the 1916 Act extended to goods obtained by any felony or misdemeanour until the Criminal Law Act 1967, and thereafter to goods obtained by any offence. Thus it was sufficient to prove that the goods had been obtained through a conspiracy to defraud. This is no longer so. Goods which have been obtained through such a conspiracy will, generally, have been obtained by deception but this is not invariably so. Suppose D receives from E money which E and F have obtained from P by backing a winning horse after inducing P to bet with them by deception.[4] E and F are guilty of a conspiracy to defraud and of obtaining a pecuniary advantage by deception[5] but they have not obtained the money by deception. Thus, while D may have been guilty of receiving[6] under the old law, he is guilty of no offence under the new.

The opinion has also been expressed[7] that s. 33 (1) of the 1916 Act might have extended to receiving goods obtained by a mere summary offence, as, for example, beer bought from a publican who had not renewed his licence. However that may be, it is quite clear that such conduct is no longer an offence.

[**438**] (ii) The second respect in which the law is narrowed concerns property stolen abroad. Under the 1916 Act, s. 33 (4), it was an offence merely to have possession of property stolen abroad and that irrespective of whether the act was an offence by the law of the place where it was committed. Now, mere

---

[4] *Clucas*, [1949] 2 K.B. 226; above, paras. [**187**] and [**277**].
[5] Contrary to s. 16 above, para. [**252**].
[6] It is submitted that this is not absolutely clear. P was defrauded by being induced to bet, not by being induced to pay out the money. See above, para. [**277**]. If so, it is arguable that, though a misdemeanour was committed, the money was not *obtained by* a misdemeanour.
[7] The *Report*, Cmnd. 2977, at p. 67.

possession is not enough[8]—there must, as in the case of property stolen in England, be proof of handling by the accused—and the "stealing" must be an offence by the law of the place where it was committed—though not necessarily the crime equivalent to stealing. These seem highly desirable reforms. It was most anomalous that the owner of property stolen abroad should have been afforded greater protection by the English criminal law than the owner of property stolen in England;[9] and it seems wrong in principle that English Law should, in effect, attribute criminality to an act innocent by the law of the place where it is done.

[**439**] While the offence is narrowed in these two respects, it is widened in another and important respect. It was no offence under s. 33 (1) of the 1916 Act to receive goods, knowing them to have been fraudulently converted, contrary to s. 20 of that Act, since the goods were neither stolen nor *obtained* in circumstances which amounted to felony or misdemeanour,[10] as s. 33 (1) required. Now, of course, acts which amounted only to fraudulent conversion contrary to s. 20 of the Larceny Act are ordinary theft and present no problem.

(d) The "thief" must be guilty

[**440**] Section 22 does not expressly state that the goods must actually be stolen. While a person cannot *know* goods to be stolen unless this is so, he may *believe* them to be stolen although they are not. So it might be argued that, just as in perjury it is sufficient that D believes his statement on oath to be false though it is in fact true, so here it is sufficient that D believes the goods to be stolen though they are not. It is submitted, however, that no such change from the former law was intended, that the offence is "handling stolen goods", and that it would be quite wrong to attribute such a far-reaching side effect to the inclusion of the word, "believing", which was inserted for a quite different purpose.[11]

If, then, the alleged thief is not guilty, then the handler cannot be convicted for there are no *stolen* goods for him to handle. So if the alleged thief turns out to have been under the age of ten at the time of the alleged theft, then the goods appropriated cannot be stolen goods and there can be no conviction for handling them.[12] In such circumstances, however, the receiver is now guilty of theft.[13] The wider ambit of theft than larceny means that problems of this type are likely to occur less often under the new Act. Where a wife took her husband's goods and vice versa there could be no larceny unless they were not living together or the goods were taken with a view to their ceasing to live together. The abolition of this rule[14] gets rid of some difficult problems[15] which would

---

[8] But it may be theft by "keeping . . . as owner"; s. 3 (1), above, para. [**47**].

[9] For example, suppose D was in possession of two pictures, one stolen in Glasgow and the other stolen in London. He received both innocently but kept them after discovering that they were stolen. This was an offence in respect of the Glasgow picture, but no offence in respect of the London picture. Under the Theft Act it would not be handling in respect of either picture—but it might be theft in respect of both, if D was not a purchaser for value in good faith. See s. 3, above, paras. [**26**] and [**42**].

[10] *Misell* (1926), Cr. App. Rep. 109; *Bianchi*, [1958] Crim. L.R. 813.

[11] Below, para. [**488**].

[12] *Walters* v. *Lunt*, [1951] 2 All E.R. 645, thus remains good law.

[13] Above, para. [**48**].

[14] Section 30 (1), below, para. [**532**].

[15] *Cf. Creamer*, [1919] 1 K.B. 564

otherwise have arisen on a handling charge. As it is, where the goods of one spouse are appropriated by another, this is an ordinary theft and the goods are "stolen" as in any other theft.

[**441**] If the appropriator of the goods is guilty of theft, it is submitted that the goods appropriated may be the subject of handling although the appropriator is immune from prosecution by reason, for example, of diplomatic immunity.[16] The thief could be prosecuted for the theft if diplomatic immunity were waived. The handler may be convicted whether that immunity is waived or not—unless, of course, he too is entitled to diplomatic immunity.

[**442**] It is submitted that the question whether the thief was guilty must be decided on the evidence of that fact produced at the trial of the receiver. Thus the fact that the "thief" has been acquitted is no bar to the prosecution of an alleged receiver of the goods which he has been acquitted of stealing and should not even be admitted as evidence that the goods were not stolen.[17] Similarly, the fact that the "thief" has been convicted, far from being conclusive against the alleged receiver, is not even admissible evidence that the goods were stolen.[18]

B. WHEN GOODS CEASE TO BE STOLEN

[**443**] By s. 24 (3) of the Act:

"But no goods shall be regarded as having continued to be stolen goods after they have been restored to the person from whom they were stolen or to other lawful possession or custody, or after that person and any other person claiming through him have otherwise ceased as regards those goods to have any right to restitution in respect of the theft."

[**444**] It is obvious that goods which have once been stolen cannot continue to be regarded as "stolen" so long as they continue to exist thereafter. A line must be drawn somewhere; and the Act draws it in the same place as did the common law. So if the stolen goods are taken from the thief by the owner or someone acting on his behalf, or by the police, and subsequently returned to the thief so that he may hand them over to a receiver, the receiver will not be guilty of handling because the goods are no longer stolen goods.[19] Difficult questions may continue to arise whether goods have in fact been "restored to the person from whom they were stolen or to other lawful possession or custody". Thus in *King*[20] a parcel containing the stolen goods (a fur coat) was handed by E, the thief, to a policeman who was in the act of examining the contents when the telephone rang. The caller was D, the proposed receiver. The policeman discontinued his examination, D was told to come along as arranged, he did

---

[16] *Cf. Dickinson* v. *Del Solar*, [1930] 1 K.B. 376; *A.B.*, [1941] 1 K.B. 454; *Madan* (1961), 45 Cr. App. Rep. 80.

[17] The rule in *Hollington* v. *Hewthorn*, [1943] K.B. 587; [1943] 2 All E.R. 35, though abolished for civil proceedings by s. 11 of the Civil Evidence Act 1968, continues to apply in criminal cases.

[18] *Hollington* v. *Hewthorn*, [1943] K.B. 587; [1943] 2 All E.R. 35. *Cf. Humphreys and Turner*, [1965] 3 All E.R. 689; *Remillard* v. *R.* (1921), 62 S.C.R. 21.

[19] *Cf. Dolan* (1855), Dears. C.C. 436; *Schmidt* (1866), L.R. 1 C.C.R. 15; *Villensky*, [1892] 2. Q.B. 597. A conviction of attempted handling may be possible: *Curbishley* (1971), 55 Cr. App. Rep. 310; *contra, Donnally*, [1970] N.Z.L.R. 980.

[20] [1938] 2 All E.R. 662, C.C.A.

so and received the coat. It was held that D was guilty of receiving stolen goods on the ground that the coat had not been reduced into the possession of the police—though it was admitted that there was no doubt that, in a very few minutes, it would have been so reduced, if the telephone had not rung. Presumably the same result would follow under the Theft Act. The case has, however, been subjected to criticism. It is easy to see that if the police are examining a parcel to see whether it contains stolen goods they do not take possession or even custody of the contents until they decide that this is what they are looking for.[1] In *King*, however, E had admitted the theft of the coat and produced the parcel. One might have expected, therefore, that the policeman had in fact made up his mind to take charge of it before the telephone rang. The decision presumably proceeds on the assumption that he had not done so.

[**445**] It is now quite clear that the goods cease to be stolen in the case where the police are acting without the authority of the owner for they are clearly in "other lawful possession or custody of the goods."[2]

[**446**] Section 24 (3) also provides that the goods lose their character of stolen goods if the person from whom they were stolen has ceased to have any *right to restitution* in respect of the theft.

Whether a "right to restitution" exists is a question of civil law. A right to literal restitution is rather rare in English law. The owner of a chattel which has been wrongfully appropriated may sue, according to the circumstances, in conversion or in detinue or both. In an action of conversion he cannot obtain the specific restitution of his chattel and in detinue the court has a discretion which will normally be exercised against specific restitution.[3] Generally the owner will have to be content with damages. It is quite clear that the phrase, "right to restitution", in s. 24 (3) is not intended to be confined to those cases in which the owner would be able to obtain specific restitution in a civil court and it is submitted that it extends to all cases in which he could succeed in an action based upon his proprietary rights in the thing in question, whether in conversion or in detinue or for the protection of an equitable interest.

[**447**] The provision seems to have been intended to bear a still wider meaning. The Criminal Law Revision Committee explained it as follows:[4]

"This is because, if the person who owned the goods when they were stolen no longer has any title to them, there will be no reason why the goods should continue to have the taint of being stolen goods. For example, the offence of handling stolen goods will . . . apply also to goods obtained by criminal deception under [section 15]. If the owner of the goods who has been deceived chooses on discovering the deception to ratify his disposal of the goods he will cease to have any title to them."

---

[1] *Cf. Warner* v. *Metropolitan Police Commissioner*, [1969] 2 A.C. 256; [1968] 2 All E.R. 356.

[2] *Cf.* the dictum of Cresswell, J. in *Dolan* (above, footnote 18) that goods retained their stolen character in this situation. Presumably the police in *King* were acting with the owner's authority. The point is not discussed, but it would seem likely that the theft had been reported to the police by the owner.

[3] *Whiteley* v. *Hilt*, [1919] 2 K.B. 808 at 819, *per* Swinfen Eady, M.R.

[4] The *Report*, Cmnd. 2977, para. 139.

[**448**] It is clear that "title" is here used in a broad sense to include a right to rescind. The Committee clearly has in mind a case where property passes from P to D at the moment when the goods are obtained by deception. In such a case, P, strictly, has no "title" and his right to recover the goods (or, much more likely, their value) will only arise on his rescinding the contract.[5] Such a potential right, it is submitted, is clearly a "right to restitution" within the Act.

[**449**] Goods will cease to be stolen in the following cases:—

E obtains goods by deception from P. There is a voidable contract of sale. On discovering the deception, P ratifies the contract. D, not knowing of the ratification, receives the goods believing them to be stolen. D is not guilty of handling.[6]

E obtains goods by deception from P. There is a voidable contract of sale. E sells the goods to F, a *bona fide* purchaser for value without notice of the deception. F gets a good title.[7] He delivers the goods to D who knows they have been obtained by but was not a party to the deception.[8] D is not guilty of handling.[9]

E steals goods from P. He sells them in market overt to F, a *bona fide* purchaser for value without notice of the theft. F gets a good title.[10]. D receives the goods knowing that they were stolen by E from P. He is not guilty of handling.

P entrusts his goods to E, a mercantile agent. E, dishonestly and in breach of his agreement with P, sells the goods to F who is a *bona fide* purchaser for value without notice of E's dishonesty. This is theft by E but F gets a good title to the goods.[11] D receives the goods knowing that they have been dishonestly appropriated by E. D is not guilty of handling.

P delivers goods to E under a conditional sale agreement, the price being in excess of £2,000.[12] Before E has paid all the instalments and, consequently, before the property in the goods has passed to him, he dishonestly sells them to F, who is a *bona fide* purchaser for value without notice of E's fraud. This is theft by E but F gets a good title and D who receives the goods from F does not handle stolen goods.

P delivers a motor vehicle (of any value) to E under a hire-purchase or conditional sale agreement. Before the property in the vehicle has passed to E, he dishonestly sells it to F, a *bona fide* purchaser for value without notice of the agreement and who is not a "trade or finance purchaser" as defined in s. 29 (2)

---

[5] *Cf.* above, para. [**78**] where it is argued in relation to s. 5 (4) that a person holding property under a voidable title is not "under an obligation to make restoration".

[6] Is he guilty of an attempt to handle? See above, paras. [**51**] and [**444**], footnote 19.

[7] Sale of Goods Act 1893, s. 23.

[8] *Cf. Peirce* v. *London Horse and Carriage Depository*, [1922] W.N. 170, C.A.

[9] F is not guilty of theft even if he realises the goods have been obtained by deception before he sells them to D: s. 3 (2) above. Nor, of course, is D.

[10] Sale of Goods Act 1893, s. 22.

[11] Factors' Act 1889, s. 2.

[12] *Cf.* Hire-Purchase Act 1965, s. 54. If the price is less than £2,000 the buyer cannot pass a good title. In such a case, therefore, the goods would continue to be stolen.

of the Hire-Purchase Act 1964. This is theft by E but F gets a good title to[13] the vehicle. D receives the vehicle knowing that it has been dishonestly appropriated by E. He is not guilty of handling.[14]

C. GOODS REPRESENTING THOSE ORIGINALLY STOLEN MAY BE STOLEN GOODS

[**450**] By s. 24 (2) of the Act:

"For purposes of those provisions reference to stolen goods shall include, in addition to the goods originally stolen and parts of them (whether in their original state or not)—

(a) any other goods which directly or indirectly represent or have at any time represented the stolen goods in the hands of the thief as being the proceeds of any disposal or realisation of the whole or part of the goods stolen or of goods so representing the stolen goods; and
(b) any other goods which directly or indirectly represent or have at any time represented the stolen goods in the hands of a handler of the stolen goods or any part of them as being the proceeds of any disposal or realisation of the whole or part of the stolen goods handled by him or of goods so representing them."

[**451**] The effect of the interpretation put upon the corresponding provision in the Larceny Act 1916 (s. 46 (1)) was that anything into or for which the stolen goods were converted or exchanged, whether immediately or otherwise, acquired the character of stolen goods. Thus if A stole an Austin motor car from P and exchanged it with B for a Bentley; B exchanged the Austin with C for a Citroen; and A exchanged the Bentley with D for a Daimler, all four cars would now be stolen goods even though B, C and D might be innocent. And if A, B, C and D each sold the car he had in his possession, the proceeds of each sale (as well as the cars) would be stolen, as would any property purchased with the proceeds. Thus the stolen goods might be multiplied to an alarming extent. The provision did not seem to give rise to any difficulty in practice and it seems that it was very rarely invoked; but it was clearly undesirable to re-enact a provision with such far-reaching theoretical possibilities. Section 24 (2) imposes a limitation upon the possible multiplication of stolen goods.

[**452**] The Criminal Law Revision Committee stated [15] of this provision:

"It may seem technical; but the effect will be that the goods which the accused is charged with handling must, at the time of the handling or at some previous time, (i) have been in the hands of the thief or of a handler, and (ii) have represented the original stolen goods in the sense of being the proceeds, direct or indirect, of a sale or other realization of the original goods."

---

[13] Hire-Purchase Act 1964, s. 27.
[14] In none of these examples is D guilty of theft from P, for P has no proprietary right or interest in the goods. If, however, D believes that P has such an interest, it is possible that he could be convicted of an attempt to steal.
[15] The *Report*, Cmnd. 2977, at p. 66.

[**453**] Thus, in the example above, if B, C and D were innocent (i) the Austin would continue to be stolen throughout unless P ceased to have any right to restitution of it in respect of the theft;[16] (ii) the Bentley would be stolen goods since it directly represented the goods originally stolen in the hands of the thief as the proceeds of a disposition of them; (iii) the Citroen would not be stolen since B was neither a thief nor a handler; (iv) the Daimler would be stolen since it indirectly represented the stolen goods in the hands of the thief; and the proceeds of sale of the Daimler would also be stolen goods; but the proceeds of sale of the Austin, the Bentley and the Citroen would not, since they came into the hands of C, D and B respectively, none of whom was a thief or a handler.

[**454**] The difference between the old law and the new is, of course, that a disposition or realisation of the stolen goods by a person who is neither a thief nor a handler (i.e., by one who is in fact appropriating or handling the goods but who has no *mens rea*) no longer causes the proceeds to be stolen.

(a) *Handling the proceeds of goods got by theft*

[**455**] In the vast majority of cases, stolen goods will have been got by theft,[17] contrary to s. 1 (1). Where this is the case, s. 24 (2) effects only a very slight extension of the law. That is, in almost every case where goods are notionally stolen by virtue of s. 24 (2), they are probably "stolen" by virtue of some other provision in the Act, if the original "stealing" was theft.

[**456**] There are two reasons for this:

(i) In most cases where a thief or a handler disposes of stolen goods to an innocent person he will commit an offence against that person which will result in the proceeds being stolen within the meaning of s. 24 (4). In most such cases the thief will, inevitably, represent that he has a greater interest in the goods than is in fact the case and so will be guilty of obtaining by deception. Thus, in the example of the cars, A appears to be guilty of obtaining both the Bentley and the Daimler by deception—they were "stolen" independently of s. 24 (2). The Citroen, on the other hand, which was not the subject of any offence under the Act, did not become stolen by virtue of s. 23 (2). Thus s. 24 (2) in fact adds precisely nothing in this situation.

[**457**] (ii) Section 24 (2) only operates in the case of proceeds of stolen goods which are or have been in the hands of a thief or handler. It is almost inevitable that the thief or handler will have done some act in relation to the proceeds which amounts to an appropriation of them. If, then, the proceeds are the property of another, there will be a theft of them; and it would seem that the proceeds *will* generally be the property of another. A thief does not usually obtain the proprietary interest[18] of the "owner" in the goods stolen. When a person's property is wrongfully converted into another form, he continues to own the property in its changed form: *Taylor* v. *Plumer*.[19] It is generally said that the legal owner of the property is the legal owner of the proceeds, but this has been disputed.[20] It is irrelevant, however, whether P's rights are legal

---

[16] Section 24 (3), above, para. [**443**].
[17] *Cf. D.P P.* v. *Neiser*, [1959] 1 Q.B. 254.
[18] See s. 5 (1), above, para. [**52**].
[19] (1815), 3 M. & S. 562.
[20] By Turner, [1956] Crim. L.R. at 664.

or equitable, provided only that they are proprietary rights within s. 5.[1] So, even if the thief or handler does not commit an offence against the person to whom he disposes of the stolen goods, he probably does commit theft against the owner of the original goods when he appropriates the proceeds of those goods.

[458] Suppose that A steals £1,000 in cash from P and with it buys a necklace from B who is *bona fide* and without notice of the theft. A then delivers the necklace to D who knows all the facts. There was certainly no theft of the necklace from B, nor was it obtained by deception. The necklace, however, belongs to P[2] and A's receipt of it is an appropriation of property belonging to P and is theft.

In that example, P's interest in the original property, the money, was a legal interest. The position is similar where P's interest is an equitable one. Suppose D is a trustee who holds a valuable painting on trust for P. Intending to appropriate the proceeds, he dishonestly sells the picture (theft) to E, who is *bona fide*. E gets a good title to the picture, but P can trace his equitable interest into the proceeds and D's appropriation of them is theft from him.

[459] In these examples, then, the proceeds are stolen goods independently of s. 24 (2). The cases are thus likely to be few where the original offence is theft and the proceeds are "stolen" solely by virtue of s. 24 (2) and are not the subject of an independent offence.

[460] Though it will rarely be *necessary* to rely on s. 24 (2), it may, however, be simpler to do so rather than on the doctrine of *Taylor* v. *Plumer* (which is not entirely free from obscurity) or of tracing in equity, which requires an understanding of a difficult branch of the civil law. In general, it seems to be unimportant whether goods are regarded as stolen because they are the product of other stolen goods or because they are the subject of an independent theft. Occasionally it may be thought important because the gravity of the first theft outweighs that which consists in the appropriation of the proceeds; and, when it comes to sentencing, the gravity of the handling depends to some extent on the gravity of the theft which is in issue. An obvious example is that of the man who received a large sum which came indirectly from the Great Train Robbery.[3] The large sum was no doubt the property of the owner of the original stolen money. The appropriation of the proceeds of the original stolen money would now be theft from the owner, but a much less serious theft than the original robbery. It is the original robbery which the prosecution wish to rely on.

(b) Handling the proceeds of goods got by deception or blackmail

[461] Where the goods are "stolen" within s. 24 (4), having been obtained by deception, the position is rather different. Here s. 24 (2) may have an important part to play. Where the ownership did not pass to D (i.e., it is a case of theft

---

[1] Above, para. [52].

[2] He cannot, of course, recover both the money and the necklace but, in this example, there can be no question of his having his money back since B now has a good title to it. A's only surviving proprietary interest is in the necklace.

[3] *Cf.* the *Report*, Cmnd. 2977, at p. 66.

as well as obtaining by deception), the position is the same as where the goods are stolen contrary to s. 1. Where the ownership did pass to D so that D did not commit theft, s. 24 (2) may come into its own.

[**462**] For example A induces P to sell him an Alvis by deception. A is guilty of obtaining by deception but the property passes to him, so, subject to the *Lawrence* (C.A.) principle,[4] he is not guilty of theft. He exchanges the Alvis with B, a *bona fide* purchaser, for a Buick. This is probably not obtaining of the Buick by deception, even though B does not know that the Alvis is "stolen", since A is able to give a good title to it. A now delivers the Buick[5] to D who knows all the facts. D is guilty of handling stolen goods and the Buick is stolen solely by virtue of s. 24 (2).

[**463**] Similar considerations apply where the goods have been obtained by blackmail. If the transaction is void, then subsequent dealing with the goods obtained or the proceeds is likely to amount to an independent theft. If the transaction is voidable merely so the ownership passes, subsequent dealings with the property or proceeds will not amount to theft so that the proceeds will be stolen solely by virtue of s. 24 (2).

(c) When proceeds of stolen goods cease to be stolen

[**464**] It has already been seen that stolen goods cease to be stolen when the conditions laid down by s. 24 (3) are fulfilled. What then, is the position of goods which have been stolen notionally under s. 24 (2)? Do they cease to be notionally stolen when the goods which they represent cease to be stolen? They must do so when the original goods are *restored to the possession* of the owner, for then the right to restitution of the proceeds lapses. Do the proceeds also cease to be stolen when the owner loses his *right to restitution* of the original goods? It seems clear that the answer must be in the negative. If it were otherwise, s. 24 (2) would be almost completely ineffective. In the case of the Alvis and the Buick (above, para. [**462**]) the right to recover the stolen Alvis was lost at the same instant that the Buick became the proceeds of the stolen Alvis, so that s. 24 (3) would cancel out s. 24 (2). Suppose, again, that A obtains a car by deception from P. The contract of sale is voidable, so that A gets ownership of the car. He sells it to B who knows all the facts and who re-sells it to C who is *bona fide* and without notice of A's dishonesty. C gets an unimpeachable title to the car and it ceases to be stolen goods. A then gives the proceeds of the sale to D who knows all the facts. This is just the situation in which it might be desirable to rely on s. 24 (2) but it would not be possible to do so if the money (notionally stolen, as the proceeds of the car) ceased to be stolen on the car's so ceasing. It is submitted, therefore, that the money does not cease to be stolen. It continues to be stolen until the conditions specified in s. 20 (3) are satisfied in respect of it.

[**465**] Section 24 (3) may be applicable to "stolen" proceeds since the person from whom the original goods were stolen may assert a right to restitution as

---

[4] Above, para. [**33**].
[5] P has lost his right to restitution in respect of the Alvis if B is in good faith and it has, therefore, ceased to be stolen. But P still has a right to rescind as against A and D and so has a right to restitution in respect of the Buick which, therefore, continues to be stolen. See below, para. [**466**].

against the proceeds. Suppose that some of the money stolen in the Great Train Robbery had been used to purchase a necklace from a *bona fide* seller so that the right to restitution of the money had been lost and it had ceased to be stolen. Suppose further that the necklace had been given to D who knew all the facts. The necklace would be stolen by virtue of s. 24 (2).[6] P would have a right to restitution in respect of it and there would be room for the application of s. 24 (3) in that this right might be lost in the various ways[7] in which the right to restitution of the original goods might be lost. Additionally, it would be lost if the original property were restored to the possession of the owner, since he could not recover the value of his property twice.

[**466**] To sum up, it is submitted that:

1. Goods notionally stolen as being the proceeds of other stolen goods do not necessarily cease to be notionally stolen when the original stolen goods cease, by virtue of s. 24 (3), to be stolen.

2. Goods notionally stolen cease to be notionally stolen when the conditions of s. 24 (3) are satisfied in respect of those goods.

3. Goods notionally stolen are usually also actually stolen. They cease to be actually stolen when the conditions of s. 24 (3) are satisfied in respect of them—i.e., at the same moment as they cease to be notionally stolen.

D. FORMS OF HANDLING

[**467**] The term "handling" has been adopted because "receiving"—the only way of committing the offence under s. 33 (1) of the 1916 Act—is now one of several ways in which the new offence can be committed. These are:

   (i) *Receiving* the goods.

  (ii) *Undertaking* the retention, removal, disposal or realisation of the goods by or for the benefit of another person.

 (iii) *Assisting* in the retention, removal, disposal or realisation of the goods by or for the benefit of another person.

 (iv) *Arranging* to do (i), (ii) or (iii).

[**468**] It has been decided that s. 22 creates only one offence.[8] Since that offence may be committed in four or six or even eighteen ways, a contrary decision would have had a disastrously complicating effect on the section, giving wide scope to possible objections on the ground of duplicity.

[**469**] Particulars should be given so as to enable the accused to understand the ingredients of the charge he has to meet.[9] In the case of an indictment where more than one variety of handling is alleged, it seems that the better practice is to have a separate court for each method of handling.[10]

---

[6] It would also be stolen independently of s. 24 (2); above, para. [**456**].
[7] Above, paras. [**448**]–[**449**].
[8] *Griffiths* v. *Freeman*, [1970] 1 All E.R. 1117.
[9] *Ibid.*
[10] *Ibid* ; Archbold (37th ed.), 7th Cumulative Supplement, 1540.

(a) Receiving

[**470**] All forms of handling other than receiving or arranging to receive are subject to the qualification that it must be proved that D was acting "for the benefit of another person". If there is no evidence of this—as will frequently be the case—then it must be proved that D *received* or *arranged to receive* the goods and evidence of no other form of handling will suffice. The Act does not define receiving in any way and it must be assumed that all the old authorities remain valid.

[**471**] It must be proved, then, that D took possession or control of the stolen property or joined with others to share possession or control of it. "Receiving" the thief who has the goods in his possession does not necessarily amount to receiving the goods. If the thief retains exclusive control, there is no receiving.[11] There may, however, be a joint possession in thief and receiver, so it is unnecessary to prove that the thief ever parted with possession—it is sufficient that he shared it with the alleged receiver. In *Smith*[12] it was held that a recorder had correctly directed a jury when he told them that if they believed "that the watch was then in the custody of a person with the cognizance of the prisoner, that person being one over whom the prisoner had absolute control, so that the watch would be forthcoming if the prisoner ordered it, there was ample evidence to justify them in convicting . . .". Lord Campbell, C.J. said that if the thief had been employed by D to commit larceny, so that the watch was in D's control, D was guilty of receiving. In such a case D was an accessory before the fact to larceny and today he would be guilty of theft. If the facts were as put by Lord Campbell, when did D become a receiver? As soon as the theft was committed? If so, we have the extraordinary result that D became guilty of both theft and receiving at the same moment. But, if this moment is not selected, it is difficult to see what other is appropriate. This may, however, appear less anomalous under the new law than under the old. Virtually all handling is now theft, so it is the general rule that the two offences are committed simultaneously. In the ordinary case, however, the offence is handling because there has been a previous theft. The peculiarity of the present problem is that there has been no *previous* theft; and it may be, therefore, that the requirement that the handling be "otherwise than in the course of the stealing", would prevent D from being guilty of handling until he did some act amounting to that offence, *after* the theft was complete.

[**472**] As is clear from *Smith*, actual manual possession by D need not be proved. It is enough if the goods are received by his servant or agent with his authority.[13] The receipt may be for a merely temporary purpose such as concealment from the police.[14] It is unnecessary that the receiver should receive any profit or advantage from the possession of the goods. If D took possession of the goods from the thief without his consent, this was formerly only larceny (from the thief) and not receiving.[15] There seems to be no reason why it should not be both theft and handling under the Act, since it is clear that the two offences can be committed by one and the same act.

---

[11] *Wiley* (1850), 2 Den. 37.
[12] (1855), Dears. C.C. 494.
[13] *Miller* (1854), 6 Cox C.C. 353.
[14] *Richardson* (1834), 6 C. & P. 335.
[15] *Wade* (1844), 1 Car. & Kir. 739.

[**473**] It continues to be essential for the judge to give a careful direction as to possession or control.[16] If the only evidence against D is that he ran away on being found by the police in a house where stolen property had been left, there would appear to be no case to leave to a jury. Likewise where the evidence is consistent with the view that D went to premises where stolen goods were stored with the intention of assuming possession, but had not actually done so;[17] or where the only evidence of receiving a stolen car is that D's finger-print was found on the driving mirror.[18] The mere fact that the stolen goods were found on D's premises is not sufficient evidence. It must be shown that the goods had come either by invitation or arrangement with him or that he had exercised some control over them.[19] D is not necessarily in possession of a stolen safe simply because he assists others in trying to open it.[20]

(b) *Arranging to receive*

[**474**] D's preparations to receive, not yet amounting to an attempt to do so, may constitute a sufficient "arrangement". The crime is complete as soon as the arrangement is made. It is not undone if D repents or does nothing to carry out the arrangement, or it becomes impossible of performance. So in a case like *King*[1] it might now be possible to get a conviction for handling by showing that the arrangement was made while the goods were still stolen. It is odd that the offence is committed both by arranging to receive and by actually doing so. Is it two offences or one continuing offence? The latter view is preferable, for *Griffiths* v. *Freeman*[2] by no means solves all the problems of duplicity. The arrangement must be made after the theft, since D must know or believe the goods to be stolen. Most arrangements will involve agreement with another. An arrangement with an innocent person will be enough. If the other knows the goods are stolen, there will usually be a conspiracy.

(c) *Undertaking and assisting*

[**475**] The provisions of the Act relating to handling by *undertaking and assisting* extend the law to cover cases which were formerly not criminal at all. They are far-reaching and overlapping. "Undertaking" presumably covers the case where D sets out to retain, etc., the stolen goods, on his own initiative, and "assisting", the case where he joins the thief or another handler in doing so. Some examples drawn from the old law will illustrate the kind of case to which the law will be extended.

D negotiates the sale to F of goods which he knows to have been stolen by E. D is never in possession or control of the goods.[3] He would appear to have arranged and undertaken or assisted in the disposal of stolen goods.

---

[16] *Frost and Hale* (1964), 48 Cr. App. Rep. 284.
[17] *Freedman* (1930), 22 Cr. App. Rep. 135.
[18] *Court* (1960), 44 Cr. App. Rep. 242.
[19] *Cavendish*, [1961] 2 All E.R. 856.
[20] *Tomblin*, [1964] Crim. L.R. 780.
[1] Above, para. [**444**].
[2] Above, para [**468**], footnote 8.
[3] *Cf. Watson*, [1916] 2 K.B. 385.

D assists E to lift from a van a barrel of gin which he knows to have been stolen by E or another. Even if he never has possession or control[4] he has arranged, assisted or undertaken the removal of the stolen goods.

D's fifteen-year-old son, E, brings home a bicycle which he has stolen. D assists in its retention if (i) he agrees that E may keep the bicycle in the house, or (ii) he tells the police there is no bicycle in the house, or (iii) he gives E a tin of paint so that he may disguise it.

D lights the way for E to carry stolen goods from a house to a barn so that E may negotiate the sale of the goods. D has assisted in the removal of the goods.[5]

(d) Arranging or undertaking to assist

[476] Far-reaching though the extension of the law to undertaking and assisting is, the Act goes further. A mere arrangement to do any of the acts amounting to undertaking or assisting is enough. D simply agrees or prepares to negotiate the sale of stolen goods, to lift down the barrel of stolen gin or to any act for the purpose of enabling E to retain, remove or dispose of the goods. Nothing more is required.

E. HANDLING BY OMISSION

[477] "Receiving", "undertaking" and "arranging" all suggest that an act of some kind is required. It is difficult to envisage any of these forms of handling being committed by omission. It is however possible to *assist* another by inactivity; but this will not constitute an offence except in the rather rare case where the law imposes a duty to act.

In *Brown*,[6] it was held that D's mere failure to reveal to the police the presence of stolen goods on his premises did not amount to assisting in their retention. (Nor did his advice to the police to "Get lost.") Clearly the thief was in fact assisted by D's silence in the sense that D's omission to disclose the truth delayed the finding of the stolen goods. There is, however, no duty to give information to the police.[7] No doubt the answer would have been different if D had not merely refused information but had told lies.[8]

The court thought that D's conduct was *evidence* that D was permitting the goods to remain and thereby assisting in their retention. It would obviously be an act of assistance for D, expressly or tacitly, to give a thief permission to keep stolen goods on D's premises. The court's remarks (and, indeed, decision, for they applied the proviso) seem to go farther and suggest that it would be enough if D did not communicate with the thief at all but simply allowed stolen goods which had been placed on his premises to remain there. This comes very close to making the mere omission to remove goods or report their presence an offence. But the result is perhaps reasonable. If a lorry driver were to observe that his mate had secretly inserted some stolen goods in the lorry

---

[4] *Gleed* (1916), 12 Cr. App. Rep. 32; *Hobson* v. *Impett* (1957), 41 Cr. App. Rep. 138.

[5] *Wiley* (1850), 2 Den. 37.

[6] [1970] 1 Q.B. 105; [1969] 3 All E.R. 198 (C.A.).

[7] The "duty" referred to in Appendix A to the Judges' Rules appears to be no more than a moral duty. Refusal to answer a constable is not an obstruction of the course of his duty: *Rice* v. *Connolly*, [1966] 2 Q.B. 414; [1966] 2 All E.R. 649; Smith & Hogan, 261-263.

[8] This probably is obstruction of the police: *Rice* v. *Connolly* (footnote 7, above); *Matthews* v. *Dwan*, [1949] N.Z.L.R. 1037.

and were then to drive the lorry to its destination without comment, there would be no difficulty in saying that he had assisted in the removal of the goods. Where the goods are planted on static premises, the assistance consists in the maintenance of the premises where the goods lie and the exclusion of strangers, just as in the lorry case it consists in driving the lorry.

F. OTHERWISE THAN IN THE COURSE OF THE STEALING

[478] Whatever the form of handling alleged, it must be proved it was done "otherwise than in the course of the stealing". This provision was obviously necessary if a great many instances of perfectly ordinary theft were not automatically to become handling as well. Thus, without the provision, virtually every instance of theft by two or more persons would have been handling by one or other or, more likely, both of them, since they would inevitably render mutual assistance to one another in the removal of the goods. Given the decision to keep handling as a separate crime, the provision was, then, necessary —but it adds further unfortunate complications to an already complicated offence.

[479] The position was in fact much the same under the old law of receiving, because of the rule that a principal in the felony of larceny could not be guilty of receiving as a principal in the first degree.[9] If D received the goods in the course of the stealing, it followed that he was a principal in the larceny and this necessarily meant that he could not be convicted of receiving. If a servant stole money from his master's till and handed it to an accomplice in his master's shop, the accomplice was guilty of larceny and not guilty of receiving.[10] Similarly, if a man committed larceny in the room in which he lodged and threw a bundle of stolen goods to an accomplice in the street, the accomplice was guilty of larceny and not guilty of receiving.[11] "If one burglar stands outside a window", said Alderson, B., "while another plunders the house and hands out the goods to him, he surely could not be indicted as a receiver".[12] It seems clear enough that in cases such as these, the same result must be reached under the Theft Act—i.e., in each case D is guilty of theft and not guilty of handling. This result necessarily follows from the words, "otherwise than in the course of the stealing", whether or not the rule survives (under which the cases cited were decided) that a principal in larceny cannot be a principal in the first degree in receiving.[13] These cases show that larceny was a continuing offence. As soon as the thief moved the thing a fraction of an inch the larceny was complete in the sense that, if he had been stopped at that moment, he could have been successfully indicted for the complete crime. The commission of the offence nevertheless continued at least until the point, in those cases, where the goods were put into the accomplice's hands. It has already been noted[14] that it is arguable that theft is not a continuing offence in the way that larceny was. If this argument were accepted, it might well follow that the receipt, on the

---

[9] Below, para. [486].
[10] *Coggins* (1873), 12 Cox C.C. 517.
[11] *Perkins* (1852), 5 Cox C.C. 554.
[12] *Ibid.* at 555.
[13] As to which, see below, para. [486].
[14] Above, paras. [161]–[163], and see also para. [45].

facts of these cases, is not "in the course of the stealing". On the whole, however, it is thought that such an argument is unlikely to be accepted. If theft were an instantaneous act, the words "in the course of the stealing" would be rendered virtually nugatory. They clearly contemplate that the offence may continue for at least some period of time and it is thought that the authorities on the law of larceny will continue to afford guidance on the matter. These indicate that there is some difficulty in establishing precisely where the line is to be drawn. So where E broke into a warehouse, stole butter and deposited it in the street some thirty yards from the warehouse door, D who then came to assist in carrying it off was not guilty of larceny as a principal offender.[15] Similarly where D waited half a mile from the scene of a proposed larceny and there received a horse stolen by E.[16] Doubtless, in these cases, D was guilty of receiving and would be so guilty on similar facts under the Theft Act.

[480] A similar problem arose under the now (happily) repealed s. 5 (1) (a) of the Homicide Act 1957. Under this provision "any murder done in the course or furtherance of theft" was capital. In *Jones*[17] D committed murder when he was interrupted as he was about to leave a store in which he had committed larceny. The Court of Criminal Appeal had no doubts that this was a killing "in the course . . . of theft".

[481] These cases suggest that the theft continues at least while the thief is on the premises in which he perpetrates it and while "the job" is incomplete. But is E still in the course of theft as he walks down the garden path with the swag? as he drives home? and as he shows it to his wife in the kitchen? On the other hand, is the theft necessarily in the course of commission because the stolen property has not yet been removed from the premises on which it was stolen, if E has completed "the job" and all that remains is for others to take possession of the goods? It is thought that, in such a case, E is no longer in the course of stealing. If so, some of the old cases on larceny are no longer in point. Thus in *Atwell and O'Donnell*[18] goods were left in the warehouse in which they had been stolen for *some time thereafter* and the court held that it was a continuing transaction as to those who joined in the plot *before the goods were finally carried away from the premises*. Presumably until this occurred, the asportation was incomplete. It does not necessarily follow that the course of stealing under the Theft Act continues so long. If E appropriates goods in his employer's warehouse and conceals them so that they may be taken by D who comes to the warehouse a week later, is it to be said that D's taking is in the course of the stealing? Surely not. It is thought that E must still be "on the job"—vague though that phrase may be—if the receipt is to be "in the course of the stealing".

G. FOR THE BENEFIT OF ANOTHER PERSON

[482] The Undertaking, Assisting or Arranging must be shown to be *for the benefit of another person*, and the italicised words should be included in the

---

[15] *King* (1817), Russ. & Ry. 332; *cf. Gruncell and Hopkinson* (1839), 9 C. & P. 365.
[16] *Kelly* (1820), Russ. & Ry. 421.
[17] [1959] 1 Q.B. 291; see also *H.M. Advocate* v. *Graham*, 1958 S.L.T. 167.
[18] (1801), 2 East P.C. 768.

particulars of the indictment.[19] If it were not for this qualification almost all thieves would be handlers as well. As it is, the thief may be guilty of handling (by undertaking) if he himself retains, removes, etc., the goods for the benefit of another person. It would seem to be immaterial that the third person is guilty of no offence and even unaware of what is going on.

[**483**] D steals goods, sells them to E, a *bona fide* purchaser, and keeps the purchase price for himself. D is not guilty of handling unless merely performing the contract with E amounts to acting " for the benefit of " E. D sells the goods to E, a *bona fide* purchaser, and instructs E to pay the purchase price to F. D is guilty of handling the stolen goods. He has undertaken the disposal of the goods for the benefit of another person. Presumably D is guilty when he sells the goods and receives the purchase price from E with the intention of paying it over to F. Thus an inquiry into D's motives may be necessary.

H. INNOCENT RECEIPT AND SUBSEQUENT RETENTION WITH MENS REA

[**484**] If D receives the stolen goods innocently, either, that is, believing them not to be stolen or knowing them to be stolen but intending to return them to the true owner, of course, he commits no offence. Suppose he subsequently discovers the goods to be stolen or decides not to return them to the true owner or disposes of them. He has dishonestly undertaken the retention of or has disposed of stolen goods knowing them to be stolen. Whether he is guilty of an offence depends on a number of factors.

[**485**] 1. Where D does not get ownership of the goods. (The normal situation where goods are stolen.):

    (i) D gives value for the goods.

        (*a*) D retains or disposes of the goods for his own benefit. This is not theft because of s. 3 (2);[20] nor is it handling by undertaking, assisting or arranging since it is not for the benefit of another. D might be guilty of handling by aiding and abetting the receiving by the person to whom he disposes of the goods, if that person has *mens rea*.

        (*b*) D retains or disposes of the goods for the benefit of another. This is not theft (s. 3 (2)) but is handling.

    (ii) D does not give value.

        (*a*) D retains or disposes of the goods for his own benefit. This is theft but not handling unless it amounts to aiding and abetting receipt by another.

        (*b*) D retains or disposes of the goods for the benefit of another. This is theft and handling.

2. Where D gets ownership of the goods. (Because the rogue obtained them by deception and acquired a voidable title or because of some exception to the *nemo dat* rule.)

(*a*) D gives value for the goods.

---

[19] *Sloggett*, [1971] 3 All E.R. 264; and see *Marshall*, "The Times", December 22, 1971.
[20] Above, para. [**42**].

Retention or disposal of the goods cannot be theft, since P has no property in the goods, nor handling since P has lost his right to restitution,[1] his right to rescind being destroyed on the goods coming into the hands of D who was a *bona fide* purchaser for value.

(*b*) D does not give value.

Again this cannot be theft, since P has no property in the goods, but it may be handling since P's right to rescind and secure restitution of his property is not extinguished by the goods coming into the hands of one who does not give value. It will be handling if this is so *and* D either aids and abets a guilty receipt by another or disposes of the goods for the benefit of another.

I. HANDLING BY THE THIEF

[486] The common law rules regulating the liability of a thief to a charge of receiving goods feloniously stolen by him were complicated.

1. A principal in the first or the second degree to larceny could not be convicted as a principal in the first degree of receiving the goods so stolen.[2]

2. An accessory before the fact to larceny could be convicted as a principal in the first degree (or in the second degree or as an accessory) of receiving the goods so stolen.[3]

3. A principal in the first or second degree to larceny could be convicted as a principal in the second degree or accessory before the fact to receiving the goods so stolen.[4]

[487] The distinction between principals and accessories has now been abolished and all participants in a crime are classed as principals.[5] What is the effect of this change in the law upon the rules set out above? It seems never to have been decided whether these rules applied to receiving property obtained by misdemeanour, so the old law affords no guidance on the point. There are two possibilities:

(*a*) To hold that the rules governing principals in larceny now apply to principals in theft. The effect would be that anyone guilty of theft could not be convicted of handling the goods so stolen by receiving them into his own possession or control but that he could be guilty of handling those goods by aiding and abetting, or counselling or procuring another to receive them.

(*b*) To hold that these rules were technicalities of the old law of receiving or of felonies and that they have died with it. The effect would be that any thief could be convicted of handling the goods stolen by him by receiving them—if the evidence warranted this conclusion. In the majority of cases the thief can only be guilty of handling by receiving where he is aiding and abetting the receipt by another because he is already in possession or control and therefore cannot receive as the principal offender. In some circumstances, however, a thief might be convicted of handling the stolen goods by

---

1 Above, para. [443].
2 *Perkins* (1852), 2 Den. 459; *McEvin* (1858), Bell 20; *Coggins* (1873), 12 Cox C.C. 517.
3 *Froggett*, [1965] 2 All E.R. 832; *Thompson*, [1965] Crim. L.R. 553.
4 *Carter Patersons and Pickfords, Ltd.* v. *Wessel*, [1947] K.B. 849.
5 Criminal Law Act 1967, s. 1.

receiving them as the principal offender. For example, D steals goods and, in the course of the theft, delivers them to E. Two days later E returns the goods to D.

It is submitted that the second is the preferable course. There is no reason why the old rules about receiving should be extended to handling by retention, removal, disposal or realisation of the goods and it would be unsatisfactory to have one set of rules for handling by receiving and another set for handling by other acts. The section should be construed so as to preserve, as far as possible, the unity of the offence.

2 THE MENS REA

A. KNOWLEDGE OR BELIEF

[488] It must be proved that D handled the goods, "knowing or believing them to be stolen goods". The Criminal Law Revision Committee thought that this provision would extend the law:

"It is a serious defect of the present law that actual knowledge that the property was stolen must be proved. Often the prosecution cannot prove this. In many cases indeed guilty knowledge does not exist, although the circumstances of the transaction are such that the receiver ought to be guilty of an offence. The man who buys goods at a ridiculously low price from an unknown seller whom he meets in a public house may not *know* that the goods were stolen, and he may take the precaution of asking no questions. Yet it may be clear on the evidence that he believes that the goods were stolen. In such cases the prosecution may fail (rightly, as the law now stands) for want of proof of guilty knowledge."[6]

It may be doubted, with respect, whether this was really so.[7] Generally the courts have equated "wilful blindness" of the kind here described with knowledge,[8] and it is submitted that this is right in principle. The Act now settles beyond any doubt what, it must be assumed, was previously at least a doubtful matter. There will no doubt be general agreement with the committee that such cases ought to be covered by the law of handling. A possible and undesirable side effect of the provision would be an unduly narrow construction of other provisions[9] which use only the word "knowing" and not "believing". It will be possible to point to the Theft Act and to urge that the omission of "believing" in the other provision means that wilful blindness is not enough. The present provision should, it is submitted, be regarded as a clarification of a doubtful point in a particular case and not as having any bearing on the interpretation of the requirement of knowledge in other statutes.

B. DISHONESTY

[489] Dishonesty was an essential ingredient of the old crime of receiving though it was not expressed in the statute. The inclusion of the word "dishonestly" thus makes no change in the law. D may receive goods knowing

---

[6] The *Report*, Cmnd. 2977, at p. 64. See now *Atwal* v. *Massey*, (1971) 3 All E.R. 881 (C.A.).
[7] See *White* (1859), 1 F. & F. 665 and *cf. Woods*, (1969), 1Q.B. 447 (C.A.).
[8] Smith and Hogan, 73 and cases there cited.
[9] See, for example, s. 12; above, para. [326].

or believing them to be stolen and yet not be guilty if, for example, he intends to return them to the true owner or the police.[10] A claim of right will amount to a defence, but it will be difficult to establish such a claim where D knows or believes the goods to be stolen except in the case put above, where he intends to return the goods to the owner.

C. PROOF OF MENS REA

[**490**] The common law rules concerning proof of *mens rea* on a receiving charge hold good under the Act. In particular, where D is found in possession of recently stolen property the jury may be directed that they *may* infer guilty knowledge or belief if D offers no explanation of his possession or if they are satisfied beyond reasonable doubt that any explanation he has offered is untrue. The onus of proof remains on the Crown throughout, and, whether D offers an explanation or not, he should be convicted only if the jury are satisfied beyond reasonable doubt that he had the guilty knowledge or belief.[11]

[**491**] Because of the difficulty of proving guilty knowledge, the Larceny Act provided for the admission of certain evidence on a receiving charge which would not be admissible in criminal cases generally. The Theft Act has corresponding provisions. By s. 27 (3):

"Where a person is being proceeded against for handling stolen goods (but not for any offence other than handling stolen goods), then at any stage of the proceedings, if evidence has been given of his having or arranging to have in his possession the goods the subject of the charge, or of his undertaking or assisting in, or arranging to undertake or assist in, their retention, removal, disposal or realisation, the following evidence shall be admissible for the purpose of proving that he knew or believed the goods to be stolen goods:—

(a) evidence that he has had in his possession, or has undertaken or assisted in the retention, removal, disposal or realisation of, stolen goods from any theft taking place not earlier than twelve months before the offence charged; and

(b) (provided that seven days notice in writing has been given to him of the intention to prove the conviction) evidence that he has within the five years preceding the date of the offence charged been convicted of theft or of handling stolen goods."

[**492**] In some respects this provision is narrower than that contained in the Larceny Act 1916, in other respects it is wider. It is narrower in that

(i) The evidence described in both para. (a) and para. (b) is admissible only after evidence has been given of the *actus reus* of handling by D. Under the 1916 Act, this condition precedent was applicable only to the evidence corresponding to that admitted by para. (b).

---

[10] *Cf. Matthews*, [1950] 1 All E.R. 137.
[11] *Abramovitch* (1914), 11 Cr. App. Rep. 45; *Aves* (1950), 34 Cr. App. Rep. 159; *Hepworth*, [1955] 2 Q.B. 600.

(ii) The provision corresponding to para. (*b*) in the 1916 Act allowed evidence of any offence involving fraud or dishonesty. Paragraph (*b*) is confined to convictions of theft and handling stolen goods, so that whereas, for example, a conviction for obtaining by false pretences would have been admissible on a charge of receiving under the old law, a conviction of obtaining by deception will not be admissible on a charge of handling under the new. This is very reasonable. If under the general rules of evidence a conviction of obtaining by deception is not admissible on a charge of the same nature because its prejudicial effect outweighs its probative value, it should, *a fortiori*, be inadmissible on a charge of handling where, obviously, its relevance is less.

[**493**] The new provision is wider than that in the Larceny Act in that:

(i) Paragraph (*a*) admits evidence not merely that D had stolen property in his possession, as did the Larceny Act, but also that he dealt with the property in any of the ways which now may amount to the offence of handling under the Theft Act.

(ii) Under the Larceny Act the property which D was proved to have in his possession must have been stolen in the twelve months preceding the date of the offence charged. Under the Theft Act, the other property may have been stolen *after* the offence charged, or within the twelve months preceding the commission of the offence charged. This seems to be reasonable. D's possession after the alleged theft would seem to have at least equal probative force to his possession before.

CHAPTER XIII

ENFORCEMENT AND PROCEDURE

1 SEARCH FOR STOLEN GOODS

[494] Power to issue a warrant or authority to search premises for stolen goods is given by s. 26 of the Theft Act.[1]

Under the Larceny Act a search warrant might authorise search by any person specified in the warrant. Under the Theft Act, only a policeman may be authorised to search, though the information may be sworn by any person. Other enactments authorising the issue of search warrants to persons other than police officers are, however, expressly preserved. In any such Act a reference to stolen goods shall be construed in accordance with s. 24 of the Theft Act.[2] The effect will be to widen the power of search to include goods which have been obtained by blackmail and by deception.

[495] The power given by s. 26 (2) to superintendents and above was formerly enjoyed only by Chief Constables. With the increasing size of police forces, this was thought by the Criminal Law Revision Committee to be too restrictive. A small restriction on the power given by s. 26 (2) (a) is that the occupier's offence of dishonesty must have been committed within the preceding five years whereas under the Larceny Act it might have been committed at any time.

It is submitted that the constable's authority to seize goods under s. 26 (3) extends to any goods on the premises in question which he believes to be stolen goods, whether they are named in the warrants or not.[3] Even if the section did not justify such a seizure, it would be lawful by the common law.[4]

2 JURISDICTION

A. TERRITORIAL

[496] It is a general principle of the common law that criminal jurisdiction does not extend to acts committed abroad. Parliament may, of course, extend jurisdiction so far as it pleases but it is a general rule of construction that unless there is something which points to a contrary intention, a statute will be taken to apply only to the United Kingdom. The Act expressly provides that, with one small exception, it does not extend to Scotland or Northern Ireland.[5] The majority of the House of Lords in *Treacy* v. *D.P.P.*[6] assumed that the general principle of construction applied to offences under the Act,

---

1 Below, page 208.
2 See s. 32 (2) (b), below, page 214.
3 Contrast the wording of s. 42 (1) of the Larceny Act 1916.
4 *Chic Fashions (West Wales), Ltd.* v. *Jones*, [1968] 2 Q.B 299; [1968] 1 All E.R. 229.
5 Section 36 (2).
6 [1971] A.C. 537.

with the result that they are triable only if committed in England and Wales. Lord Diplock alone expressed the opinion that the only territorial limitations to be implied are those required by the rules of international comity which "do not call for more than that each sovereign state should refrain from punishing persons for their conduct within the territory of another sovereign state where that conduct has had no harmful consequences within the territory of the state which imposes the punishment."[7] It would look a little odd that the Act should provide that conduct should be an offence under English law if committed anywhere in the world *except* Scotland and Northern Ireland; but Lord Diplock explained the exception of these areas as depending on constitutional practice, not international comity. Probably the majority opinion will prevail; but it will be recalled that the interpretation of offences such as obtaining by deception and blackmail as continuing offences,[8] goes some way to achieving the effect desired by Lord Diplock.

The exception referred to above is created by ss. 14 and 33. Where a person is charged with theft, attempted theft, robbery, attempted robbery or assault with intent to rob, with respect to the theft of a mail bag or postal packet, or the contents of either when in course of transmission in the British postal area,[9] then he may be tried in England and Wales without proof that the offence was committed there.

[**497**] By Part I of Schedule 3[10], the provisions of the Post Office Act 1953 which relate to stealing and receiving are repealed for England and Wales (but not for Scotland). Anyone prosecuted in England and Wales for stealing or handling mail bags, etc. must therefore be prosecuted under the appropriate section of the Theft Act. If the charge is one of handling mail bags, etc., then it seems that it must be proved that the offence was committed in England and Wales. The other offences under the Post Office Act, including those akin to but not amounting to theft, such as unlawfully taking away or opening a mail bag, continue in force.

B. COURTS

(a) The Crown Court

[**498**] Under the Courts Act 1971, courts of assize and quarter sessions are abolished and all proceedings on indictment are to be brought in the Crown Court. Of the indictable offences under the Theft Act, aggravated burglary, burglary in the circumstances described in S. 29 (2) (*b*) of the Act[12] blackmail and handling stolen goods from an offence not committed in the United Kingdom are "Class 3" offences and the remainder are "Class 4" offences[13]. The effect is that all the offences may be listed for trial by a High Court judge or by a circuit judge or recorder but the Class 4 offences will normally be listed for trial by a circuit judge or recorder.

---

[7] [1971] A.C. at 564.
[8] Above, paras. [**173**]–[**175**] and [**339**].
[9] Section 14 (2).
[10] Below, page 221.
[11] See S. 1(2), s. 3 and s. 6.
[12] Below, para [**449**].
[13] Practice Note, [1971] 3 All E.R. 829.

(b) Magistrates' Courts

[**499**] Any of the indictable offences under the Theft Act is triable summarily with the consent of the accused except:

"(a) robbery, aggravated burglary, blackmail and assault with intent to rob; and

(b) burglary comprising the commission of, or an intention to commit, an offence which is not included in [the Schedule 1 to the Magistrates' Courts Act 1952 (which lists the indictable offences by adults which may be tried summarily with the consent of the accused)]; and

(c) burglary in a dwelling if entry to the dwelling or the part of it in which the burglary was committed, or to any building or part of a building containing the dwelling, was obtained by force or deception or by the use of any tool, key or appliance, or if any person in the dwelling was subjected to violence or the threat of violence; and

(d) handling stolen goods from an offence not committed in the United Kingdom."[14]

[**500**] The only provision likely to give rise to any difficulty here is the rather complicated one relating to burglary. "Dwelling" is wider than "dwelling house" in the Larceny Act in that it will no doubt extend to inhabited vehicles or vessels; but in other respects it is narrower, since "dwelling house" was defined to include buildings connected with it by a covered and enclosed passage.[15] So D will be triable summarily if he commits burglary on the ground floor of a large commercial building in which the caretaker has a flat on the top floor. Probably the same is true where D commits burglary in a shop with living quarters above or at the back. The burglary is committed in a "building containing the dwelling" but not in the dwelling.

[**501**] The word "force" has been interpreted in some magistrates' courts to include the opening of a closed door or unfastened window. This view has been taken partly because of the meaning of "breaking" under the old law; but it is a very strained interpretation of "force" and, if the Act had meant "breaking", it would have said so. The reference to "tool, key or appliance" suggests that, where a door or window is opened without the use of one of these, the case is triable summarily. If D breaks the window with a brick, that is presumably the use of an "appliance". If he does so with his elbow, is that the use of "force"? The conjunction of "force" and "deception" suggests that the draftsman had in mind the old cases of "constructive breaking", where D caused P to admit him by force or deception; and, if this is so, "force" means force against the person. Whatever the answer, these factors scarcely amount to satisfactory criteria for determining whether a case is suitable for

---

[14] Theft Act, s. 29 (2).
[15] Larceny Act 1916, s. 46 (2).

summary trial and it would have been much better if the legislature had trusted magistrates to use their discretion.

3 RESTITUTION[16]

[**502**] Section 28 provides a summary procedure whereby the court before which a person is convicted of certain offences may order that the property concerned be restored to the owner. Under the old law, conviction might affect the title to goods. This is no longer so.[17] Who is the owner of property is a question for the civil law and the fact that there has been a conviction of any criminal offence with respect to the property is irrelevant, so far as title is concerned.

[**503**] Section 28 (1) provides:

"Where goods have been stolen, and a person is convicted of any offence with reference to the theft (whether or not the stealing is the gist of his offence), the court by or before which the offender is convicted may on the conviction exercise any of the following powers:—

(*a*) the court may order anyone having possession or control of the goods to restore them to any person entitled to recover them from him; or

(*b*) on the application of a person entitled to recover from the person convicted any other goods directly or indirectly representing the first-mentioned goods (as being the proceeds of any disposal or realisation of the whole or part of them or of goods so representing them), the court may order those other goods to be delivered or transferred to the applicant; or

(*c*) on the application of a person who, if the first-mentioned goods were in the possession of the person convicted, would be entitled to recover them from him, the court may order that a sum not exceeding the value of those goods shall be paid to the applicant out of any money of the person convicted which was taken out of his possession on his apprehension."

A. STOLEN GOODS

[**504**] "Goods" are defined in s.34 (2) (*b*) which is considered above.[18] "Stolen" bears the same meaning as in s. 24 (4)[19] and thus extends to goods obtained by blackmail or by deception.[20]

B. THE CONVICTION

[**505**] The court's power arises on a conviction "of any offence with reference to the theft[1] (whether or not the stealing is the gist of his offence)". The power would thus arise on a conviction for handling the stolen goods, robbery,

---

[16] Macleod, "Restitution under the Theft Act", [1968] Crim. L.R. 577.
[17] Section 31 (2), below, page 213.
[18] See para. [**431**].
[19] Above, para. [**435**].
[20] Sections 24 (4) and 28 (6).
[1] I.e., the theft, blackmail or deception.

burglary and aggravated burglary. The two latter offences do not necessarily involve theft and it would, of course, be necessary for the court to be satisfied on the evidence admissible under s. 28 (4)[2], that a theft of the goods which were the object of the burglary had in fact been committed. It is not necessary that the conviction should be an offence against the Act. It might be, for example, a conviction of assisting an arrestable offender under s. 4 (1) of the Criminal Law Act 1967 or of concealing an arrestable offence under s. 5 (1) of that Act; of conspiracy or an attempt to commit theft where there is proof that the theft was actually committed; or of a forgery done for the purpose of committing the theft in question.

C. AGAINST WHOM THE ORDER MAY BE MADE

[506] An order under s. 28 (1) (*a*) may be made against anyone having possession or control of the goods. A *bona fide* purchaser may thus be ordered to surrender the goods to someone with a better title. The order may be made against a person holding the goods on behalf of another as, for example, a servant who has custody of goods, possession being in the employer.

An order under s. 28 (1) (*b*)[3] or (*c*) may be made only against the person convicted.

D. IN WHOSE FAVOUR THE ORDER MAY BE MADE

[507] An order may be made in favour of any person entitled to recover the goods from the person in possession or control (para. (*a*)); any *applicant* entitled to recover the *proceeds* of the stolen goods from the person convicted (para. (*b*)); and any *applicant* who would be entitled to recover the goods if they were in the possession of the person convicted (para. (*b*)).

[508] As has been pointed out above,[4] it is only in exceptional cases that the owner of goods has a literal right to recover them, even from a thief, in civil law. Generally his remedy is an action in detinue or conversion in which he will be awarded damages. It is submitted that, as with "right to restitution", so also "entitled to recover" must be given a broad interpretation to extend to cases in which the claimant would be able to succeed in an action based upon his proprietary rights in the thing in question. This would therefore extend to cases in which the ownership has passed to the rogue under a voidable transaction[5] which the owner has rescinded.

[509] The person entitled will generally be the victim of the theft or someone standing in his shoes, as his executor, administrator or trustee in bankruptcy. If the victim has received compensation for the loss of the stolen goods under an insurance policy, then the insurance company may be subrogated to his rights.[6] If the victim had not the best right to possession of the goods (as, for example, if he himself had stolen them from another) the person with that right is the person entitled.

---

[2] Below, para. [514].
[3] *Cf.* the *Report*, Cmnd. 2977, para. 165.
[4] In discussing the meaning of "a right to restitution" in s. 24 (3); para. [446].
[5] Above, para. [446].
[6] *Church* (1970), 55 Cr. App. Rep. 65 at 71.

E. THE PROPERTY IN RESPECT OF WHICH THE ORDER MAY BE MADE

[**510**] The property in respect of which the order may be made is as follows:

Section 28 (1) (*a*): such of the goods[7] which have been stolen as are in the possession or control of the person against whom the order is made.

Section 28 (1) (*b*): such of the proceeds of the goods which have been stolen as are in the possession or control of the person against whom the order is made.

Section 28 (1) (*c*): any *money* of the person convicted which was taken out of his possession on his apprehension, not exceeding the value of the stolen goods.

Two questions arise here. The first relates to the meaning of "taken out of his possession on his apprehension". This is not confined, as might have been supposed, to money which is taken from D's person when he is arrested. In *Ferguson*[8], it was held to include money in a safe deposit box at Harrods, of which D had the key, which was properly appropriated by the police as the suspected proceeds of the theft, ten days after D's arrest. This decision seems to attribute to "possession" its legal rather than its popular meaning but the court said that it was "difficult to think of a clearer case of money being in the possession" of the accused and that, giving "'on his apprehension' a common-sense meaning", the money was so taken. If the money had been deposited in a bank account, the result would have been different since D would have been only a creditor of the bank and not in possession. It seems then that money at D's home or in his car is in his possession for this purpose.

Presumably the taking must be lawful. The police have no right to seize money which they do not reasonably believe to be the proceeds of a crime or evidence of its commission. It is submitted that money unlawfully seized, though literally taken from the accused on his apprehension, could not be used to compensate the victim. The provision may thus work somewhat capriciously. Money wrongly but reasonably suspected to be the proceeds of the theft may be taken and used to compensate, but other money in the possession of the accused may not. It is odd that a wrong, though reasonable, suspicion should make the difference.

Any provision containing the word "possession" is likely to present problems. In *Parker*,[9] D apparently threw away a wallet containing money shortly before his arrest, and this was found in a garden by the police the following day; the court refused to answer the question whether the money was taken from his possession on his apprehension. On one view, he had abandoned possession by throwing the wallet away; but so to hold would seem to depart from the broad "commonsense" view taken in *Ferguson*.[8]

Finally, the money must be "money of the person convicted" so that if, as in *Ferguson*, any doubt is raised as to D's ownership of the money, no order may be made.

[**511**] The second problem concerns the extent to which D may be required to make compensation. Section 28 (1) (*c*) says to the extent of "a sum not exceeding the value of those goods"—i.e., the goods which have been stolen. This

---

[7] *Cf.* s. 34 (2) (*b*), above, paras. [**431**]–[**434**].
[8] [1970] 2 All E.R. 820 (C.A.).
[9] [1970] 2 All E.R. 458 (C.A.).

presents no difficulty where D is convicted of the theft. He may, however, be convicted of an offence "with reference to the theft" and his participation may relate only to a small part of the stolen property. For example, it may be proved that £1,000 was stolen from a bank and that D dishonestly received £10 of that money which was taken from him when he was arrested. On a literal reading, it would seem that D might be ordered to pay £990 out of other money taken from him on his arrest which was not the proceeds of the theft. However, in *Parker*[10] the court held that, whatever the proper construction of the section:

> "If a man is charged with handling stolen goods and the whole of the goods in respect of which he has been convicted are recovered, then it must, we hold, be an incorrect exercise of any discretion which exists under the section to make him pay compensation in addition in respect of other goods which are not the subject of a charge against him".

F. COMPENSATION TO A THIRD PARTY

[512] By s. 28 (3):
> "Where under subsection (1) above[11] the court on a person's conviction makes an order under paragraph (*a*) for the restoration of any goods, and it appears to the court that the person convicted has sold the goods to a person acting in good faith, or has borrowed money on the security of them from a person so acting, then on the application of the purchaser or lender the court may order that there shall be paid to the applicant, out of any money of the person convicted which was taken out of his possession on his apprehension, a sum not exceeding the amount paid for the purchase by the applicant or, as the case may be, the amount owed to the applicant in respect of the loan."

[513] Thus if D has stolen a necklace from P and pawned it with Q for a loan of £100, on D's conviction, Q may be ordered to restore the necklace to P and be compensated out of the money taken from D on his apprehension. The provision is confined to money taken from D on his apprehension so Q will have no remedy under s. 28 if D, when apprehended, is wearing a gold watch but carrying no money, though he has large sums in his bank. Q, may, however, be compensated by an order made under s. 4 of the Forfeiture Act 1870 or s. 34 of the Magistrates' Courts Act 1952.[12]

G. WHEN AN ORDER SHOULD BE MADE

[514] It is provided by s. 28 (4)[13] that "The court shall not exercise the powers conferred by this section unless in the opinion of the court the relevant facts sufficiently appear from the evidence given at the trial or the available documents, together with admissions made by or on behalf of any person in connection with any proposed exercise of the powers . . ."

---

[10] [1970] 2 All E.R. at 462–463.
[11] See above, para. [503].
[12] Below, para. [524].
[13] Below, page 211.

The court must be satisfied on the evidence given *at the trial* that an order should be made; and the trial concludes when sentence is passed.[14] The court may not embark on a new inquiry at the end of the trial. The words, "on the conviction" in s. 28 (1) mean the same as "immediately after the conviction" in the Forfeiture Act 1870, s. 4.

The court is never bound to make an order under s. 28; when the condition in s. 28 (4) is satisfied it is a matter for the discretion of the court. Clearly, however, when the relevant facts do sufficiently appear, an order should generally be made unless there is a real dispute as to the title to the goods. Even when the facts are absolutely clear the question of entitlement to the goods may involve difficult questions of law. Where they have been transferred to a third party, many of the subtleties of the old law of larceny by a trick and false pretences may arise. If there is any real dispute or any doubt as to title, then an order should not be made; the parties should be left to their civil remedies. Only in the plainest cases, where there is no doubt of fact or law, should an order be made.[15]

> "In practice the power will be exercisable only where there is no real dispute as to ownership. It would seriously hamper the work of the criminal courts if at the end of a trial they had to investigate disputed titles."[16]

[**515**] No right to be heard is given to a third party against whom an order might be made—and it has been said that he has no *locus standi*[17]—but it is submitted that it would be improper to make an order against a party without allowing him to be heard on the subject[18]—particularly since, where the order is made by the Crown Court, the third party has no right of appeal.[19] An order made against a person not afforded a hearing would seem to offend against the rules of natural justice and, where made by a magistrates' court, liable to be quashed by *certiorari*; but *certiorari* will not lie to the Crown Court, which is part of the Supreme Court.

H. EXERCISE OF MORE THAN ONE POWER

[**516**] The question may arise as to whether the court may exercise more than one of its powers in respect of the same theft.[20] Though paras. (*a*), (*b*) and (*c*) of s. 28 (1) are expressed in the alternative, s. 28 (2) contemplates that an order may be made against the thief under both (*b*) and (*c*). The situation contemplated is that where the thief has disposed of the goods for less than their true value. If power is exercised under (*b*) to award these proceeds to the applicant, the balance may be made up from money taken from D on his apprehension. Normally, where the power under (*a*) is exercised to restore the

---

[14] *Church* (1971), 55 Cr. App. Rep. 65.
[15] *Ferguson*, [1970] 2 All E.R. 820 (C.A.).
[16] The *Report*, Cmnd. 2977, para. 164: "it would probably be impracticable (as well as being undesirable) that an order should be made in any but straightforward cases.
[17] *Ferguson*, [1970] 2 All E.R. at 822.
[18] ". . . certainly it is intended that he should be heard, either in person or through counsel"—Parl. Debate Official Report (H.L.) 290, col. 865, *per* Lord Stonham. *Cf. Macklin* (1850), 5 Cox C.C. 216.
[19] Below, para. [**521**].
[20] *Cf.* Macleod, [1968] Crim. L.R. at 586–587.

goods to the owner, no further compensation will be required. If, however, only a part of the goods can be restored by exercising power (*a*), there seems to be no reason why power (*b*) or (*c*) should not be exercised in relation to the remainder.

Where P gets the whole of his goods back under (*a*) but they are damaged, he might succeed in an application for compensation under (*c*). If a count for criminal damage were included in the indictment and the accused convicted, the court might, on application or otherwise, order the payment of up to £400 compensation under the Criminal Damage Act 1971, s. 8; and, if there were no such count, then the similar power under the Forfeiture Act might be exercised on application. There seems to be nothing to prevent the court exercising these various statutory powers on the same occasion and in combination if it thinks it just to do so.

Where D has succeeded in passing a good title to a *bona fide* purchaser (B), and the court, in the exercise of power (*a*), consequently orders possession to be given to B, may it then exercise power (*c*) in favour of the original owner, A? This is the converse of the more usual situation expressly provided for in s. 28 (3)[1] where the *bona fide* purchaser gets no title and consequently is ordered to surrender the goods to A. It is submitted that the above question should be answered in the affirmative. If the goods were in the possession of D, A "would be entitled to recover them from him". The superior right of B would not defeat an action by A against D. A therefore satisfies the condition in para. (*c*), and it seems entirely right that he should be compensated out of money taken from D where D has succeeded in depriving him of his title to the goods. The situation will probably rarely arise, since it will not often be absolutely clear that D has passed a good title to B; and where there is a doubt, the court must refrain from making orders.[2]

I. ENFORCEMENT OF AN ORDER

[517] The Act makes no provision for the enforcement of orders made under s. 28.

> "Disobedience to an order made by a court of assize or quarter sessions for the handing over of goods could, we think, be dealt with as contempt. Disobedience to a similar order made by a magistrates' court could be dealt with under s. 54 (3) of the Magistrates' Courts Act 1952." [3]

J. THE EFFECT OF AN ORDER

[518] The Act contains no provision similar to that in the Police (Property) Act 1897, protecting the person in whose favour an order is made against claims to the property on the expiration of six months from the order.[4] It is submitted that an order should have no effect whatever on the rights under the civil law of any claimant to the property, except possibly where those rights consist in a merely possessory title.[5]

---

[1] Above, para. [512].
[2] Above, para. [514].
[3] The *Report*, Cmnd. 2977, para. 168.
[4] Below, para. [527].
[5] *Cf. Irving* v. *National Provincial Bank, Ltd.*, [1962] 2 Q.B. 73 (C.A.), below, para. [527].

[**519**] It may frequently happen that a magistrates' court is in a position to order the return of the property either under the Police (Property) Act or under the Theft Act and, when this is so, the court should make it clear under which provision it is acting since there is the difference in effect referred to.[6] In general it is thought that it would be better to utilise the power under the Theft Act, since the 1897 Act may interfere in a rather arbitrary fashion with the rights at civil law, even of persons who are unaware that the proceedings are taking place.[7]

K. APPEAL

(a) *From an order in the Crown Court*

[**520**] It has now been decided[8] that where an order is made against a person convicted on indictment, he may appeal against it to the Court of Appeal. Though the point has not been made clear by the courts, it seems that the appeal is an appeal against sentence under s. 9 of the Criminal Appeal Act 1968; for, by s. 50 (1) of that Act:

". . . 'sentence', in relation to an offence, includes any order made by a court when dealing with an offender . . ."

It has been held that this is wide enough to include an order made under s. 4 of the Forfeiture Act 1870 for payment of money by way of satisfaction or compensation,[9] and it would seem to follow that an order made under s. 24 is also part of the sentence.[10] Leave to appeal against sentence must be obtained from the Court of Appeal.

[**521**] Where an order is made against a person other than the person convicted no appeal by him will lie[11]; though if the convicted person appeals, the court may then annul or vary[12] a restitution order made against a third party. This is anomalous—particularly since it is possible for an order to be made against a third party who has not been heard; but it will be of no practical importance if orders are made only in undisputed and straightforward cases.

(b) *From an order in the Magistrates' Court*

[**522**] Section 83 of the Magistrates' Courts Act 1952 gives a right of appeal against sentence to the Crown Court and sentence includes (with inapplicable exceptions) "any order made on conviction". This clearly gives a right of appeal to the convicted person against an order made under s. 28. Both the convicted person and a third party against whom an order has been made might appeal

---

[6] Moreover the order under the Theft Act does not take effect if the conviction is quashed (below, para. [**523**]) whereas that under the Police (Property) Act is quite unaffected by the quashing of any conviction since the power does not depend upon the existence of a conviction, but only of a charge.
[7] Below, para. [**529**].
[8] *Parker*, [1970] 2 All E.R. 458; *Ferguson*, [1970] 2 All E.R. 820.
[9] *Jones*, [1929] 1 K.B. 211; [1928] All E.R. Rep. 532.
[10] In *Thebith* (1969), 54 Cr. App. Rep. 35 at 37, it was stated that there was (unspecified) authority that a restitution order was not part of the sentence, and consequently there was no appeal. The author has been unable to trace the authority, and it would appear to be overruled by the cases cited above.
[11] *Cf. Elliott*, [1908] 2 K.B. 452; *JJ. of the Central Criminal Court* (1886), 18 Q.B.D. 314.
[12] Criminal Appeal Act 1968, s. 30 (4).

by way of case stated to the High Court on a question of law or jurisdiction, under s. 87 (1) of the Magistrates' Courts Act which applies to any person aggrieved by an order.

L. SUSPENSION OF ORDERS MADE ON INDICTMENT

[**523**] The operation of an order for restitution is suspended for 28 days after the date of conviction on indictment unless, "in any case in which, in their opinion, the title to the property is not in dispute,"[13] the court directs otherwise. Where notice of appeal or leave to appeal is given within those 28 days, then the operation of the order is suspended until the conviction is quashed or, if it is not quashed, until time for applying for leave to the House of Lords has run out or so long as any appeal to that House is pending.[14] If the conviction is quashed by the Court of Appeal or the House of Lords then the order does not take effect. When a conviction is quashed by the Court of Appeal and restored by the House of Lords, the House may make any order for restitution which could have been made by the court which convicted the respondent.[15]

M. OTHER POWERS TO AWARD COMPENSATION

(a) Under the Forfeiture Act 1870 and the Magistrates' Courts Act 1952

[**524**] Other powers to award compensation exist which may be used in conjunction with s. 24. Section 4 of the Forfeiture Act 1870 and s. 34 of the Magistrates' Courts Act 1952, both as amended by the Criminal Law Act 1967, empower the court before which a person is convicted on indictment and a magistrates' court respectively to order compensation to be paid by the convicted person for loss of or damage to property up to the amount of £400 to be paid to any person aggrieved by the offence.

Unlike s. 28 of the Theft Act, these provisions do not relate to any particular property. They may thus be relied on where neither the stolen property nor its proceeds has been recovered and nothing has been taken from D on his apprehension. An order may indeed be made even though the offender has no means and is being sent to prison.[16] Compensation under the Forfeiture Act 1870 may be awarded only on the application of the person aggrieved[17] and prosecuting counsel cannot be considered an agent for the aggrieved person.[18]

(b) Under the Police (Property) Act 1897

[**525**] Where any property has come into the possession of the police in connection with any criminal charge, a court of summary jurisdiction may, under s. 1 (1) of the Police (Property) Act 1897, make an order for the delivery of the property to the person appearing to be the owner, or, if the owner cannot be ascertained, make "such order with respect to the property as to the magistrate or court may seem meet."

---

[13] *Ibid.*, s. 30; and Theft Act 1968, s. 28 (4).
[14] Criminal Appeal Act 1968, s. 42 (1).
[15] *Ibid.*, s. 42 (3).
[16] *Ironfield*, [1971] 1 All E.R. 202.
[17] *Taylor* (1969), 53 Cr. App. Rep. 357; *Melksham* (1971), 55 Cr. App. Rep. 400.
[18] *Forest JJ., ex parte Coppin*, [1969] 2 All E.R. 668; see *Melksham* (footnote 17 above) at 402.

[526] The property must not be restored to the person who is the owner in the strict sense, if it appears that there is some person with a better right to immediate possession, such as a person with a valid lien on the property. It was so held in *Marsh* v. *Commissioner of Police*,[19] though, curiously, in that case the court declined to decide whether the lienor was the "owner" for this purpose. It is submitted that, if it is wrong to deliver to the owner in the strict sense where there is another with a better right to possession, this can only be because the owner in the strict sense is not "the owner" for the purposes of the Act; and that it should follow that "the owner" is the person with the best right to possession.[20]

[527] It is provided by s. 1 (2) of the Police (Property) Act 1897 that an order made under s. 1 (1) does not affect any person's right to bring legal proceedings to recover the property from the person to whom it has been delivered under the order of the court; but on the expiration of those six months, the right shall cease. An order may, however, affect the onus of proof: *Irving* v. *National Provincial Bank Ltd.*[1] where it was held that, in the absence of any evidence as to the ownership of the money, the defendant bank's title arising from an order made under the Act was superior to that of the plaintiff from whose possession the money had been taken by the police; the onus was on the plaintiff and not on the defendant to establish actual ownership in the money.

[528] It is submitted that this provision should defeat the title only of one who might have asserted a better right to possess before the magistrates' court. If, for example, D steals a car from P and, on D's conviction, the magistrates order that it be returned to P, the rights of Q, from whom P had the car on hire or hire purchase, should not be affected. If, after the expiration of six months, Q seeks to recover the car in accordance with the terms of the contract he should not be debarred from doing so by the order made under the Act.

[529] Even thus limited, the provision could lead to arbitrary and unjust interference with civil rights. Suppose that the court makes an order in favour of P from whom goods have been stolen. The goods had been the subject of an earlier theft from Q. More than six months after the order, Q discovers that the goods are in the possession of P. His right to recover them would appear to be barred. It is not obvious why P should have this windfall arising out of the dishonest intervention of a third party.

[530] It has been held by a metropolitan magistrate that "property" includes anything into or for which the property has been converted or exchanged, by analogy to s. 46 (1) of the Larceny Act 1916.[2] It is submitted that this was the correct decision, though it would be better to rely on the common law concerning ownership[3] than on the analogy of a criminal statute. Difficult questions might arise where the property has been converted into a more valuable thing by the expenditure of skill and labour.[4]

---

[19] [1945] K.B. 43 (D.C.).
[20] Howard argues that the property must in all cases be awarded to the owner in the strict sense: [1958] Crim. L.R. 744.
[1] [1962] 2 Q.B. 73 (C.A.).
[2] (1959), 123 J.P.J. 640.
[3] *Taylor* v. *Plumer* (1815), 3 M. & S. 562. *Cf.* above, para. **[457]**.
[4] See 104 L.J. 296.

[**531**] The Theft Act provides that the 1897 Act shall apply to any property seized by the police under the authority of s. 26 of the Theft Act.[5]

4 HUSBAND AND WIFE[6]

[**532**] Under the Larceny Act 1916, a husband could steal from a wife and *vice versa* only if, at the time of the theft, *either*, they were not living together *or* the property was taken with a view to their ceasing to live together. So where a wife took her husband's property and gave it to her lover, the lover was not guilty of receiving stolen goods.[7] This rule is abolished by s. 30 (1) of the Theft Act which provides:

> "This Act shall apply in relation to the parties to a marriage, and to property belonging to the wife or husband whether or not by reason of an interest derived from the marriage, as it would apply if they were not married and any such interest subsisted independently of the marriage."

The effect is that wives and husbands can steal, or commit any other offence under the Act in relation to, the property of each other.

A. PROCEEDINGS INSTITUTED BY INJURED SPOUSE

[**533**] The proceedings may be instituted by the injured spouse. Section 30 (2) provides:

> "Subject to subsection (4) below, a person shall have the same right to bring proceedings against that person's wife or husband for any offence (whether under this Act or otherwise) as if they were not married, and a person bringing any such proceedings shall be competent to give evidence for the prosecution at every stage of the proceedings."

This subsection is not confined to offences under the Act but applies to "any offence". Thus, for example, a wife may prosecute her husband for stealing or damaging the property of a third party, for an offence against the person of a third party, or for perjury; and in any such prosecution the wife would now be a competent witness for the prosecution. The Act does not say whether the wife would be compellable and it might be argued that, since there is a proviso to s. 30 (3) (*b*) that the spouse shall not be compellable and no such proviso to s. 30 (2), the spouse *is* compellable under s. 30 (2).[8] Presumably it is very unlikely that the problem will arise, since the spouse who is bringing the proceedings is unlikely to be unwilling to give evidence. The problem could arise where the prosecuting spouse declines to give evidence and the court wishes to compel him to do so. It is submitted that such a spouse should be compellable.

B. PROCEEDINGS INSTITUTED BY THIRD PARTY

[**534**] Section 30 (3) makes provision for the competence of a spouse in

---

[5] Section 26 (4).
[6] The *Report*, Cmnd. 2977, paras. 189–199.
[7] *Creamer*, [1919] 1 K.B. 564.
[8] *Cf. Tilley* v. *Tilley*, [1949] P. 240.

proceedings instituted by a third party for an offence committed by a person "with reference to" his spouse or his spouse's property:

> "Where a person is charged in proceedings not brought by that person's wife or husband with having committed any offence with reference to that person's wife or husband or to property belonging to the wife or husband, the wife or husband shall be competent to give evidence at every stage of the proceedings, whether for the defence or for the prosecution, and whether the accused is charged solely or jointly with any other person:

Provided that—

> (*a*)   the wife or husband (unless compellable at common law) shall not be compellable either to give evidence or, in giving evidence, to disclose any communication made to her or him during the marriage by the accused; and

> (*b*)   her or his failure to give evidence shall not be made the subject of any comment by the prosecution."

[**535**] This follows the form of earlier statutes which make one spouse competent for the prosecution or defence on the trial of the other. The effect is the same as that of s. 4 (1) of the Criminal Evidence Act 1898 in relation to the offences mentioned in the Schedule to that Act or of s. 39 of the Sexual Offences Act 1956 to offences under that Act, other than those expressly excluded from its provisions.

(a) Where spouse is compellable

[**536**] Where the alleged crime is one of personal violence by one spouse against the other, the aggrieved spouse is a compellable witness at common law.[9] It is this rule that the words in brackets in proviso (a) are intended to preserve. So if a husband is charged with robbery of his wife, at all events if actual violence is alleged, he will be a compellable witness. The position in the case of robbery by threats is less clear. In *Yeo*[10] it was held by Gorman, J. that the rule was inapplicable to a charge of sending to a spouse a letter threatening to kill, contrary to s. 16 of the Offences against the Person Act 1861. *Yeo* might well be distinguishable on a charge of robbery by threats of force, since the threats have a much more direct effect on the person of the victim than in the case of a letter. If *Yeo* is correct, however, it means that one spouse would not be a compellable witness against the other on a charge of blackmailing the former spouse by a letter even though the menaces amounted to threats of force. Some doubt was cast on *Yeo* by Melford Stevenson, J. in *Verolla*[11] where the rule was held applicable on a charge of attempting to cause the accused's wife to take poison with intent to murder her.[12]

---

[9] *Lapworth*, [1931] 1 K.B. 117.
[10] [1951] 1 All E.R. 864.
[11] [1963] 1 Q.B. 285.
[12] Cross submits that *Yeo* was wrongly decided: *Evidence* (3rd ed.), 150; and see Olive Stone, 14 M.L.R. 341.

(b) Where spouse is competent but not compellable for the prosecution

[537] Where D is prosecuted by a third party for stealing his wife's property, obtaining it by deception or handling it when stolen, the wife is clearly a competent but not compellable witness for the prosecution. Likewise where the prosecution is for burglary of a building of which his wife is in possession[13] or of a building of which she is not in possession, if the burglary is committed with the intention of stealing or inflicting damage on her property, doing her grievous bodily harm or raping her.[14] Other cases are where one spouse is blackmailed by the other or where the one takes the other's motor vehicle or conveyance contrary to s. 12, or abstracts his electricity, contrary to s. 13, etc. If a spouse, robbed by threats, is not compellable at common law,[15] he is at least competent under this subsection.

[538] Offences committed "with reference to" a spouse would include such cases as that where the husband lives on the earnings of his wife's prostitution, or where he wilfully neglects to maintain her. There is corresponding provision for the former of these two cases in the Sexual Offences Act 1956 and for the latter under the Criminal Evidence Act 1898. The spouse's competence in such prosecutions could now be justified by reference to either the Theft Act or the earlier statute.

If *Yeo* was rightly decided, the wife, though still not compellable, would now be competent under this subsection, since the offence was undoubtedly committed "with reference" to her.

C. RESTRICTIONS ON PROSECUTION

[539] Section 30 (4) provides:

"Proceedings shall not be instituted against a person for any offence of stealing or doing unlawful damage to property which at the time of the offence belongs to that person's wife or husband, or for any attempt, incitement or conspiracy to commit such an offence, unless the proceedings are instituted by or with the consent of the Director of Public Prosecutions:

Provided that—

(a) this subsection shall not apply to proceedings against a person for an offence—

(i) if that person is charged with committing the offence jointly with the wife or husband; or

---

13 If D burgled a building occupied by P as tenant of D's wife, would the wife be a competent witness for the prosecution? Strictly the offence is committed "with reference to" the wife's property, since she owns the freehold of the burgled premises; but the trespass is committed against P and unless there is an intention to damage the wife's property (e.g., the fabric of the building) her ownership of the freehold might be thought insufficient to bring the offence within the subsection.

14 A husband may be guilty of rape upon his wife where they are judicially separated (*Clarke*, [1949] 2 All E.R. 448) and probably also where they have separated by agreement or after a decree nisi of divorce or nullity. See *Miller*, [1954] 2 Q.B. 282; Smith and Hogan, 288–290.

15 Above, para. **[536]**.

(ii) if by virtue of any judicial decree or order (wherever made) that person and the wife or husband are at the time of the offence under no obligation to cohabit; and

(*b*) this subsection shall not prevent the arrest, or the issue of a warrant for the arrest, of a person for an offence, or the remand in custody or on bail of a person charged with an offence, where the arrest (if without a warrant) is made, or the warrant of arrest issues on an information laid, by a person other than the wife or husband."

[**540**] Where it is a case of stealing or the doing of unlawful damage by one spouse to the property of the other, consent is required whether the proceedings are to be instituted by the aggrieved spouse or by a third party. Outside these cases, however, no consent is required whether the proceedings be instituted by the aggrieved spouse or by a third party. If a wife alleges, or a third party alleges, that her husband has obtained her property by deception, blackmailed her, wounded her or committed sodomy with her, no consent is required. Presumably consent will be required on a robbery charge since this is within "any offence of stealing". It is not obvious why this clause (which was not in the draft bill produced by the Criminal Law Revision Committee) should be thus limited.

[**541**] Proviso (*a*) (i) is not very clear. It is a proviso to a subsection dealing with a case of a person who steals or damages his spouse's property; and so one would expect a proviso to qualify the rule that *such a person* cannot be prosecuted except with the consent of the Director. That is, the natural meaning of "that person" in the proviso is the person who has stolen or damaged the property of his wife or husband.

If that be correct, proviso (*a*) (i) deals with the case where the husband and wife are jointly charged with theft of or criminal damage to property which belongs to one of them. This looks a little curious; but it will be recalled[16] that it is perfectly possible for a person to be convicted of stealing his own property where some third person has a proprietary interest in it. Suppose that a husband has pawned his watch. While his wife engages the pawnbroker's attention, he secretly takes the watch back again. Proceedings may be brought against the couple without the consent of the Director. It is very reasonable that consent should not be necessary in this case; and perhaps the proviso is required because the proceeding, literally, is for an offence of stealing property belonging to the husband.

[**542**] The position would seem to be much the same in the case of criminal damage. Generally a man may damage property which is his own with impunity, no matter how barbarous his action may be.[17] But if another has a proprietary interest in the property, this would surely be an offence. For example, D has mortgaged a valuable painting to P by bill of sale. If he deliberately destroys the painting, he is surely guilty of an offence of criminal damage. If then, his wife destroys the painting with his connivance, they may both be prosecuted without consent.

---

[16] Above, para. [**57**].
[17] Smith and Hogan, 458–461.

If this interpretation is correct, it follows that if, in the above examples, the wife had taken the watch and destroyed the painting, without the husband's connivance, the Director's consent would have been required, for proceedings instituted by P. This looks strange because, though it is the husband's property which is destroyed, the *offence* is committed against a third party.

Moreover, property may "belong" to one of the spouses, at least for the purposes of theft,[18] although the ownership in the strict sense is in a third party. Suppose that H has a television set on hire or hire-purchase from P. If his wife, W, sells the television set without H's consent, it is clearly right that he should have to get consent to prosecute her for stealing from him. The same should apply if she smashes the set and he alleges that she has criminally damaged his property. On the other hand, it looks distinctly odd that P has to get the consent of the Director to prosecute W; but that appears to be the effect.

[**543**] It may well be that the proviso was not actually intended to deal with this situation at all, but to apply to the case where D, a third party, assists H to steal or destroy W's property and D and H are prosecuted jointly. It may be intended to say that, in those circumstances, no consent shall be required so far as the proceedings against D are concerned. If that is the intention, the proviso is not strictly necessary because D is not within the main part of the subsection. It would mean, moreover, that consent would still be necessary for the proceedings against H; so that joint proceedings would still have to wait on consent. That would not be very sensible; so probably the better course (if not the only proper course) is to assume that the proviso means what it says. In that event, the situation envisaged in this paragraph is the same as if the proviso did apply to it. No consent is required so far as D is concerned (because he is not a person charged with an offence against his wife's property) but consent is required so far as H is concerned. There must either be separate trials or the Director's consent obtained.

[**544**] Proviso (*a*) (ii) means that if H and W have been judicially separated and one of them steals or damages the other's property, proceedings may be brought without the consent of the Director, whether they were in fact living together at the time of the offence or not. If the parties have merely separated in pursuance of an agreement, the Director's consent is required even if they are in fact living apart at the time of the alleged offence.

---

[18] See s. 5, above, para. [**52**].

APPENDIX

THEFT ACT 1968

(1968 c. 60)

ARRANGEMENT OF SECTIONS

Section 2

An Act to revise the law of England and Wales as to theft and similar or associated offences, and in connection therewith to make provision as to criminal proceedings by one party to a marriage against the other, and to make certain amendments extending beyond England and Wales in the Post Office Act 1953 and other enactments; and for other purposes connected therewith.

[26th July, 1968]

Definition of "theft"

1. Basic definition of theft

(1) A person is guilty of theft if he dishonestly appropriates property belonging to another with the intention of permanently depriving the other of it; and "thief" and "steal" shall be construed accordingly.

(2) It is immaterial whether the appropriation is made with a view to gain, or is made for the thief's own benefit.

(3) The five following sections of this Act shall have effect as regards the interpretation and operation of this section (and, except as otherwise provided by this Act, shall apply only for purposes of this section).

EFFECT OF SECTION
For the effect of this section see above, Chapter II, paras. [18]-[149].

PREVIOUS CORRESPONDING OFFENCES
This offence replaces the offences of larceny, embezzlement and fraudulent conversion under ss. 1, 17 and 20 of the Larceny Act 1916 (5 Halsbury's Statutes (2nd ed.) 1012, 1021, 1022).

PUNISHMENT
For the maximum punishment for this offence, see s. 7, below.

"PERSON"
Under the Interpretation Act 1889, s. 2 (32 Halsbury's Statutes (3rd ed.), 435) "person" includes a body corporate unless a contrary intention appears. It seems that a corporation may be guilty of any offence under the Act, other than under ss. 18, 19 and, probably, 25. (A corporation does not have a "place of abode".)

"THIEF" AND "STEAL"
For the meaning of "thief" and "steal" for the purpose of offences relating to stolen goods, see s. 24 (4), below.

EXCEPT AS OTHERWISE PROVIDED BY THIS ACT
See ss. 15 (3), 34 (1), below, in relation to offences under s. 15, below.

2. "Dishonestly"

(1) A person's appropriation of property belonging to another is not to be regarded as dishonest—

    (a) if he appropriates the property in the belief that he has in law the right to deprive the other of it, on behalf of himself or of a third person; or

(b) if he appropriates the property in the belief that he would have the other's consent if the other knew of the appropriation and the circumstances of it; or

(c) (except where the property came to him as trustee or personal representative) if he appropriates the property in the belief that the person to whom the property belongs cannot be discovered by taking reasonable steps.

(2) A person's appropriation of property belonging to another may be dishonest notwithstanding that he is willing to pay for the property.

EFFECT OF SECTION
For the effect of this section see above, paras. [**118**]-[**129**].

3. "Appropriates"

(1) Any assumption by a person of the rights of an owner amounts to an appropriation, and this includes, where he has come by the property (innocently or not) without stealing it, any later assumption of a right to it by keeping or dealing with it as owner.

(2) Where property or a right or interest in property is or purports to be transferred for value to a person acting in good faith, no later assumption by him of rights which he believed himsef to be acquiring shall, by reason of any defect in the transferor's title, amount to theft of the property.

EFFECT OF SECTION
For the effect of this section see above, paras. [**19**]-[**51**], [**112**]-[**115**].

4. "Property"

(1) "Property" includes money and all other property, real or personal, including things in action and other intangible property.

(2) A person cannot steal land, or things forming part of land and severed from it by him or by his directions, except in the following cases, that is to say—

(a) when he is a trustee or personal representative, or is authorised by power of attorney, or as liquidator of a company, or otherwise, to sell or dispose of land belonging to another, and he appropriates the land or anything forming part of it by dealing with it in breach of the confidence reposed in him; or

(b) when he is not in possession of the land and appropriates anything forming part of the land by severing it or causing it to be severed, or after it has been severed; or

(c) when, being in possession of the land under a tenancy, he appropriates the whole or part of any fixture or structure let to be used with the land.

For purposes of this subsection "land" does not include incorporeal hereditaments; "tenancy" means a tenancy for years or any less period and includes an agreement for such a tenancy, but a person who after the end of a tenancy remains in possession as statutory tenant or otherwise is to be treated as having possession under the tenancy, and "let" shall be construed accordingly.

(3) A person who picks mushrooms growing wild on any land, or who picks flowers, fruit or foliage from a plant growing wild on any land, does not (although not in possession of the land) steal what he picks, unless he does it for reward or for sale or other commercial purpose.

For purposes of this subsection "mushroom" includes any fungus, and "plant" includes any shrub or tree.

(4) Wild creatures, tamed or untamed, shall be regarded as property; but a person cannot steal a wild creature not tamed nor ordinarily kept in captivity, or the carcase of any such creature, unless either it has been reduced into possession by or on behalf of another person and possession of it has not since been lost or abandoned, or another person is in course of reducing it into possession.

EFFECT OF SECTION
  For the effect of this section see above, paras. [**83**]-[**111**].

5. "Belonging to another"

(1) Property shall be regarded as belonging to any person having possession or control of it, or having in it any proprietary right or interest (not being an equitable interest arising only from an agreement to transfer or grant an interest).

(2) Where property is subject to a trust, the persons to whom it belongs shall be regarded as including any person having a right to enforce the trust, and an intention to defeat the trust shall be regarded accordingly as an intention to deprive of the property any person having that right.

(3) Where a person receives property from or on account of another, and is under an obligation to the other to retain and deal with that property or its proceeds in a particular way, the property or proceeds shall be regarded (as against him) as belonging to the other.

(4) Where a person gets property by another's mistake, and is under an obligation to make restoration (in whole or in part) of the property or its proceeds or of the value thereof, then to the extent of that obligation the property or proceeds shall be regarded (as against him) as belonging to the person entitled to restoration, and an intention not to make restoration shall be regarded accordingly as an intention to deprive that person of the property or proceeds.

(5) Property of a corporation sole shall be regarded as belonging to the corporation notwithstanding a vacancy in the corporation.

EFFECT OF SECTION
  For the effect of this section see above, paras. [**52**]-[**82**].

HUSBAND AND WIFE
  As to property belonging to a husband or wife see s. 30 (1), below.

H

6. "With the intention of permanently depriving the other of it"

(1) A person appropriating property belonging to another without meaning the other permanently to lose the thing itself is nevertheless to be regarded as having the intention of permanently depriving the other of it if his intention is to treat the thing as his own to dispose of regardless of the other's rights; and a borrowing or lending of it may amount to so treating it if, but only if, the borrowing or lending is for a period and in circumstances making it equivalent to an outright taking or disposal.

(2) Without prejudice to the generality of subsection (1) above, where a person, having possession or control (lawfully or not) of property belonging to another, parts with the property under a condition as to its return which he may not be able to perform, this (if done for purposes of his own and without the other's authority) amounts to treating the property as his own to dispose of regardless of the other's rights.

EFFECT OF SECTION
  For the effect of this section see above, paras. [**130**]-[**149**].

Theft, robbery, burglary, etc.

7. Theft

A person guilty of theft shall on conviction on indictment be liable to imprisonment for a term not exceeding ten years.

"THEFT"
  For the definition of "theft" see s. 1, above.
TRIAL
  This offence is triable summarily with the consent of the accused: see s. 29 (2), below.

8. Robbery

(1) A person is guilty of robbery if he steals, and immediately before or at the time of doing so, and in order to do so, he uses force on any person or puts or seeks to put any person in fear of being then and there subjected to force.

(2) A person guilty of robbery, or of an assault with intent to rob, shall on conviction on indictment be liable to imprisonment for life.

EFFECT OF SECTION
  For the effect of this section see above, Chapter III, paras. [**150**]-[**169**].
PREVIOUS CORRESPONDING OFFENCES
  This offence replaces the offences of robbery and aggravated robbery punishable under s. 23 of the Larceny Act 1916 (5 Halsbury's Statutes (2nd ed.) 1025).
"STEALS"
  For the meaning of "steals" see s. 1 (1) above.
TRIAL
  Offences under this section are triable only on indictment: see s. 29 (2), below.

9. Burglary

(1) A person is guilty of burglary if—

    (*a*) he enters any building or part of a building as a trespasser and with intent to commit any such offence as is mentioned in subsection (2) below; or

    (*b*) having entered any building or part of a building as a trespasser he steals or attempts to steal anything in the building or that part of it or inflicts or attempts to inflict on any person therein any grievous bodily harm.

(2) The offences referred to in subsection (1) (*a*) above are offences of stealing anything in the building or part of a building in question, of inflicting on any person therein any grievous bodily harm or raping any woman therein, and of doing unlawful damage to the building or anything therein.

(3) References in subsections (1) and (2) above to a building shall apply also to an inhabited vehicle or vessel, and shall apply to any such vehicle or vessel at times when the person having a habitation in it is not there as well as at times when he is.

(4) A person guilty of burglary shall on conviction on indictment be liable to imprisonment for a term not exceeding fourteen years.

EFFECT OF SECTION
    For the effect of this section see above, paras. [**369**]-[**411**].

PREVIOUS CORRESPONDING OFFENCES
    This section and s. 10 below replace offences of burglary, housebreaking etc. under ss. 24-27 of the Larceny Act 1916 (5 Halsbury's Statutes (2nd ed.)1026, 1027).

"STEALS"
    For the meaning of "steals" and "stealing" see s. 1 (1), above.

TRIAL
    For offences under this section which may be tried summarily with the consent of the accused, see s. 29 (2), below.

10. Aggravated burglary

(1) A person is guilty of aggravated burglary if he commits any burglary and at the time has with him any firearm or imitation firearm, any weapon of offence, or any explosive; and for this purpose—

    (*a*) "firearm" includes an airgun or air pistol, and "imitation firearm" means anything which has the appearance of being a firearm, whether capable of being discharged or not; and

    (*b*) "weapon of offence" means any article made or adapted for use for causing injury to or incapacitating a person, or intended by the person having it with him for such use; and

    (*c*) "explosive" means any article manufactured for the purpose of producing a practical effect by explosion, or intended by the person having it with him for that purpose.

(2) A person guilty of aggravated burglary shall on conviction on indictment be liable to imprisonment for life.

EFFECT OF SECTION
    For the effect of this section see above, paras. [**412**]-[**421**].

PREVIOUS CORRESPONDING OFFENCES
    See notes to s. 9, above.

''STEALS''
    For the meaning of "steals", "stealing" see s. 1 (1), above.

TRIAL
    Offences under this section are triable only on indictment: see s. 29 (2), below.

11. Removal of articles from places open to the public

(1) Subject to subsections (2) and (3) below, where the public have access to a building in order to view the building or part of it, or a collection or part of a collection housed in it, any person who without lawful authority removes from the building or its grounds the whole or part of any article displayed or kept for display to the public in the building or that part of it or in its grounds shall be guilty of an offence.

For this purpose "collection" includes a collection got together for a temporary purpose, but references in this section to a collection do not apply to a collection made or exhibited for the purpose of effecting sales or other commercial dealings.

(2) It is immaterial for purposes of subsection (1) above, that the public's access to a building is limited to a particular period or particular occasion; but where anything removed from a building or its grounds is there otherwise than as forming part of, or being on loan for exhibition with, a collection intended for permanent exhibition to the public, the person removing it does not thereby commit an offence under this section unless he removes it on a day when the public have access to the building as mentioned in subsection (1) above.

(3) A person does not commit an offence under this section if he believes that he has lawful authority for the removal of the thing in question or that he would have it if the person entitled to give it knew of the removal and the circumstances of it.

(4) A person guilty of an offence under this section shall, on conviction on indictment, be liable to imprisonment for a term not exceeding five years.

EFFECT OF SECTION
    For the effect of this section see above, Chapter VI, paras. [**296**]-[**311**].

TRIAL
    This offence is triable summarily with the consent of the accused: see s. 29 (2), below.

12. Taking motor vehicle or other conveyance without authority

(1) Subject to subsections (5) and (6) below, a person shall be guilty of an offence if, without having the consent of the owner or other lawful authority, he takes any conveyance for his own or another's use or, knowing that any conveyance has been taken without such authority, drives it or allows himself to be carried in or on it.

(2) A person guilty of an offence under subsection (1) above shall on conviction on indictment be liable to imprisonment for a term not exceeding three years.

(3) Offences under subsection (1) above and attempts to commit them shall be deemed for all purposes to be arrestable offences within the meaning of section 2 of the Criminal Law Act 1967.

(4) If on the trial of an indictment for theft the jury are not satisfied that the accused committed theft, but it is proved that the accused committed an offence under subsection (1) above, the jury may find him guilty of the offence under subsection (1).

(5) Subsection (1) above shall not apply in relation to pedal cycles; but, subject to subsection (6) below, a person who, without having the consent of the owner or other lawful authority, takes a pedal cycle for his own or another's use, or rides a pedal cycle knowing it to have been taken without such authority, shall on summary conviction be liable to a fine not exceeding fifty pounds.

(6) A person does not commit an offence under this section by anything done in the belief that he has lawful authority to do it or that he would have the owner's consent if the owner knew of his doing it and the circumstances of it.

(7) For purposes of this section—

    (*a*) "conveyance" means any conveyance constructed or adapted for the carriage of a person or persons whether by land, water or air, except that it does not include a conveyance constructed or adapted for use only under the control of a person not carried in or on it, and "drive" shall be construed accordingly; and

    (*b*) "owner", in relation to a conveyance which is the subject of a hiring agreement or hire-purchase agreement, means the person in possession of the conveyance under that agreement.

EFFECT OF SECTION
    For the effect of this section see above, Chapter VII, paras. [**312**]-[**327**].

PREVIOUS CORRESPONDING OFFENCES
    This section replaces offences against s. 217 of the Road Traffic Act 1960, and the Vessels Protection Act 1967.

TRIAL
    Offences under sub-s. (1) of this section are triable summarily with the consent of the accused: see s. 29 (2), below.

13. Abstracting of electricity

A person who dishonestly uses without due authority, or dishonestly causes to be wasted or diverted, any electricity shall on conviction on indictment be liable to imprisonment for a term not exceeding five years.

EFFECT OF SECTION
    For the effect of this section see above, Chapter VIII, paras. [**328**]-[**332**].

PREVIOUS CORRESPONDING OFFENCES
    This section replaces offences against s. 10 of the Larceny Act 1916 (5 Halsbury's Statutes (2nd ed.) 1018).

TRIAL
    This offence is triable summarily with the consent of the accused: see s. 29 (2), below.

14. Extension to thefts from mails outside England and Wales, and robbery etc. on such a theft

(1) Where a person—

(a) steals or attempts to steal any mail bag or postal packet in the course of transmission as such between places in different jurisdictions in the British postal area, or any of the contents of such a mail bag or postal packet; or

(b) in stealing or with intent to steal any such mail bag or postal packet or any of its contents, commits any robbery, attempted robbery or assault with intent to rob;

then, notwithstanding that he does so outside England and Wales, he shall be guilty of committing or attempting to commit the offence against this Act as if he had done so in England or Wales, and he shall accordingly be liable to be prosecuted, tried and punished in England and Wales without proof that the offence was committed there.

(2) In subsection (1) above the reference to different jurisdictions in the British postal area is to be construed as referring to the several jurisdictions of England and Wales, of Scotland, of Northern Ireland, of the Isle of Man and of the Channel Islands.

(3) For purposes of this section "mail bag" includes any article serving the purpose of a mail bag.

EFFECT OF SECTION
For the effect of this section see above, para. [**496**].

"STEALS"
For the meaning of "steals" see s. 1 (1), above.

Fraud and blackmail

15. Obtaining property by deception

(1) A person who by any deception dishonestly obtains property belonging to another, with the intention of permanently depriving the other of it, shall on conviction on indictment be liable to imprisonment for a term not exceeding ten years.

(2) For purposes of this section a person is to be treated as obtaining property if he obtains ownership, possession or control of it, and "obtain" includes obtaining for another or enabling another to obtain or to retain.

(3) Section 6 above shall apply for purposes of this section, with the necessary adaptation of the reference to appropriating, as it applies for purposes of section 1.

(4) For purposes of this section "deception" means any deception (whether deliberate or reckless) by words or conduct as to fact or as to law, including a deception as to the present intentions of the person using the deception or any other person.

EFFECT OF SECTION
For the effect of this section see above, paras. [170]-[251].

PREVIOUS CORRESPONDING OFFENCES
The principal offence replaced by this section is obtaining by false pretences under s. 32 (1) of the Larceny Act 1916 (5 Halsbury's Statutes (2nd ed.) 1031).

PROPERTY BELONGING TO ANOTHER
See the definitions in ss. 4 (1) and 5 (1), above, which apply for the purposes of this section by virtue of s. 34 (1), below.

TRIAL
The offences under this section are triable summarily with the consent of the accused: see s. 29 (2), below.

16. Obtaining pecuniary advantage by deception

(1) A person who by any deception dishonestly obtains for himself or another any pecuniary advantage shall on conviction on indictment be liable to imprisonment for a term not exceeding five years.

(2) The cases in which a pecuniary advantage within the meaning of this section is to be regarded as obtained for a person are cases where—

(a) any debt or charge for which he makes himself liable or is or may become liable (including one not legally enforceable) is reduced or in whole or in part evaded or deferred; or

(b) he is allowed to borrow by way of overdraft, or to take out any policy of insurance or annuity contract, or obtains an improvement of the terms on which he is allowed to do so; or

(c) he is given the opportunity to earn remuneration or greater remuneration in an office or employment, or to win money by betting.

(3) For purposes of this section "deception" has the same meaning as in section 15 of this Act.

EFFECT OF SECTION
For the effect of this section see above, paras. [252]-[282].

PREVIOUS CORRESPONDING OFFENCES
This offence replaces the offence of obtaining credit by fraud under s. 13 (1) of the Debtors Act 1869 (3 Halsbury's Statutes (3rd ed.) 10).

TRIAL
Offences under this section are triable summarily with the consent of the accused: see s. 29 (2), below.

17. False accounting

(1) Where a person dishonestly, with a view to gain for himself or another or with intent to cause loss to another,—

(a) destroys, defaces, conceals or falsifies any account or any record or document made or required for any accounting purpose; or

(b) in furnishing information for any purpose produces or makes use of any account, or any such record or document as aforesaid, which to his knowledge is or may be misleading, false or deceptive in a material particular;

he shall, on conviction on indictment, be liable to imprisonment for a term not exceeding seven years.

(2) For purposes of this section a person who makes or concurs in making in an account or other document an entry which is or may be misleading, false or deceptive in a material particular, or who omits or concurs in omitting a material particular from an account or other document, is to be treated as falsifying the account or document.

EFFECT OF SECTION
    For the effect of this section see above, paras. [**283**]-[**289**].

PREVIOUS CORRESPONDING OFFENCES
    This section replaces offences under ss. 82 and 83 of the Larceny Act 1861 (5 Halsbury's Statutes (2nd ed.) 741) and the Falsification or Accounts Act 1875 (5 Halsbury's Statutes (2nd ed.) 878).

''GAIN''; ''LOSS''
    For the meaning of "gain" and "loss" see s. 34 (2) (*a*), below.

OFFENCES BY COMPANY OFFICERS
    For offences under this section by company officers see s. 18, below.

TRIAL
    Offences under this section are triable summarily with the consent of the accused: see s. 29 (2), below.

18. Liability of company officers for certain offences by company

(1) Where an offence committed by a body corporate under section 15, 16 or 17 of this Act is proved to have been committed with the consent or connivance of any director, manager, secretary or other similar officer of the body corporate, or any person who was purporting to act in any such capacity, he as well as the body corporate shall be guilty of that offence, and shall be liable to be proceeded against and punished accordingly.

(2) Where the affairs of a body corporate are managed by its members, this section shall apply in relation to the acts and defaults of a member in connection with his functions of management as if he were a director of the body corporate.

EFFECT OF SECTION
    For the effect of this section see above, paras. [**290**]–[**291**].

19. False statements by company directors, etc.

(1) Where an officer of a body corporate or unincorporated association (or person purporting to act as such), with intent to deceive members or creditors of the body corporate or association about its affairs, publishes or concurs in publishing a written statement or account which to his knowledge is or may be misleading, false or deceptive in a material particular, he shall on conviction on indictment be liable to imprisonment for a term not exceeding seven years.

(2) For purposes of this section a person who has entered into a security for the benefit of a body corporate or association is to be treated as a creditor of it.

(3) Where the affairs of a body corporate or association are managed by its members, this section shall apply to any statement which a member publishes or concurs in publishing in connection with his functions of management as if he were an officer of the body corporate or association.

EFFECT OF SECTION
For the effect of this section see above, paras. [**292**]-[**294**].

PREVIOUS CORRESPONDING OFFENCES
This section replaces s. 84 of the Larceny Act 1861.

TRIAL
Offences under this section are triable summarily with the consent of the accused: see s. 29 (2), below.

20. Suppression, etc. of documents

(1) A person who dishonestly, with a view to gain for himself or another or with intent to cause loss to another, destroys, defaces or conceals any valuable security, any will or other testamentary document or any original document of or belonging to, or filed or deposited in, any court of justice or any government department shall on conviction on indictment be liable to imprisonment for a term not exceeding seven years.

(2) A person who dishonestly, with a view to gain for himself or another or with intent to cause loss to another, by any deception procures the execution of a valuable security shall on conviction on indictment be liable to imprisonment for a term not exceeding seven years; and this subsection shall apply in relation to the making, acceptance, indorsement, alteration, cancellation or destruction in whole or in part of a valuable security, and in relation to the signing or sealing of any paper or other material in order that it may be made or converted into, or used or dealt with as, a valuable security, as if that were the execution of a valuable security.

(3) For purposes of this section "deception" has the same meaning as in section 15 of this Act, and "valuable security" means any document creating, transferring, surrendering or releasing any right to, in or over property, or authorising the payment of money or delivery of any property, or evidencing the creation, transfer, surrender or release of any such right, or the payment of money or delivery of any property, or the satisfaction of any obligation.

EFFECT OF SECTION
For the effect of this section see above, para. [**295**].

PREVIOUS CORRESPONDING OFFENCES
This section replaces offences under ss. 27-30 of the Larceny Act 1861.

TRIAL
Offences under this section are triable summarily with the consent of the accused: see s. 29 (2), below.

21. Blackmail

(1) A person is guilty of blackmail if, with a view to gain for himself or another or with intent to cause loss to another, he makes any unwarranted demand

with menaces; and for this purpose a demand with menaces is unwarranted unless the person making it does so in the belief—

> (*a*) that he has reasonable grounds for making the demand; and
>
> (*b*) that the use of the menaces is a proper means of reinforcing the demand.

(2) The nature of the act or omission demanded is immaterial, and it is also immaterial whether the menaces relate to action to be taken by the person making the demand.

(3) A person guilty of blackmail shall on conviction on indictment be liable to imprisonment for a term not exceeding fourteen years.

EFFECT OF SECTION
> For the effect of this section see above, Chapter IX, paras. [**333**]-[**368**].

PREVIOUS CORRESPONDING OFFENCES
> This section replaces offences against ss. 29-31 of the Larceny Act 1916 (5 Halsbury's Statutes (2nd ed.) 1028-1030).

"GAIN"; "LOSS"
> For the meaning of "gain" and "loss", see s. 34 (2) (*a*), below.

TRIAL
> Offences under this section are triable only on indictment: see s. 29 (2), below.

Offences relating to goods stolen, etc.

22. Handling stolen goods

(1) A person handles stolen goods if (otherwise than in the course of the stealing) knowing or believing them to be stolen goods he dishonestly receives the goods, or dishonestly undertakes or assists in their retention, removal, disposal or realisation by or for the benefit of another person, or if he arranges to do so.

(2) A person guilty of handling stolen goods shall on conviction on indictment be liable to imprisonment for a term not exceeding fourteen years.

EFFECT OF SECTION
> For the effect of this section see above, Chapter XII, paras. [**430**]-[**493**].

PREVIOUS CORRESPONDING OFFENCES
> The section replaces offences under s. 97 of the Larceny Act 1861 (5 Halsbury's Statutes (2nd ed.) 743) and s. 33 of the Larceny Act 1916 (5 Halsbury's Statutes (2nd ed.) 1032).

"STOLEN GOODS"
> For the meaning of stolen goods see s. 24, below.

TRIAL
> Offences under this section are triable summarily with the consent of the accused provided the stolen goods are not from an offence committed outside the United Kingdom: see s. 29 (2) below.

23. Advertising rewards for return of goods stolen or lost

Where any public advertisement of a reward for the return of any goods which have been stolen or lost uses any words to the effect that no questions will be asked, or that the person producing the goods will be safe from apprehension or inquiry, or that any money paid for the purchase of the goods or advanced by way of loan on them will be repaid, the person advertising the reward and any person who prints or publishes the advertisement shall on summary conviction be liable to a fine not exceeding one hundred pounds.

PREVIOUS CORRESPONDING OFFENCE
This section replaces offences under s. 102 of the Larceny Act 1861 (5 Halsbury's Statutes (2nd ed.) 744).

STOLEN GOODS
For the meaning of "stolen goods" see s. 24, below.

24. Scope of offences relating to stolen goods

(1) The provisions of this Act relating to goods which have been stolen shall apply whether the stealing occurred in England or Wales or elsewhere, and whether it occurred before or after the commencement of this Act, provided that the stealing (if not an offence under this Act) amounted to an offence where and at the time when the goods were stolen; and references to stolen goods shall be construed accordingly.

(2) For purposes of those provisions reference to stolen goods shall include, in addition to the goods originally stolen and parts of them (whether in their original state or not),—

    (*a*) any other goods which directly or indirectly represent or have at any time represented the stolen goods in the hands of the thief as being the proceeds of any disposal or realisation of the whole or part of the goods stolen or of goods so representing the stolen goods; and

    (*b*) any other goods which directly or indirectly represent or have at any time represented the stolen goods in the hands of a handler of the stolen goods or any part of them as being the proceeds of any disposal or realisation of the whole or part of the stolen goods handled by him or of goods so representing them.

(3) But no goods shall be regarded as having continued to be stolen goods after they have been restored to the person from whom they were stolen or to other lawful possession or custody, or after that person and any other person claiming through him have otherwise ceased as regards those goods to have any right to restitution in respect of the theft.

(4) For purposes of the provisions of this Act relating to goods which have been stolen (including subsections (1) to (3) above) goods obtained in England or Wales or elsewhere either by blackmail or in the circumstances described in section 15 (1) of this Act shall be regarded as stolen; and "steal", "theft" and "thief" shall be construed accordingly.

EFFECT OF SECTION
For the effect of this section see above, paras. [**435**]-[**439**].

"GOODS"
For the meaning of "goods" see s. 34 (2) (*b*), below.

PROVISIONS OF THIS ACT RELATING TO GOODS WHICH HAVE BEEN STOLEN
I.e. ss. 22-23, 26-28 and 32.

Possession of housebreaking implements, etc.

25. Going equipped for stealing, etc.

(1) A person shall be guilty of an offence if, when not at his place of abode, he has with him any article for use in the course of or in connection with any burglary, theft or cheat.

(2) A person guilty of an offence under this section shall on conviction on indictment be liable to imprisonment for a term not exceeding three years.

(3) Where a person is charged with an offence under this section, proof that he had with him any article made or adapted for use in committing a burglary, theft or cheat shall be evidence that he had it with him for such use.

(4) Any person may arrest without warrant anyone who is, or whom he, with reasonable cause, suspects to be, committing an offence under this section.

(5) For purposes of this section an offence under section 12 (1) of this Act of taking a conveyance shall be treated as theft, and "cheat" means an offence under section 15 of this Act.

EFFECT OF SECTION
>For the effect of this section see above, Chapter XI, paras. [**422**]-[**429**].

PREVIOUS CORRESPONDING OFFENCES
>The section replaces offences against s. 28 of the Larceny Act 1916 (5 Halsbury's Statutes (2nd ed.) 1028).

"BURGLARY"
>For the meaning of "burglary" see ss. 9, 10, above.

"THEFT"
>For the meaning of theft see s. 1, above.

TRIAL
>Offences under this section are triable summarily with the consent of the accused. see s. 29 (2), below.

Enforcement and procedure

26. Search for stolen goods

(1) If it is made to appear by information on oath before a justice of the peace that there is reasonable cause to believe that any person has in his custody or possession or on his premises any stolen goods, the justice may grant a warrant to search for and seize the same; but no warrant to search for stolen goods shall be addressed to a person other than a constable except under the authority of an enactment expressly so providing.

(2) An officer of police not below the rank of superintendent may give a constable written authority to search any premises for stolen goods—

  (a) if the person in occupation of the premises has been convicted within the preceding five years of handling stolen goods or of any offence involving dishonesty and punishable with imprisonment; or

  (b) if a person who has been convicted within the preceding five years of handling stolen goods has within the preceding twelve months been in occupation of the premises.

(3) Where under this section a person is authorised to search premises for stolen goods, he may enter and search the premises accordingly, and may seize any goods he believes to be stolen goods.

(4) The Police (Property) Act 1897 (which makes provision for the disposal of property in the possession of the police) shall apply to property which has come into the possession of the police under this section as it applies to property which has come into the possession of the police in the circumstances mentioned in that Act.

(5) This section is to be construed in accordance with section 24 of this Act; and in subsection (2) above the references to handling stolen goods shall include any corresponding offence committed before the commencement of this Act.

EFFECT OF SECTION
For the effect of this section see above, paras. [**494**]-[**495**].

POLICE PROPERTY ACT 1897
See 25 Halsbury's Statutes (3rd ed.) 280.

27. Evidence and procedure on charge of theft or handling stolen goods

(1) Any number of persons may be charged in one indictment, with reference to the same theft, with having at different times or at the same time handled all or any of the stolen goods, and the persons so charged may be tried together.

(2) On the trial of two or more persons indicted for jointly handling any stolen goods the jury may find any of the accused guilty if the jury are satisfied that he handled all or any of the stolen goods, whether or not he did so jointly with the other accused or any of them.

(3) Where a person is being proceeded against for handling stolen goods (but not for any offence other than handling stolen goods), then at any stage of the proceedings, if evidence has been given of his having or arranging to have in his possession the goods the subject of the charge, or of his undertaking or assisting in, or arranging to undertake or assist in, their retention, removal, disposal or realisation, the following evidence shall be admissible for the purpose of proving that he knew or believed the goods to be stolen goods:—

(a) evidence that he has had in his possession, or has undertaken or assisted in the retention, removal, disposal or realisation of, stolen goods from any theft taking place not earlier than twelve months before the offence charged; and

(b) (provided that seven days' notice in writing has been given to him of the intention to prove the conviction) evidence that he has within the five years preceding the date of the offence charged been convicted of theft or of handling stolen goods.

(4) In any proceedings for the theft of anything in the course of transmission (whether by post or otherwise), or for handling stolen goods from such a theft, a statutory declaration made by any person that he despatched or received or failed to receive any goods or postal packet, or that any goods or postal packet when despatched or received by him were in a particular state or condition,

shall be admissible as evidence of the facts stated in the declaration, subject to the following conditions:—

    (*a*) a statutory declaration shall only be admissible where and to the extent to which oral evidence to the like effect would have been admissible in the proceedings; and

    (*b*) a statutory declaration shall only be admissible if at least seven days before the hearing or trial a copy of it has been given to the person charged, and he has not, at least three days before the hearing or trial or within such further time as the court may in special circumstances allow, given the prosecutor written notice requiring the attendance at the hearing or trial of the person making the declaration.

(5) This section is to be construed in accordance with section 24 of this Act; and in subsection (3) (*b*) above the references to handling stolen goods shall include any corresponding offence committed before the commencement of this Act.

EFFECT OF SECTION
    For the effect of this section see above, paras. [**490**]–[**493**].

TRANSITIONAL PROVISIONS
    This section applies in relation to offences committed before the commencement of the Act: see s. 35 (2), below.

28. Orders for restitution

(1) Where goods have been stolen, and a person is convicted of any offence with reference to the theft (whether or not the stealing is the gist of his offence), the court by or before which the offender is convicted may on the conviction exercise any of the following powers:—

    (*a*) the court may order anyone having possession or control of the goods to restore them to any person entitled to recover them from him; or

    (*b*) on the application of a person entitled to recover from the person convicted any other goods directly or indirectly representing the first-mentioned goods (as being the proceeds of any disposal or realisation of the whole or part of them or of goods so representing them), the court may order those other goods to be delivered or transferred to the applicant; or

    (*c*) on the application of a person who, if the first-mentioned goods were in the possession of the person convicted, would be entitled to recover them from him, the court may order that a sum not exceeding the value of those goods shall be paid to the applicant out of any money of the person convicted which was taken out of his possession on his apprehension.

(2) Where under subsection (1) above the court has power on a person's conviction to make an order against him both under paragraph (*b*) and under paragraph (*c*) with reference to the stealing of the same goods, the court may

make orders under both paragraphs provided that the applicant for the orders does not thereby recover more than the value of those goods.

(3) Where under subsection (1) above the court on a person's conviction makes an order under paragraph (*a*) for the restoration of any goods, and it appears to the court that the person convicted has sold the goods to a person acting in good faith, or has borrowed money on the security of them from a person so acting, then on the application of the purchaser or lender the court may order that there shall be paid to the applicant, out of any money of the person convicted which was taken out of his possession on his apprehension, a sum not exceeding the amount paid for the purchase by the applicant or, as the case may be, the amount owed to the applicant in respect of the loan.

(4) The court shall not exercise the powers conferred by this section unless in the opinion of the court the relevant facts sufficiently appear from evidence given at the trial or the available documents, together with admissions made by or on behalf of any person in connection with any proposed exercise of the powers; and for this purpose "the available documents" means any written statements or admissions which were made for use, and would have been admissible, as evidence at the trial, the depositions taken at any committal proceedings and any written statements or admissions used as evidence in those proceedings.

(5) Any order under this section shall be treated as an order for the restitution of property within the meaning of sections 30 and 42 of the Criminal Appeal Act 1968 (which relate to the effect on such orders of appeals).

(6) References in this section to stealing are to be construed in accordance with section 24 (1) and (4) of this Act.

EFFECT OF SECTION
For the effect of this section see above, paras. [**502**]-[**531**].

TRANSITIONAL PROVISIONS
This section applies in relation to offences committed before the commencement of the Act: see s. 35 (2), below.

29. Jurisdiction of quarter sessions, and summary trial

(1) In Schedule 1 to the Criminal Law Act 1967 there shall cease to have effect paragraph 13 (*a*) and (*b*) of List B (which exclude from the jurisdiction of quarter sessions the theft etc. of court records and documents of title to land).

(2) In Schedule 1 to the Magistrates' Courts Act 1952 (which lists the indictable offences by adults which may be tried summarily with the consent of the accused) for paragraph 11 there shall be substituted:—

"11. Any indictable offence under the Theft Act 1968 except—

(*a*) robbery, aggravated burglary, blackmail and assault with intent to rob; and

(*b*) burglary comprising the commission of, or an intention to commit, an offence which is not included in this Schedule; and

(c) burglary in a dwelling if entry to the dwelling or the part of it in which the burglary was committed, or to any building or part of a building containing the dwelling, was obtained by force or deception or by the use of any tool, key or appliance, or if any person in the dwelling was subjected to violence or the threat of violence; and

(d) handling stolen goods from an offence not committed in the United Kingdom."

EFFECT OF SECTION
For the effect of this section see above, paras. [**498**]-[**501**].

CRIMINAL LAW ACT 1967, SCHEDULE 1
This Schedule was repealed by the Courts Act 1971, s. 56 and Sched. 2, Part IV.

MAGISTRATES' COURTS ACT 1952, SCHEDULE 1
21 Halsbury's Statutes (3rd ed.) 292.

General and consequential provisions

30. Husband and wife

(1) This Act shall apply in relation to the parties to a marriage, and to property belonging to the wife or husband whether or not by reason of an interest derived from the marriage, as it would apply if they were not married and any such interest subsisted independently of the marriage.

(2) Subject to subsection (4) below, a person shall have the same right to bring proceedings against that person's wife or husband for any offence (whether under this Act or otherwise) as if they were not married, and a person bringing any such proceedings shall be competent to give evidence for the prosecution at every stage of the proceedings.

(3) Where a person is charged in proceedings not brought by that person's wife or husband with having committed any offence with reference to that person's wife or husband or to property belonging to the wife or husband, the wife or husband shall be competent to give evidence at every stage of the proceedings, whether for the defence or for the prosecution, and whether the accused is charged solely or jointly with any other person:
Provided that—

(a) the wife or husband (unless compellable at common law) shall not be compellable either to give evidence or, in giving evidence, to disclose any communication made to her or him during the marriage by the accused; and

(b) her or his failure to give evidence shall not be made the subject of any comment by the prosecution.

(4) Proceedings shall not be instituted against a person for any offence of stealing or doing unlawful damage to property which at the time of the offence belongs to that person's wife or husband, or for any attempt, incitement or conspiracy to commit such an offence, unless the proceedings are instituted by or with the consent of the Director of Public Prosecutions:

Provided that—

(a) this subsection shall not apply to proceedings against a person for an offence—

    (i) if that person is charged with committing the offence jointly with the wife or husband; or

    (ii) if by virtue of any judicial decree or order (wherever made) that person and the wife or husband are at the time of the offence under no obligation to cohabit; and

(b) this subsection shall not prevent the arrest, or the issue of a warrant for the arrest, of a person for an offence, or the remand in custody or on bail of a person charged with an offence, where the arrest (if without a warrant) is made, or the warrant of arrest issues on an information laid, by a person other than the wife or husband.

EFFECT OF SECTION
For the effect of this section see above, paras. [**532**]-[**544**].

31. Effect on civil proceedings and rights

(1) A person shall not be excused, by reason that to do so may incriminate that person or the wife or husband of that person of an offence under this Act—

(a) from answering any question put to that person in proceedings for the recovery or administration of any property, for the execution of any trust or for an account of any property or dealings with property; or

(b) from complying with any order made in any such proceedings;

but no statement or admission made by a person in answering a question put or complying with an Order made as aforesaid shall, in proceedings for an offence under this Act, be admissible in evidence against that person or (unless they married after the making of the statement or admission) against the wife or husband of that person.

(2) Notwithstanding any enactment to the contrary, where property has been stolen or obtained by fraud or other wrongful means, the title to that or any other property shall not be affected by reason only of the conviction of the offender.

32. Effect on existing law and construction of references to offences

(1) The following offences are hereby abolished for all purposes not relating to offences committed before the commencement of this Act, that is to say—

(a) any offence at common law of larceny, robbery, burglary, receiving stolen property, obtaining property by threats, extortion by colour of office or franchise, false accounting by public officers, concealment of treasure trove and, except as regards offences relating to the public revenue, cheating; and

(b) any offence under an enactment mentioned in Part I of Schedule 3 to this Act, to the extent to which the offence depends on any section or part of a section included in column 3 of that Schedule;

but so that the provisions in Schedule 1 to this Act (which preserve with modifications certain offences under the Larceny Act 1861 of taking or killing deer and taking or destroying fish) shall have effect as there set out.

(2) Except as regards offences committed before the commencement of this Act, and except in so far as the context otherwise requires,—

(*a*) references in any enactment passed before this Act to an offence abolished by this Act shall, subject to any express amendment or repeal made by this Act, have effect as references to the corresponding offence under this Act, and in any such enactment the expression "receive" (when it relates to an offence of receiving) shall mean handle, and "receiver" shall be construed accordingly; and

(*b*) without prejudice to paragraph (*a*) above, references in any enactment, whenever passed, to theft or stealing (including references to stolen goods), and references to robbery, blackmail, burglary, aggravated burglary or handling stolen goods, shall be construed in accordance with the provisions of this Act, including those of section 24.

33. Miscellaneous and consequential amendments and repeal

(1) The Post Office Act 1953 shall have effect subject to the amendments provided for by Part I of Schedule 2 to this Act and (except in so far as the contrary intention appears) those amendments shall have effect throughout the British postal area.

(2) The enactments mentioned in Parts II and III of Schedule 2 to this Act shall have effect subject to the amendments there provided for, and (subject to subsection (4) below) the amendments made by Part II to enactments extending beyond England and Wales shall have the like extent as the enactment amended.

(3) The enactments mentioned in Schedule 3 to this Act (which include in Part II certain enactments related to the subject matter of this Act but already obsolete or redundant apart from this Act) are hereby repealed to the extent specified in column 3 of that Schedule; and, notwithstanding that the foregoing sections of this Act do not extend to Scotland, where any enactment expressed to be repealed by Schedule 3 does so extend, the Schedule shall have effect to repeal it in its application to Scotland except in so far as the repeal is expressed not to extend to Scotland.

(4) No amendment or repeal made by this Act in Schedule 1 to the Extradition Act 1870 or in the Schedule to the Extradition Act 1873 shall affect the operation of that Schedule by reference to the law of a British possession; but the repeal made in Schedule 1 to the Extradition Act 1870 shall extend throughout the United Kingdom.

POST OFFICE ACT 1953
    25 Halsbury's Statutes (3rd ed.) 413.

EXTRADITION ACT 1870, SCHEDULE 1
    13 Halsbury's Statutes (3rd ed.) 266.

EXTRADITION ACT 1873, SCHEDULE
13 Halsbury's Statutes (3rd ed.) 272.

Supplementary

34. Interpretation

(1) Sections 4 (1) and 5 (1) of this Act shall apply generally for purposes of this Act as they apply for purposes of section 1.

(2) For purposes of this Act—

    (*a*) "gain" and "loss" are to be construed as extending only to gain or loss in money or other property, but as extending to any such gain or loss whether temporary or permanent; and—

        (i) "gain" includes a gain by keeping what one has, as well as a gain by getting what one has not; and

        (ii) "loss" includes a loss by not getting what one might get, as well as a loss by parting with what one has;

    (*b*) "goods", except in so far as the context otherwise requires, includes money and every other description of property except land, and includes things severed from the land by stealing.

35. Commencement and transitional provisions

(1) This Act shall come into force on the 1st January 1969 and, save as otherwise provided by this Act, shall have effect only in relation to offences wholly or partly committed on or after that date.

(2) Sections 27 and 28 of this Act shall apply in relation to proceedings for an offence committed before the commencement of this Act as they would apply in relation to proceedings for a corresponding offence under this Act, and shall so apply in place of any corresponding enactment repealed by this Act.

(3) Subject to subsection (2) above, no repeal or amendment by this Act of any enactment relating to procedure or evidence, or to the jurisdiction or powers of any court, or to the effect of a conviction, shall affect the operation of the enactment in relation to offences committed before the commencement of this Act or to proceedings for any such offence.

36. Short title, and general provisions as to Scotland and Northern Ireland

(1) This Act may be cited as the Theft Act 1968.

(2) The restrictions imposed by the Government of Ireland Act 1920 on the powers of the Parliament of Northern Ireland shall not be treated as precluding that Parliament from enacting in relation to Northern Ireland, by any Act passed for purposes similar to this Act, a provision corresponding to any provision of this Act or, in connection therewith, from repealing or amending in relation to Northern Ireland any provision of Part I of Schedule 2 to this Act.

(3) This Act does not extend to Scotland or, apart from subsection (2) above, to Northern Ireland, except as regards any amendment or repeal which in accordance with section 33 above is to extend to Scotland or Northern Ireland.

GOVERNMENT OF IRELAND ACT 1920
23 Halsbury's Statutes (3rd ed.) 843.

SCHEDULES

Section 32

SCHEDULE 1

OFFENCES OF TAKING, ETC. DEER OR FISH

Taking or killing deer

1.—(1) A person who unlawfully takes or kills, or attempts to take or kill, any deer in inclosed land where deer are usually kept shall on summary conviction be liable to a fine not exceeding fifty pounds, or, for an offence committed after a previous conviction of an offence under this paragraph, to imprisonment for a term not exceeding three months or to a fine not exceeding one hundred pounds or to both.

(2) Any person may arrest without warrant anyone who is, or whom he, with reasonable cause, suspects to be, committing an offence under this paragraph.

Taking or destroying fish

2.—(1) Subject to subparagraph (2) below, a person who unlawfully takes or destroys, or attempts to take or destroy, any fish in water which is private property or in which there is any private right of fishery shall on summary conviction be liable to a fine not exceeding fifty pounds or, for an offence committed after a previous conviction of an offence under this subparagraph, to imprisonment for a term not exceeding three months or to a fine not exceeding one hundred pounds or to both.

(2) Subparagraph (1) above shall not apply to taking or destroying fish by angling in the daytime (that is to say, in the period beginning one hour before sunrise and ending one hour after sunset); but a person who by angling in the daytime unlawfully takes or destroys, or attempts to take or destroy, any fish in water which is private property or in which there is any private right of fishery shall on summary conviction be liable to a fine not exceeding twenty pounds.

(3) The court by which a person is convicted of an offence under this paragraph may order the forfeiture of anything which, at the time of the offence, he had with him for use for taking or destroying fish.

(4) Any person may arrest without warrant anyone who is, or whom he, with reasonable cause, suspects to be, committing an offence under subparagraph (1) above, and may seize from any person who is, or whom he, with reasonable cause, suspects to be, committing any offence under this paragraph anything which on that person's conviction of the offence would be liable to be forfeited under subparagraph (3) above.

PREVIOUS CORRESPONDING OFFENCES
This Schedule reproduces in a modified form offences under ss. 12 and 13 of the Larceny Act 1861 (5 Halsbury's Statutes (2nd ed.) 729, 730).

SCHEDULE 2

Miscellaneous and Consequential Amendments

Part I

Amendments of Post Office Act 1953

1. The Post Office Act 1953 shall have effect subject to the amendments provided for by this Part of this Schedule (and, except in so far as the contrary intention appears, those amendments have effect throughout the British postal area).

2. Sections 22 and 23 shall be amended by substituting for the word "felony" in section 22 (1) and section 23 (2) the words "a misdemeanour", and by omitting the words "of this Act and" in section 23 (1).

3. In section 52, as it applies outside England and Wales, for the words from "be guilty" onwards there shall be substituted the words "be guilty of a misdemeanour and be liable to imprisonment for a term not exceeding ten years".

4. In section 53 for the words from "be guilty" onwards there shall be substituted the words "be guilty of a misdemeanour and be liable to imprisonment for a term not exceeding five years".

5. In section 54, as it applies outside England and Wales,—

   (a) there shall be omitted the words "taking, embezzling", and the words "taken, embezzled", where first occurring;

   (b) for the words "a felony" there shall be substituted the words "an offence" and the word "feloniously" shall be omitted;

   (c) for the words from "be guilty" to "secreted it" there shall be substituted the words "be guilty of a misdemeanour and be liable to imprisonment for a term not exceeding fourteen years".

6. In sections 55 and 58 (1), after the word "imprisonment", there shall in each case be inserted the words "for a term not exceeding two years".

7. In section 57—

   (a) there shall be omitted the words "steals, or for any purpose whatever embezzles," and the words from "or if" onwards;

   (b) for the word "felony" there shall be substituted the words "a misdemeanour".

8. After section 65 there shall be inserted as a new section 65A—

"65A. Fraudulent use of public telephone or telex system

If any person dishonestly uses a public telephone or telex system with intent to avoid payment (including any such system provided, under licence, otherwise than by the Postmaster General), he shall be guilty of a misdemeanour and be liable on summary conviction to imprisonment for a term not exceeding three months or to a fine not exceeding one hundred pounds or to both, or on conviction on indictment to imprisonment for a term not exceeding two years."

9. Section 69 (2) shall be omitted.

10. For section 70 there shall be substituted the following section—

"70. Prosecution of certain offences in any jurisdiction of British postal area

(1) Where a person—

(*a*) steals or attempts to steal any mail bag or postal packet in the course of transmission as such between places in different jurisdictions in the British postal area, or any of the contents of such a mail bag or postal packet; or

(*b*) in stealing or with intent to steal any such mail bag or postal packet or any of its contents, commits any robbery, attempted robbery or assault with intent to rob;

then, in whichever of those jurisdictions he does so, he shall by virtue of this section be guilty in each of the jurisdictions in which this subsection has effect of committing or attempting to commit the offence against section 52 of this Act, or the offence referred to in paragraph (*b*) of this subsection, as the case may be, as if he had done so in that jurisdiction, and he shall accordingly be liable to be prosecuted, tried and punished in that jurisdiction without proof that the offence was committed there.

(2) In subsection (1) above the reference to different jurisdictions in the British postal area is to be construed as referring to the several jurisdictions of England and Wales, of Scotland, of Northern Ireland, of the Isle of Man, and of the Channel Islands; and that subsection shall have effect in each of those jurisdictions except England and Wales."

11. In section 72 there shall be added as a new subsection (3)—

"(3) In any proceedings in England or Wales for an offence under section 53, 55, 56, 57 or 58 of this Act, section 27 (4) of the Theft Act 1968 shall apply as it is expressed to apply to proceedings for the theft of anything in the course of transmission by post; and in the case of proceedings under section 53 of this Act a statutory declaration made by any person that a vessel, vehicle or aircraft was at any time employed by or under the Post Office for the transmission of postal packets under contract shall be admissible as evidence of the facts stated in the declaration subject to the same conditions as under section 27 (4) (*a*) and (*b*) of the Theft Act 1968 apply to declarations admissible under section 27 (4)"."

12. In section 87 (1), the definition of "valuable security" shall be omitted but, except in relation to England and Wales, there shall be substituted :—

" 'valuable security' means any document creating, transferring, surrendering or releasing any right to, in or over property, or authorising the payment of money or delivery of any property, or evidencing the creation, transfer, surrender or release of any such right, or the payment of money or delivery of any property, or the satisfaction of any obligation."

PART II

Other amendments extending beyond England and Wales

Act amended	Amendment
The Extradition Act 1873 (36 & 37 Vict. c. 60)	In the Schedule (additional list of extradition crimes) for the words "the Larceny Act 1861" there shall be substituted the words "the Theft Act 1968".
The Public Stores Act 1875 (38 & 39 Vict. c. 25)	For section 12 (incorporation of **parts** of Larceny Act 1861) there shall be substituted:— "(1) Any person may arrest without warrant anyone who is, or whom he, with reasonable cause,

Schedule 2

suspects to be, in the act of committing or attempting to commit an offence against section 5 or 8 of this Act.

(2) If it is made to appear by information on oath before a justice of the peace that there is reasonable cause to believe that any person has in his custody or possession or on his premises any stores in respect of which an offence against section 5 of this Act has been committed, the justice may issue a warrant to a constable to search for and seize the stores as in the case of stolen goods, and the Police (Property) Act 1897 shall apply as if this subsection were among the enactments mentioned in section 1 (1) of that Act."

The Army Act 1955 (3 & 4 Eliz. 2. c. 18)

For section 44 (1) (b) there shall be substituted—
"(b) handles any stolen goods, where the property stolen was public or service property, or".

For section 45 (b) there shall be substituted—
"(b) handles any stolen goods, where the property stolen belonged to a person subject to military law, or".

In section 138 (1) for the words from "receiving" to "stolen" there shall be substituted the words "handling it".

In section 225 (1) after the definition of "Governor" there shall be inserted—
" 'handles' has the same meaning as in the Theft Act 1968";
and for the definition of "steals" there shall be substituted—
" 'steals' has the same meaning as in the Theft Act 1968, and references to 'stolen goods' shall be construed as if contained in that Act".

The Air Force Act 1955 (3 & 4 Eliz. 2. c. 19)

The same amendments shall be made in sections 44, 45, 138 and 223 as are above directed to be made in the corresponding sections of the Army Act 1955, except that in the amendment to section 45 (b) "air-force law" shall be substituted for "military law".

The Naval Discipline Act 1957 (5 & 6 Eliz. 2. c. 53)

For section 29 (b) there shall be substituted—
"(b) handles any stolen goods, where the property stolen was public or service property, or".

In section 76 (1) for the words from "receiving" to "embezzling" there shall be substituted the word "handling".

In section 135 (1) the same amendments shall be made as are above directed to be made in section 225 (1) of the Army Act 1955.

The Army and Air Force Act 1961 (9 & 10 Eliz. 2. c. 52)

Section 21 shall be omitted.

Act amended	*Amendment*
The Road Traffic Act 1962 (10 & 11 Eliz. 2. c. 59)	In Part II of Schedule 1 (offences involving discretionary disqualification for a driving licence), in paragraph 24 there shall be substituted for the words in the first column the words "An offence, or attempt to commit an offence, in respect of a motor vehicle under section 12 of the Theft Act 1968 or, in Scotland, section 217 (1) of the principal Act (taking, etc., without authority)", and in the second column after the words "paragraph (*a*)" there shall be inserted the words "(that is, of the said section 217 (1))"; and for paragraph 26 there shall be substituted in the first column— "26. Stealing or attempting to steal a motor vehicle.
The Road Traffic Act 1962 (10 & 11 Eliz. 2 c. 59)—*cont.*	26A. An offence under section 25 of the Theft Act 1968 committed with reference to the theft or taking of motor vehicles."

PART III

Amendments limited to England and Wales

The Gaming Act 1845 (8 & 9 Vict. c. 109)	In section 17 (punishment for cheating at play etc.) for the words "be deemed guilty of obtaining such money or valuable thing from such other person by a false pretence" and the following words there shall be substituted the words— "(*a*) on conviction on indictment be liable to imprisonment for a term not exceeding two years; or (*b*) on summary conviction be liable to imprisonment for a term not exceeding six months or to a fine not exceeding two hundred pounds or to both".
The Pawnbrokers Act 1872 (35 & 36 Vict. c. 93)	In section 38 (cesser of pawnbroker's licence on conviction of certain offences) for the words "receiving stolen goods knowing them to be stolen" there shall be substituted the words "handling stolen goods".
The Bankruptcy Act 1914 (4 & 5 Geo. 5. c. 59)	In section 166 (admissions on compulsory examination etc. not to be admissible as evidence in proceedings for certain offences) for the words following "against that person" there shall be substituted the words "or (unless they married after the making of the statement or admission) against the wife or husband of that person in any proceeding in respect of an offence under the Theft Act 1968".
The House to House Collections Act 1939 (2 & 3 Geo. 6. c. 44)	In the Schedule (offences for which a conviction is a ground for refusing or revoking a licence under the Act to promote a collection for charity) for the entry relating to the Larceny Act 1916 there shall be substituted:— "Robbery, burglary and blackmail".

Schedule 3

Act amended	*Amendment*
The Magistrates' Courts Act 1952 (15 & 16 Geo. 6. & 1 Eliz. 2. c. 55)	In Schedule 1 for paragraph 8 there shall be substituted— "8. Offences under sections 53 and 55 to 58 of the Post Office Act 1953".
The Visiting Forces Act 1952 (15 & 16 Geo. 6. & 1 Eliz. 2. c. 67)	In the Schedule there shall be inserted in paragraph 1 (*a*) after the word "buggery" the word "robbery", and in paragraph 3 there shall be added at the end— "(*g*) the Theft Act 1968, except section 8 (robbery)".
The Finance Act 1965 (1965 c. 25)	In Schedule 10, in the Table in paragraph 1, for the words "Sections 500 to 505" there shall be substituted the words "Sections 500 to 504".
The Finance Act 1966 (1966 c. 18)	In Schedule 6, in paragraph 13, for the words "Sections 500 to 505" there shall be substituted the words "Sections 500 to 504", and the words from "together with" to "the said section 505" shall be omitted.
The Criminal Law Act 1967 (1967 c. 58)	In Schedule 1, for paragraph 2 in List A Division I (whereby certain offences replaced by this Act are, with others not so replaced, made triable by all courts of quarter sessions) there shall be substituted— "2. Offences against sections 53 and 55 to 58 of the Post Office Act 1953".
The Firearms Act 1968 (1968 c. 27)	Schedule 1 (offences in connection with which possession of a firearm is an offence under section 17 (2)) shall be amended, except in relation to a person's apprehension for an offence committed before the commencement of this Act, by substituting for paragraph 4— "4. Theft, burglary, blackmail and any offence under section 12 (1) (taking of motor vehicle or other conveyance without owner's consent) of the Theft Act 1968": by omitting paragraph 7: and by substituting in paragraph 8 for the words "paragraphs 1 to 7" the words "paragraphs 1 to 6".

Section 33 (3)

SCHEDULE 3

REPEALS

PART I

PENAL ENACTMENTS SUPERSEDED BY THIS ACT

Session and Chapter	Short Title	Extent of Repeal
3 Edw. 1.	The Statute of Westminster the First	Chapters 26 and 31.
15 Geo. 2 c. 33	The Starr and Bent Act 1741	The whole Act.
22 Geo. 2 c. 27	The Frauds by Workmen Act 1748	The whole Act.

Session and Chapter	Short Title	Extent of Repeal
17 Geo. 3 c. 11	The Worsted Act 1776	In section 12 the words from "or shall conceal" to "other purposes".
17 Geo. 3 c. 56	The Frauds by Workmen Act 1777	The whole Act.
50 Geo. 3 c. 59	The Embezzlement by Collectors Act 1810	The whole Act, so far as unrepealed.
55 Geo. 3 c. 50	The Gaol Fees Abolition Act 1815	The whole Act.
5 Geo. 4 c. 83	The Vagrancy Act 1824	In section 4 the words from "having in his or her custody" to "outbuilding, or," together with the words "and every such picklock key, crow, jack, bit, and other implement."
7 Geo. 4 c. 16	The Chelsea and Kilmainham Hospitals Act 1826	Section 25. Section 34 from "and, if any pensioner" onwards, except the words from "such mark, stamp or brand" to "commissioners", where next occurring. Section 38.
2 & 3 Vict. c. 47	The Metropolitan Police Act 1839	Sections 26, 27, 28, 30 and 31.
2 & 3 Vict. c. 71	The Metropolitan Police Courts Act 1839	Section 26.
3 & 4 Vict. c. 50	The Canals (Offences) Act 1840	Sections 7 and 8.
3 & 4 Vict. c. 84	The Metropolitan Police Courts Act 1840	Section 11.
6 & 7 Vict. c. 40	The Hosiery Act 1843	The whole Act, except sections 18 to 20.
10 & 11 Vict. c. 16	The Commissioners Clauses Act 1847	In section 67 the words "exact or".
24 & 25 Vict. c. 96	The Larceny Act 1861	The whole Act.
24 & 25 Vict. c. 98	The Forgery Act 1861	Section 3.
26 & 27 Vict. c. 103	The Misappropriation by Servants Act 1863	The whole Act.
28 & 29 Vict. c. 124	The Admiralty Powers, &c. Act 1865	Sections 6 to 9, together with the words "of all offences specified in this Act, and" in section 5.
32 & 33 Vict. c. 62	The Debtors Act 1869	In section 13, paragraph (1).
33 & 34 Vict. c. 58	The Forgery Act 1870	The whole Act, so far as unrepealed.

Schedule 3

Session and Chapter	Short Title	Extent of Repeal
34 & 35 Vict. c. 41	The Gas Works Clauses Act 1871	In section 38, as incorporated in the Electric Lighting Act 1882, the words "or fraudulently abstracts, consumes or uses gas of the undertakers", the words "or for abstracting, consuming or using gas of undertakers" and the words "abstraction or consumption".
37 & 38 Vict. c. 36	The False Personation Act 1874	The whole Act.
38 & 39 Vict. c. 24	The Falsification of Accounts Act 1875	The whole Act.
38 & 39 Vict. c. 89	The Public Works Loans Act 1875	Section 44.
47 & 48 Vict. c. 55	The Pensions and Yeomanry Pay Act 1884	Section 3.
50 & 51 Vict. c. 55	The Sheriffs Act 1887	In section 29, subsection (2) (b) and in subsection (6) the words from "or demands" to "office".
50 & 51 Vict. c. 71	The Coroners Act 1887	In section 8 (2) the words "of extortion or".
54 & 55 Vict. c. 36	The Consular Salaries and Fees Act 1891	Section 2 (3).
57 & 58 Vict. c. 60	The Merchant Shipping Act 1894	In section 154 paragraph (d), and in paragraph (e) the words "or representation" and the words "or made." In section 180 paragraph (d), and in paragraph (e) the words "or representation" and the words "or made." In section 197 (8) paragraph (d). Section 248. Section 388 (5) from "and if" onwards. In section 724 (4) the words "demands or".
61 & 62 Vict. c. 57	The Elementary School Teachers (Superannuation) Act 1898	Section 10.
62 & 63 Vict. c. 19	The Electric Lighting (Clauses) Act 1899	In the Schedule, in section 38 of the Gasworks Clauses Act 1871 as set out in the Appendix, the words "or fraudulently abstracts, consumes or uses gas of the undertakers", the words "or for abstracting, consuming or using gas of

Session and Chapter	Short Title	Extent of Repeal
62 & 63 Vict. c. 19—*cont.*	The Electric Lighting (Clauses) Act 1899—*cont.*	undertakers" and the words "abstraction or consumption" (these repeals having effect for the purposes of the Schedule as incorporated with the Electricity Act 1947 or any other enactment).
6 Edw. 7 c. 48	The Merchant Shipping Act 1906	Section 28 (10) from "and if" onwards.
4 & 5 Geo. 5 c. 59.	The Bankruptcy Act 1914	In section 154 (1), paragraphs (13) and (14). In section 156, paragraph (*a*). Section 160.
5 & 6 Geo. 5 c. 83	The Naval and Military War Pensions, etc. Act 1915	Section 5.
6 & 7 Geo. 5 c. 50	The Larceny Act 1916	The whole Act (but the repeal of section 39(2) and (3) shall not extend to Scotland).
9 & 10 Geo. 5 c. 75	The Ferries (Acquisition by Local Authorities) Act 1919	Section 4 from "If any" onwards.
10 & 11 Geo. 5 c. 36	The Pensions (Increase) Act 1920	Section 5.
11 & 12 Geo. 5 c. 39	The Admiralty Pensions Act 1921	Section 1 (2).
11 & 12 Geo. 5 c. 49	The War Pensions Act 1921	Section 7 (2).
19 & 20 Geo. 5 c. 29	The Government Annuities Act 1929	Section 34. Section 61 (2). Section 64.
23 & 24 Geo. 5 c. 51	The Local Government Act 1933	In section 123, in subsection (2), the words "exact or" and, in subsection (3), the words "any of".
2 & 3 Geo. 6 c. 82	The Personal Injuries (Emergency Provisions) Act 1939	Section 6.
2 & 3 Geo. 6 c. 83	The Pensions (Navy, Army, Air Force and Mercantile Marine) Act 1939	Section 8.
5 & 6 Geo. 6 c. 28	The War Damage (Amendment) Act 1942	Section 3.
6 & 7 Geo. 6 c. 21	The War Damage Act 1943	Section 112
7 & 8 Geo. 6 c. 21	The Pensions (Increase) Act 1944	Sections 6 and 7.

Session and Chapter	Short Title	Extent of Repeal
8 & 9 Geo. 6 c. 42	The Water Act 1945	In Schedule 3, section 65 (2): in section 66 (1) the words "or fraudulently abstracts or uses water of the undertakers": in section 66 (2) the words "or for enabling him fraudulently to abstract or use water" and the words from "or as" onwards.
10 & 11 Geo. 6 c. 41	The Fire Services Act 1947	In section 26 (4) the words from "by means of" to "infirmity or", where next occurring, and the words "or by any other fraudulent conduct".
11 & 12 Geo. 6 c. 24	The Police Pensions Act 1948	In section 7 (2) the words from "by means of" to "infirmity or", where next occurring, and the words "or by any other fraudulent conduct".
11 & 12 Geo. 6 c. 38	The Companies Act 1948	Section 84. In section 328 (1), paragraphs (*m*) and (*n*) and any reference to either of those paragraphs. Section 330 (*a*).
11 & 12 Geo. 6 c. 67	The Gas Act 1948	In Schedule 3, in paragraph 29 (1), the words "or fraudulently abstracts, consumes or uses gas of the Board," and in paragraph 29 (3) the words "or for abstracting, consuming or using gas of the Board" and the words "abstraction or consumption".
14 Geo. 6 c. 36	The Diseases of Animals Act 1950	Section 78 (2) (x).
15 & 16 Geo. 6 & 1 Eliz. 2 c. 10	The Income Tax Act 1952	Section 505 (but this repeal shall not extend to Scotland).
15 & 16 Geo. 6 & 1 Eliz. 2 c. 25	The National Health Service Act 1952	In section 6 the words from "he shall" to "section".
15 & 16 Geo. 6 & 1 Eliz. 2 c. 43	The Disposal of Uncollected Goods Act 1952	In section 3 (3) the words from "or who" to "particular".
1 & 2 Eliz. 2 c. 36	The Post Office Act 1953	Sections 52 and 54 and in section 57 the words "steals, or for any purpose whatever embezzles" (but these repeals shall not extend to Scotland).
1 & 2 Eliz. 2 c. 50	The Auxiliary Forces Act 1953	Section 29 (2).
4 & 5 Eliz. 2 c. 16	The Food and Drugs Act 1955	Section 60, so far as unrepealed.

Session and Chapter	Short Title	Extent of Repeal
7 & 8 Eliz. 2 c. 28	The Income Tax (Repayment of Post-War Credits) Act 1959.	Section 1 (6) (but this repeal shall not extend to Scotland).
8 & 9 Eliz. 2 c. 16	The Road Traffic Act 1960	Section 217 (but this repeal shall not extend to Scotland).
1964 c. 28	The Agriculture and Horticulture Act 1964	In the Schedule, paragraph 3 from the words "or on conviction on indictment" onwards.
1966 c. 32	The Selective Employment Payments Act 1966	Section 8 (2) (*a*), (*b*) and (*d*) and (ii).
1966 c. 34	The Industrial Development Act 1966	Section 9.
1967 c. 1	The Land Commission Act 1967	Section 81 (5) (*a*). Section 93.
1967 c. 9	The General Rate Act 1967	Section 49 (8).
1967 c. 12	The Teachers' Superannuation Act 1967	Section 14.
1967 c. 22	The Agriculture Act 1967	Section 69 (1) (ii).
1967 c. 29	The Housing Subsidies Act 1967	Section 31.
1967 c. 34	The Industrial Injuries and Diseases (Old Cases) Act 1967	Section 11 (1). In section 12 (2) the words "section 11 (1) of this Act and".
1967 c. 85	The Vessels Protection Act 1967	The whole Act.

Part II

Obsolete and redundant enactments

Session and Chapter	Short Title	Extent of Repeal
34 & 35 Hen. 8 c. 26	The Laws in Wales Act 1542	Section 47 from "Item, that no person" onwards.
36 Geo. 3 c. 88	The Hay and Straw Act 1796	The whole Act.
5 Geo. 4 c. 83	The Vagrancy Act 1824	Sections 16 and 21.
4 & 5 Will. 4 c. 21	The Hay and Straw Act 1834	The whole Act.
3 & 4 Vict. c. 50	The Canals (Offences) Act 1840	Sections 13, 15, 17 and 19.
14 & 15 Vict. c. 19	The Prevention of Offences Act 1851	Sections 12 and 13.
18 & 19 Vict. c. 126	The Criminal Justice Act 1855	The whole Act, so far as unrepealed.
19 & 20 Vict. c. 114	The Hay and Straw Act 1856	The whole Act.

Schedule 3

Session and Chapter	Short Title	Extent of Repeal
32 & 33 Vict. c. 57	The Seamen's Clothing Act 1869	The whole Act.
33 & 34 Vict. c. 65	The Larceny (Advertisements) Act 1870	The whole Act.
34 & 35 Vict. c. 112	The Prevention of Crimes Act 1871	Sections 10 and 11.
39 & 40 Vict. c. 20	The Statute Law Revision (Substituted Enactments) Act 1876	Section 4.
59 & 60 Vict. c. 25	The Friendly Societies Act 1896	Section 87 (2).
61 & 62 Vict. c. 36	The Criminal Evidence Act 1898	In the Schedule, the entries for the Vagrancy Act 1824 and for the Prevention of Cruelty to Children Act 1894.
4 & 5 Geo. 5 c. 14	The Currency and Bank Notes Act 1914	The whole Act.

PART III

CONSEQUENTIAL REPEALS

Session and Chapter	Short Title	Extent of Repeal
2 & 3 Vict. c. 47	The Metropolitan Police Act 1839	Section 66 from "and any person" onwards.
2 & 3 Vict. c. 71	The Metropolitan Police Courts Act 1839	Section 25.
3 & 4 Vict. c. 50	The Canals (Offences) Act 1840	Section 11 from the beginning to "law; and". Section 12.
33 & 34 Vict. c. 52	The Extradition Act 1870	In Schedule 1 the entries relating to embezzlement and larceny, to obtaining money or goods by false pretences, to fraud by bailees and others, to burglary and housebreaking, to robbery with violence and to threats by letter or otherwise with intent to extort.
35 & 36 Vict. c. 93	The Pawnbrokers Act 1872	In section 30, paragraph (2) (but this repeal shall not extend to Scotland).
38 & 39 Vict. c. 83	The Local Loans Act 1875	Section 32.
40 & 41 Vict. c. 59	The Colonial Stock Act 1877	Section 21.

Session and Chapter	Short Title	Extent of Repeal
45 & 46 Vict. c. 75	The Married Women's Property Act 1882	Sections 12 and 16, so far as unrepealed.
47 & 48 Vict. c. 14	The Married Women's Property Act 1884	The whole Act.
47 & 48 Vict. c. 44	The Naval Pensions Act 1884	In section 2 the words "or the Admiralty (Powers, etc.) Act 1865".
56 & 57 Vict. c. 71	The Sale of Goods Act 1893	Section 24.
60 & 61 Vict. c. 30	The Police (Property) Act 1897	In section 1 (1) the words "section 103 of the Larceny Act 1861".
61 & 62 Vict. c. 36	The Criminal Evidence Act 1898	In the Schedule the entry for the Married Women's Property Act 1882.
16 & 17 Geo. 5 c. 7	The Bankruptcy (Amendment) Act 1926	In section 5 the words "(13), (14) and" wherever occurring.
25 & 26 Geo. 5 c. 30	The Law Reform (Married Women and Tortfeasors) Act 1935	In Schedule 1 the entries amending section 12 of the Married Women's Property Act 1882 and the Larceny Act 1916.
11 & 12 Geo. 6 c. 58	The Criminal Justice Act 1948	In section 41, subsection (3), in subsection (4) the words "or statutory declaration", and in subsection (5) the words "or statutory declaration" and the words from "or the person" onwards.
12, 13 & 14 Geo. 6 c. 36	The War Damage (Public Utility Undertakings, etc.) Act 1949	Section 10 (9) (e).
14 & 15 Geo. 6 c. 39	The Common Informers Act 1951	In the Schedule the entry relating to the Larceny Act 1861 section 102
15 & 16 Geo. 6 & 1 Eliz. 2 c. 45	The Pensions (Increase) Act 1952	In Schedule 3 the entries for sections 6 and 7 of 7 & 8 Geo. 6 c. 21.
15 & 16 Geo. 6 & 1 Eliz. 2 c. 55	The Magistrates' Courts Act 1952	Section 33. In Schedule 1, entries Nos. 1, 5 and 6.
15 & 16 Geo. 6 & 1 Eliz. 2 c. 67	The Visiting Forces Act 1952	In the Schedule, paragraph 1 (b) (v) and paragraph 3 (a), (d) and (e).
1 & 2 Eliz. 2 c. 36	The Post Office Act 1953	In section 23 (1), the words "and of the Larceny Act 1916".
8 & 9 Eliz. 2 c. 44	The Finance Act 1960	Section 55 (but this repeal shall not extend to Scotland).

Session and Chapter	Short Title	Extent of Repeal
10 & 11 Eliz. 2 c. 15	The Criminal Justice Administration Act 1962	In Schedule 3, paragraphs 4, 5, 6 and 8.
10 & 11 Eliz. 2 c. 46	The Transport Act 1962	In Part I of Schedule 2 the entry for the Criminal Justice Act 1948.
10 & 11 Eliz. 2 c. 59	The Road Traffic Act 1962	Section 44 (but this repeal shall not extend to Scotland).
1964 c. 26	The Licensing Act 1964	Section 100 (4) (*d*).
1967 c. 58	The Criminal Law Act 1967	Section 4 (7). In Schedule 1, in List A, item 1 in Division II, and, in List B, item 13. In Schedule 2, paragraph 2 (1) (*a*); in paragraph 4 the word "embezzlement"; paragraph 12, except in subparagraph (2) the words from "in the Bankruptcy Act" onwards and except subparagraph (6); and paragraph 13 (1) (*b*).
1968 c. 19	The Criminal Appeal Act 1968	In section 30, in subsection (1) the words from "and the operation" to "on conviction", in subsection (2) the words "or of section 24 (1) of the Sale of Goods Act 1893" and the words "or that subsection, as the case may be", and in subsection (3) the words "or of the said section 24 (1)". Section 42 (4).
1968 c. 27	The Firearms Act 1968	In section 17, subsection (3) and in subsection (5) the words from "and" onwards.

INDEX

A

ACCOUNTING,
  false, 283

ACTUS REUS,
  accounting, false, 284
  blackmail, 334
  burglary, 371
  criminal deception, 225
  housebreaking implements, possession of, 423
  motor vehicle or conveyance, taking, 324, 325
  public places, articles removed from, 300 *et seq.*
  stolen goods, 431
  theft, of, 19 *et seq.*

ANIMALS. *See* POACHING *and* WILD

ANNUITIES
  pecuniary advantage, 273

APPROPRIATION,
  actions not amounting to theft, 69
  act or omission an element of, 47
  animal maintenance trustee, 66
  attempted theft, 49 *et seq.*
  bailee at will, 58
      by, 25
  body, parts of, 55
  charitable trustee, 65
  conditional, 137
  consent, effect of owner's, 51
  continuing act, is not, 45
  control, 57
  conversion by trustee, 65
      compared with, 21
  co-owners, 64
  corpse, 53
  criminal damage, 103
  deception, obtaining by, 78
  definition, 20-22, 45
  dishonest, notwithstanding payment, 149
  "dishonestly", 118 *et seq.*
  equitable interests, 61-63
  finding, 126
  hereditaments, incorporeal, 90
  intention an element of, 46
  intimidation, property obtained by, 37-40
  land, theft of, 83, 84 *et seq.*
      thing severed from, 86
  monument maintenance trustee, 66
  necessary element, 73
  not a continuing act, 45
  obligation, 67, 79
      meaning, 76
  ownership, 57, 70
  partners, 64
  permanently depriving, meaning, 29
  persons not in possession, by, 28, 29
  poaching, 99
      generally, 102

All references are to paragraph numbers

All references are to paragraph numbers

Index

BURGLARY. *See also* HOUSEBREAKING IMPLEMENTS
  actus reus, 371
  aggravated—
    articles of aggravation, 414
    "at the time", meaning, 418
    definition, 412
    explosive, 416
    firearm, 414
    "has with him", meaning, 419
    incapacitation, article for, 415
    punishment, 413
    weapon of offence, 415
  building, extent of, 395
      meaning, 389
      part of, 393-398
      parts, and, extent of, 395
  caravans, 399
  damage, unlawful, 411
  entering, 371
      common law interpretation, 372
      for purpose alien to licence to enter, 384
      innocent agent, use of, 374
      intended as trespasser, 403
      involuntary, 376
      under false pretences, 379
  flats, 395-397
  generally, 369
  grievous bodily harm, 407
  houseboat, 399
  inhabited vehicle or vessel, 399
  lodgers, 387
  master and servant, 386
  mens rea, 402, 403 *et seq.*
  offence, nature of, 370
      ulterior, 404
  outbuildings, 391
  part of building, from, 393-398
  rape, 409
  shoplifting, 385
  stealing, 406
  trespass, 375
      ab initio, 377
      intention of, 403
      knowledge of, 403
  victim, 386

C

CHARGES, *See* DEBT

CHEQUES,
  theft of, 140

COMPANIES,
  false statements by directors, 292
  offences by officers, 290

CONTRACT,
  voidable, 79, 81

CONTROL,
  appropriation, 57

CONVERSION,
  appropriation, compared with, 21
  fraudulent, 16, 67

All references are to paragraph numbers

All references are to paragraph numbers

Index

D

DAMAGE,
  criminal, 103
  unlawful in burglary, 411

DEBT,
  charge, meaning, 268
          reduction, evasion or deferment, 268
  credit, meaning, 262
      obtaining, 262
  evasion or deferment, 256-269
              deception, by, 256-263
              means other than deception, by, 264
  liability for, 256
  overdraft, 273
  payment, evasion or deferment, 256
  reduction, 256, 257, 266, 269
  unenforceable debts or charges, 270
        obligation, 270
  voidness and illegality, 271

DECEPTION. *And see* CRIMINAL DECEPTION
  obtaining property by, 78
          penalty, 7

DEPRIVING,
  cheques, 140
  permanently, intention of, 130, 132
  persons with limited interests, 131
  virtue of property, 141

DIPLOMATIC IMMUNITY,
  stolen goods, 441

DISHONESTY,
  "dishonestly", significance, 121
  law or fact, 125
  necessity no defence, 123
  right in law, 120
     to deprive, belief in, 119

DOCUMENTS,
  suppression of, 295

E

ELECTRICITY,
  abstracting, 328 *et seq.*
  fraudulent benefit of use obtained, 331
  mains or other source, 330
  offences, 328, 329

EMBEZZLEMENT,
  former legislation, 15

EQUITABLE INTERESTS,
  appropriations, 61, 62

EXHIBITIONS,
  articles removed from, 305

F

FALSE PRETENCES. *And see* CRIMINAL DECEPTION
  obtaining by, former legislation, 17, 30

All references are to paragraph numbers

All references are to paragraph numbers

Index

All references are to paragraph numbers

MOTOR VEHICLES AND CONVEYANCES—*continued*
  conveyance, meaning, 319
  driven away, former significance, 316
  driving, meaning, 324
  hirers, 315
  lawful authority, taking without, 322
  mens rea of theft, 323
  milk floats, 319
  punishment for taking, 327
  taking, meaning, 313
          without authority, 312 *et seq.*
                consent of owner, 321
                lawful authority, 322

N

NULLA POENA SINE LEGE
  penal provisions, 12

O

OBTAINING. *See* CRIMINAL DECEPTION

OVERDRAFT,
  liability for deferred debt, 273

OWNERSHIP,
  appropriation, 57

P

PARTNERS,
  appropriation, 64

PAWNING,
  goods of another, 144

PECUNIARY ADVANTAGE. *See* CRIMINAL DECEPTION

POACHING,
  abandonment and resumption of possession, 100
  condition of regarding as theft, 99
  generally, 102

POSSESSION,
  appropriation, 57
  freedom from concept of, 22

POSSESSOR,
  appropriation by, 26, 27

POWER,
  distinguished from right, 113
  exercise of more than one, 516

PROFIT MAKING,
  dishonest, 110

PROPERTY. *See also* APPROPRIATION
  abandonment, 147
  appropriation permitted, 112
  conditional intention to return, 137
  criminal deception, meaning in cases of, 189
                obtained by, 171
  defined, 83
  disposition as one's own, 132
  obtained by mistake, 70
  parting with under condition of return, 143

All references are to paragraph numbers

All references are to paragraph numbers

STOLEN GOODS—*continued*
assisting, 475, 477
constable's authority to seize, 495
diplomatic immunity, 441
goods ceasing to be stolen, 443, 449
   meaning, 432
   representative of goods stolen, 450
handling, 430
   by thief, 486
   dishonesty involved, 489
   for benefit of another, 482
   forms of, 467
   mens rea, 488
      proof of, 490
   omission, by, 477
   otherwise than in course of stealing, 478
   undertaking or assisting, by 475, 476
hire-purchase transactions, 449
innocent receipt, 484
land, 434
multiplication, 451
principals and accessories no longer distinguished, 487
proceeds ceasing to be stolen, 464
   handling of, 455
      where goods obtained by deception or blackmail, 461
receiving, 470
restitution, 446, 502 *et seq.*
search for, 494
stolen, meaning, 435
thief must be guilty, 440
things in action, 432
title, 448
undertaking, assisting, and arranging, 474, 475, 476

T

TELEPHONE,
dishonest use of, 332

TENANCY,
appropriation during, 87
defined, 84

THEFT. *See also* APPROPRIATION; ROBBERY; STEALING
actus reus, 19 *et seq.*
attempted, 49 *et seq.*
borrowing, 139
concept simplified, 3, 6
"dishonestly", significance, 118 *et seq.*
duration of, 163
land, of, 83, 84 *et seq.*
mens rea, 116 *et seq.*
nature, 4
penalty, 6
restitution, 502
things in action, 104
victim, presence of, 168

THIRD PERSON,
force or threat against, 165

THREAT. *See* ROBBERY

TRESPASS,
burglary, 375
theft, no longer required for, 51

All references are to paragraph numbers

Index

All references are to paragraph numbers